Errata and regrets:

(1) In *True to His Ways,* written when I was a young believer, I quoted many authors. That never meant nor could mean that I endorse everything they say – even if I were competent to judge everything, which I am not. But some I now have real concerns about. Also, I quoted from bible versions that I would not now use. Please bear these things in mind.

(2) My understanding was wrong at pages 254-255 where I speak of the "good" of the tree of the knowledge of good and evil. I asked a few pastors to review my script, and even paid a Christian editor, but this escaped all eyes. (Pastor Holmes, to whom I dedicated the book, read it before I inserted that comment, and is not responsible for letting it pass.)

(3) I have come to believe that the "blessing" of the spirit given in occult practice is perhaps above all a counterfeit of that Spirit which is so sweetly found in the sacrament of Holy Communion, especially (I have found) when celebrated with the traditional Book of Common Prayer of Thomas Cranmer. I wish I had referred to this sacrament in chapter 6 dealing with the right ways to seek God.

Thankfully these things do not affect the central message of my book and warning against the occultism of Charismatic practices. *R. Davis*

65 –
69 –

P13 – Alpha Course
P47 – latter Rain.
P49 + P50
P55 – 'Light`

True to His Ways

Purity & Safety in Christian Spiritual Practice

R. DAVIS

P80 – Prayer : Communication with God.

ACW Press
Ozark, AL 36360

The author gratefully acknowledges permission granted by Dr. J.I. Packer and Pastor Bill Randles to quote from their works.

True to His Ways
Copyright ©2006 R. Davis
All rights reserved

Cover Design by Alpha Advertising. Calligraphy by Dan North.
Interior Design by Pine Hill Graphics.

Packaged by ACW Press
1200 HWY 231 South #273
Ozark, AL 36360
www.acwpress.com
The views expressed or implied in this work do not necessarily reflect those of ACW Press. Ultimate design, content, and editorial accuracy of this work are the responsibility of the author(s).

Publishers Cataloging-in-Publication Data
(Provided by Cassidy Cataloguing Services, Inc.)

Davis, R.

   True to His ways : purity & safety in Christian spiritual practice / R.
   Davis. -- 1st ed. -- Ozark, AL : ACW Press, 2005.

      p. ; cm.

      Includes bibliographical references.
      ISBN: 1-932124-61-6
      ISBN-13: 978-1-932124-61-3

      1. Pentecostalism. 2. Toronto blessing. 3. Christian life.
   4. Spirituality. I. Title.

BR1644 .D38 2005
270.8/2--dc22   0509

Printed in the United States of America.

Dedication

To Pastor Holmes, who struggled valiantly
through an early manuscript and provided the
advice and encouragement I needed to persevere.

Contents

Introduction

This book is the result of detailed research, hours of Bible study, much prayer and, I believe, the leading of the Holy Spirit. As I progressed, each answer raised new questions. In the end I was led to conclusions I had not anticipated, and to research new and strange areas of religious practice.

When I began enquiring into the signs, wonders and manifestations I experienced as a new believer in a charismatic church, I had no idea my work would result in a book. Nor did I begin with any preconceived theory to prove. I only wanted to know the truth. Eventually I realized my discoveries and conclusions should be made available for others. I felt like Josiah who "rediscovered" the Law as I began to understand the full import of God's injunction against the occult and His hatred of spiritual adultery. I praised Him as I grew in understanding about true Christian spiritual practice and experienced the fruits of it in my own life.

I have endeavored to explain in these pages the "hows" and "whys," and "how nots" and "why nots," of Christian spiritual practice, with much-needed explanations, along with examples of how Satan comes as an angel of light.

I did not strive for "balance" when I reviewed the teaching of other authors, although I tried to avoid presumption as to their motives or the state of their souls. I wrote plainly because I do not read Scripture as exhorting us to be anything but firmly, clearly and single-mindedly on the side of truth. We are commanded to cling to the doctrines taught by the apostles, to stand firm against winds of false doctrine and to refute false teaching. I have attempted to do all these things—with compassion, but without apology. This said, however, I offer my book with apprehension. It is no slight responsibility to presume to teach.

For illustration purposes I have occasionally referred to leaders and pastors I know personally. I want to make it clear that despite their errors I appreciate most of them, love some of them and I am glad God placed me with them when I was a new believer. I pray He will use my work to bless them.

So, I commit my book to the judgment of those who are sincere and, above all, to the blessing of Him who alone can use it to grow us in understanding of His eternal truth.

R. Davis

Chapter One

The Wondering
Never Ceased

*A*n enthusiastic pastor from Liverpool, England, wrote:

> I had a mighty power encounter with God. I've been
> intoxicated—completely drunk with the Holy Spirit. He's a
> person, and he's so wonderful. When I was baptized in the
> Holy Spirit some 20 years ago, it made Jesus real to me.
> This move has made the Holy Spirit and the Father's heart
> real. It has completely turned us around as a church. It's
> given us a real hunger for souls, a love for people, and a
> desire to be relevant to the community where we live—to
> show them the love of God.[1]

An Australian pastor joins in this glad praise:

> In November '94 God began to pour out His Spirit in such
> a powerful way that in the first service 300 people were lit-
> erally swept off their feet. Because people are responding
> in faith, we are seeing a great move across the country not

---

1. John Scotland, Liverpool, England, posted at
   http://www.tacf.org/stf/archive/2-4/testimonies.html.

only in Pentecostal churches, but in charismatic and main-
line churches as well. We're seeing a tremendous response
even from the unsaved.[2]

These pastors, and thousands like them, are sincerely devoted
to sharing the "Father's heart" and the love of God with other
people. But, in the midst of it all, strange things are happening
too. At meetings where God's love is "called down," people sometimes sob, giggle wildly for no apparent reason or fall to the floor.
The spiritual drunkenness referred to by the pastor from
Liverpool is commonplace; it is an odd state of altered consciousness that causes people to stagger, and sometimes renders them
unable to speak. Charismatics refer to these, and other supernatural phenomena, as "manifestations."

OVERVIEW OF THE MANIFESTATIONS

Charismatics believe their practices bring them into communion with God's Holy Spirit, and that manifestations are evidence
of the Spirit's presence among them. They say God is doing a new
thing and talk a lot about the "river," "wind" or "move of the
Spirit," and about "new wine values." All this is part and parcel of
the so-called charismatic movement, which gained prominence in
Vineyard churches but has since reached into most of the
Christian church. (I am mindful that if we adopt biblical terminology, all Christians could aptly be called "charismatic" because
all receive *charismata*—gifts of grace—from God. I use the term
in the popular sense.)

The Toronto Airport Church in Toronto, Canada, is interna-
tionally known for the frequent occurrence of manifestations. It
is so well-known that over a million curious, hopeful people
have traveled there to receive "blessings" through the manifestations, an experience which has come to be known as the
"Toronto Blessing," or "TB" for short. Similar manifestations are
reported at many other churches including Holy Trinity Brompton

---

2. Adrian Gray, Campelltown, New S. Wales, Australia, posted at
   http://www.tacf.org/stf/archive/2-4/testimonies.html.

ANGLICAN,
CHARISMATIC.

Jeremy James ↗ www.zephania.eu

"*The Great Pentecostal - Charismatic Error*" (17 pages)

in London, England, which is pastored by Nicky Gumbel of the Alpha Course. → since 1977

Following are practices and manifestations typically considered charismatic:

- falling down under prayer, touch or even at the word of a leader (also known as being "slain in the Spirit")
- "soaking in the Spirit," a trance state of spiritual communion
- giving words or visions believed to be from God
- trembling hands during worship or prayer
- involuntary weeping or laughter
- prophesying about people or events

and more extreme manifestations such as:

- getting "drunk in the Spirit" ("new wine" experience)
- gatherings as party time with the Lord
- miracles like gold dust and gold fillings
- shaking, jerking and strange movements
- people growling, roaring or making other animal and bird noises

The more extreme TB manifestations are common at the Toronto church and Holy Trinity Brompton, from which have come many reports of people barking like dogs and roaring like lions. Although some charismatics are not comfortable with all the bizarre behaviors, they turn a blind eye to them because they do not want to be negative or divisive.

MY EXPERIENCES

As a new Christian, I was taken under the wing of TB enthusiasts, sincere and loving people. I will share some of my experiences with them throughout the book, to show that I really do understand both the good and the bad in charismatic practice.

Initially, I was uncomfortable with and confused by the manifestations. Members of my new church would hold trembling hands high into the air during worship, and it seemed to me they were trying to prove how spiritual they were. Some leaders stood at the back waving flags, and I wished they would stop. (A friend I brought to church refused to return because of the flag-waving.) During ministry time after Sunday worship, people fell down after prayer or after receiving a touch to the forehead; the floor was littered with bodies as people lay there, soaking in the Spirit or "doing carpet time" as it is sometimes called. This seemed weird to me. Mats and blankets were kept handy so people could lay in comfort and modesty while God did a "work" in them.

The Spirit of love

As time went on, however, I grew more tolerant of the manifestations, partly because I was sure God was with us, and also because I trusted my leaders when they told me I should not be judgmental and opinionated. They taught me that God works through wounded vessels—that is, people who are less than perfect—and I had to agree, when I looked at myself! Also, many of my leaders were respectable, generous people who acted normal most of the time. I figured they were good role models.

Also important to me was that my pastors were very anointed. Often, when they prayed, I felt holiness literally "fall" down upon me from the heavens, shedding love abroad in my heart and filling me with compassion toward others. When I received this spirit I just knew it was God, and I longed for more. Sometimes the feeling of a holy presence stayed with me for hours.

Visions and prophetic words

During church services, people often came before the congregation to describe visions or words from God. One woman described visions of Jesus walking down the aisle, shimmering like gold. Prophets would lurch to a microphone as if bearing a great burden, or deliver messages with loud sobs, mostly on themes of God's love and the coming revival. People were sometimes encouraged to participate in "prophetic acts"; a woman sincerely and joyfully told me once that God had burned a hole in her jacket as she passed through a "prophetic tunnel"! I found it difficult to believe God destroyed her clothing, but she really thought it was true and I did not doubt that it happened.

Dancing and celebration

One evening Pastor John Arnott from the Toronto Airport Church visited my town for a large, multi-church meeting. That was one of the most extreme evenings I ever saw. A local pastor preached about how God keeps our microwaves functioning. (I'll call him the "Microwave Preacher" since I will need to refer to him later.) This preacher spilled water from a glass onto the front of his trousers and laughed as the dark stain widened, declaring himself "drunk in the Spirit." Eerie wails pierced the atmosphere from time to time. A member of the worship team fell onto his back and began to pedal in the air as though riding a bicycle. The Microwave Preacher chastised those of us who were sitting quietly, exhorting us to get up, dance and "celebrate properly." Indeed there was much revelry, hopping about and dancing. The meeting became so noisy that when it was Pastor Arnott's turn, no one could hear him. I was so disgusted I left before the meeting was over, but when one of my leaders later told me he had remained and received a wonderful blessing I was disappointed because I had missed out. It was confusing.

Doing the crunch

At another meeting, during ministry time, I went forward for prayer but was not receiving anything at all. I so wanted a touch from God! Then a person touched me on the belly and to my astonishment I felt a "force" hit me there. An invisible force! I doubled over as though kicked and was knocked backwards to the floor where I lay feeling chilled and unhappy. I doubted this was from God, but could not deny the reality of it. Others thought I was having a spiritual experience and put a blanket over me while I struggled to "feel" the Holy Spirit. It was extremely confusing. Later I learned that the doubling-over phenomenon happens so often at the Toronto church that they have a name for it: it is called "crunching" or "doing the crunch."

The prophetic anointing

As time went on I grew in a "prophetic anointing." One day at a prayer meeting I felt a subtle electrical energy in my forearms. I somehow knew that if I laid hands on a woman I would transfer this energy to her. I felt urged to do so, and I did. Sure enough, a warm, supernatural surge of tingling energy passed through my hands and she slumped under the power of it. But then I "prophesied," and spoke words which I must say were not my own because I did not believe them. To my own surprise I called—in a new, deep voice—for an increase of this woman's gift of teaching. These assuredly were not my words because, in my privately held opinion, she was a poor teacher. Again, it was confusing.

Another time, with the same prayer group, I had a confident sense of "knowing" and power, and I spoke a prophecy over a woman that came to pass that very day. She called to tell me how accurate my prophecy had been and what a wonderful day she had. Now it really seemed God was using me and everyone was impressed by my strength in prayer. Indeed, I became known as a prayer warrior and was invited to join a group of prophets-in-training.

"New Wine" practices

John White, a psychologist and enthusiastic charismatic, published a book in 1988 called *When the Spirit Comes With Power*. In it he attempted to explain TB experiences and practice. His book was and remains popular, and is considered a helpful resource for those seeking to understand the manifestations; I will refer to it frequently in the pages to come. Following are descriptions from Mr. White's book of charismatic experiences during meetings and prayer:

> In meetings where the Holy Spirit's power is strongly manifest, some people may seem a little drunk. However, I have never seen them noisy or obstreperous in this state. They may describe a "heaviness" that is on them. Their speech may be slightly slurred, their movements uncoordinated.

They may need support to walk. They show little concern
about what anyone will think of their condition and are
usually a little dazed.[3]

Not infrequently when I pray for someone in a meeting,
the person will immediately go into a trancelike state. Eyes
may roll back, the person may fall, may begin to make
epileptiform [jerky] movements...[4]

I know a woman who trembles frequently (as with
Parkinsonism) when she prays for other people...She
describes the experience in terms of energy coursing through
her. The phenomenon began in a meeting she attended
where the Holy Spirit was powerfully present. While she cannot as it were produce the trembling or the "energy," when it
comes she has the choice either of resisting it, or else of
directing it (into prayer, for example). If she does the latter,
she experiences a sensation of pulsating energy extending to
her finger tips, along with a slight tremor in her hands. Her
impression is of energy flowing through her.[5]

Following are eyewitness accounts of manifestations at the
Toronto Airport Church from a Pentecostal pastor, Bill Randles,
who went there to see for himself:

After the sermon, the chairs were stacked and removed
for ministry time. You could feel the sense of expectation,
something was about to happen. The ground rules were
announced, "No one who doesn't have an approved ministry team badge can pray for people," also, "You are here
to receive, so when you are getting prayed for, don't pray,
in tongues or English for you are here to receive and that

---

3. John White, *When the Spirit Comes With Power: Signs & Wonders among
   God's People* (Downers Grove, IL: InterVarsity, 1988), 100-101.
4. White, 100.
5. White, 91-92.

can hinder your reception." Hmmm. After the rules of engagement were announced, Dupont calmly invoked the Holy Spirit, "Come, Holy Spirit," and immediately people all over began to twitch, tremble, compulsively bend over, face forward, and straighten up, over and over. Knees would give, arms would thrash, and some people would violently shake and quake. A few would become intensely cold and others feverishly hot! I saw a woman in her 50's laying on her back, suddenly convulse into a form of a sit up, rapidly and repetitively. Each time she would come up, out of her mouth would come the word "cuckoo"![6]

At another service I attended, spiritual drunkenness seemed to be the predominant manifestation. After the invocation, "Come, Holy Spirit," the receptive congregation began to stagger and sway. Loud, raucous laughter rolled over portions of the congregation, like a wave…People are stumbling and falling over each other by the dozens. Most are flat on their backs with a silly dazed grin on their faces or trying to get up and unable to. One man was yelling at the top of his voice, another laying on the ground, feet straight up in the air, laughing and trying to get his feet down. The ministry team is going around "swishing" the wave on people, getting intoxicated themselves…the young man from Ohio is telling me, "This is God," his eyes are bloodshot, he is swaying as he stands there, and he's breathing heavily, just about to fall over![7]

Prophetic practices

Charismatics usually emphasize receiving "prophetic words" from God, which are then given to the congregation. This practice

---

6. Bill Randles, *Weighed and Found Wanting: The Toronto Experience Examined in the Light of the Bible*, 2nd ed. (Cambridge, Great Britain: St Matthew Publications, 1996), 134-135.
7. Randles, *Weighed*, 137.

is common in the charismatic house church movement, where members are taught to meet and wait quietly to receive "words from God," usually mental impressions which are then shared with the rest of the group. Such "prophetic words" often involve foretelling (predicting the future, especially revival), visions and encouragement for everyone to "open up and accept what the Lord has to offer."

Charismatics also emphasize "growing in the prophetic," meaning that we should increasingly seek—and expect—direct revelation from God about various issues, personal or for the church body. By way of example, Carol Arnott, wife of Pastor Arnott of the Toronto church, published the following "word" claiming revelation knowledge about God's desire for women today:

> In these days of refreshing, God is breathing new life into our hearts, and is waking the Church to the vast potential of women as soldiers in His spiritual army. He is preparing us to take up the sword of His Spirit and go forth as warriors, anointed and empowered alongside our male companions.[8]

Mrs. Arnott closed her "word" with an exhortation to continue in soaking prayer, meaning the practice of waiting for and "soaking" in manifested supernatural, spiritual presence:

> Let God fill you with Himself, marinate you and rub you all over with His perfume so that you will look like Jesus, act like Jesus and minister like Jesus.

WONDERING ABOUT THESE EXPERIENCES

I never stopped wondering about some of these things. Do you wonder? Just a little, even, at the back of your mind?

My doubts were never completely resolved, but at the same time I was convinced that God was with us intimately and

---

8. Carol Arnott, "Women—The Anointing Makes Room For You," *http://www.tacf.org/stf/archive/4-4/feature4.html.*

powerfully—at my church in particular. However, as time went on and I grew in biblical understanding, I began to think that some of the teaching did not line up with Scripture. Could it be so? I began to pray about leaving, torn by the issue. On one hand, I found myself hungry for deep Bible teaching. On the other, I had frequent, precious experiences of God's peace and love. I did not want to leave God behind at the church!

After more than a month of prayer, a Bible verse jumped out at me one morning during devotions. It was, "*Cease, my son, to hear the instruction that causeth to err from the words of knowledge*" (Proverbs 19:27 KJV). My strong impression was that the Lord had spoken to me through this Scripture.

Shortly thereafter I left my church, in search of His will. I felt regret, even fear, about losing the more wonderful experiences of the Holy Spirit. However, I reasoned the fear away by reminding myself of Jesus' promise which seemed especially for me: He would always be with me, even until the end of the age.

At the time I had no idea about the discoveries to which I would eventually be led, discoveries that would show me just how far I (and my beloved pastors) had strayed from the truth.

Some months later I discovered something that alarmed me, something that merited further enquiry. I learned that many charismatic experiences of the "Holy Spirit" are similar—in fact, almost completely identical—with mystic Hindu experiences of something called "kundalini power." *What on earth is kundalini?* Good question. We also have to ask, *Are similarities between Hindu and charismatic experience something we really need to worry about?* I didn't know the answer, and that is the question I will try to answer in this book.

Chapter Two

Enchantments of
the Serpent God

Kali's devotees are...full of unending joy. When you see that at the very name of the Lord tears begin to flow and hair on the body stand on end, know it that...one has attained God.
                                            —Sri Ramakrishna, Kali devotee

Several years before I became a Christian, I spent an afternoon with my boyfriend in Chinatown, exploring some of the quirky shops. We loved bookstores, and browsed a while in a little New Age place. I was always looking, always searching, always hoping for books that might shed light on the mystery of life.

I soon found a book entitled *Chakras: Wheels of Life*, or something like that. It was big and fat with lots of drawings, and talked about something called "kundalini yoga." I was asking the salesclerk about it when another customer standing in the shop interrupted us, and volunteered an enthusiastic explanation from her own experience.

"It's all about a kundalini awakening," she told us in a loud, unpleasant voice. "The energy rises up, and 'wham,' you come alive! It's a real awakening!" As if to demonstrate, she bent her torso forward, hung her arms to the floor and shook herself while a gurgling sound issued from her mouth.

I decided kundalini yoga wasn't for me.

But later I realized I needed to learn about it. Bear with me through the following pages, and you will soon understand why.

WHAT IS KUNDALINI, AND WHY DO I CARE?

The classic definition of kundalini (or, the Kundalini) is as the "primordial energy of the universe." It is known as the "serpent force," also "shakti," and in Hindu thought is considered the key that opens the door to hidden "spiritual" truths. Kundalini is also called a "creative life force" or "divine energy."

The Kundalini is accessed or awakened through yoga and meditation, practices which are believed to lead the seeker into communion with Brahman (God). Once the seeker has achieved yoga—complete union with God—he or she will remain forever in that state, fully enlightened and not required to suffer through another reincarnation on Earth. (Reincarnation is romanticized in Western New Age teachings, but is feared by orthodox Hindus because of the threat of coming back to a hard or painful life, and because they hold natural life in low esteem.)

Kundalini yoga is actually orthodox Hinduism, though few know it in the West where yoga is promoted as exercise for relaxation and health. The real purpose of yoga is religious: it is to "raise the Kundalini" so a person can grow in intimacy with God.

Some say the Hindu goddess Kali brings kundalini, or arouses it in a person. You have probably seen pictures of Kali, with black skin, mouth open and tongue protruding far down her chin. She usually has four or six arms, and is holding the severed head of at least one man in a fist, blood dripping from the neck. Legends about her are contradictory; she is known as a goddess of evil and destruction, but also as a heroine who wars against demons. Here is what her followers say about Kali, the kundalini goddess:

- "Kali…is oriented towards spiritual evolution."
- "She will destroy your ego so that you can be reborn."

- "Her force awakens Kundalini…purification of the subtle force centers (chakras) and the ascension of the Divine Energy Kundalini, which lies dormant at the base of the spine…"[1]

I was surprised to discover that biblical language abounds in yoga teachings, which often refer to kundalini as the Holy Spirit, or even "Mother Mary." Guru Solomae Sananda writes:

> Kundalini is known as the Great Comforter, the Holy Spirit and the Divine Mother within us. It is the driving force behind our creative abilities and our soul's expression. Kundalini is the missing link to the mystery of our creation…it is the force and process by which we come to experience total communion with God.[2]

Yoga devotees share a strong desire for blissful kundalini experiences, which can apparently be very pleasurable. Solomae Sananda again:

> The desire to know God and to be one with God is felt like an ache, sending you into hours of meditation, intense devotion and deeper commitment. Nothing less will do, the Kundalini requires that you give everything… You will merge your awareness into that of God and become the Christ Consciousness/Divine Presence in and through the filter of your body.[3]

KUNDALINI AWAKENING: WHEN THE SERPENT RISES

In Hindi, kundalini literally means "coiled one." Westerners who do yoga may recognize the term. The serpent force is usually

---

1. "Kali, the Terrible Face of God," TantraMag.Com, *http://sivasakti.com/local/art-kali.html.*
2. Solomae Sananda, "What is Kundalini?," Living Spirit Foundation, *http://www.geocities.com/HotSprings/Villa/i555/bab1.htm#whatiskundalini.*
3. Sananda, "Kundalini."

pictured as a snake coiled at the base of the human spine, await-ing the right moment to "rise up" through ascending locations on the spine called "chakras" or "chakra points," which are points through which the power supposedly travels. Other chakra points on the body include the forehead, crown of the head and hands. Although many experience what feels like an upsrising of kun-dalini power from the spine, others also feel the power fall down upon them, as if given by a deity, or rise up from their feet.

Kundalini
and the Chakras

Yoga students strive to arouse the force of the serpent through a kundalini awakening, a religious experience that marks the beginning of a process believed to purify the spirit and free the soul from earthly bondages as the seeker reaches for God. An awakening is sometimes referred to as a "baptism." Following is a teaching on kundalini awakenings from guru Shri Devi:

> Now I would like to tell the secret knowledge of our inner being which was known in India thousands of years back. For our evolution and spiritual ascent there is a residual power within us which is located in the triangular bone at the base of our spine…When this Kundalini rises it connects you to the All-pervading Power, which is vital and which is an ocean of knowledge as well as an ocean of bliss. After the awakening of Kundalini, you experience many coincidences which are miraculous and extremely blissful. Above all, Kundalini is the ocean of forgiveness.[4]

There is no doubt that the experience of awakened kundalini is very real and often life-changing. Another testimony confirms the lasting delight it can bring:

> Since this awakening I have lived in this state where everything that happens is just the pure and natural expression of the will of God which one is in constant awe and gratitude for. … It is beyond beautiful. It is cosmic perfection, it is perfect harmony and integration of a magnificent diversity that is beyond all human description. It is all the expression of the will of God and it is our very own Self. And the universe sings the praise of your existence in the eternal light and glory of God.[5]

4. Shri Mataji Nirmala Devi, quoted in "Human Subtle System (Tree of Life)," *http://www.adishakti.org/subtle_system/kundalini.htm*.
5. posted at *http://www.kundalini-support.com./forums*, removed.

Yoga exercises and meditation are often used to arouse kundalini. However, there are other ways. One is by contact with an empowered yoga master. Kundalini/shakti can be aroused by a touch from a guru, especially a touch to the forehead. Shri Devi again:

> in India, the awakening of the Kundalini was done, traditionally, on an individual basis only. One guru would give awakening to one disciple...[6]

It is this transferability of kundalini by touch that first caught my attention.

Shaktipat and Samadhi

I need to write just a little longer about yoga, but only for a short time. If you need to refresh your understanding of the terminology, please refer to the glossary (p. 299).

Pat is a Hindi word meaning to "transfer" or "descend." A *shakti pat* (or, as one word, *shaktipat*) is a touch, usually on the forehead or crown, which transfers kundalini/shakti power from one person to another. Gurus give shaktipats to bless their disciples, often at meetings held for this purpose. See this advertisement:

> come to this rare and special evening with Grand Master Choa Kok Sui...we shall request him to give a Shakti Pat to each attendee. One Shakti Pat from him is equal to 20 years of spiritual practice...WOW!...It has been known that when we are in the presence of those who are highly developed spiritually and partake of the Divine energies that they can access and bring down, we have only to make the necessary wishes and, if we are entitled to it, these will manifest. This phenomenon has been observed, particularly, in relation to those who are seeking healing for different aspects of their lives.[7]

---

6. Devi, "Human Subtle."
7. For a meeting held April 2003, posted at
   http://www.aiis.com.au/AISS%20Subweb/hot%20news.htm.

Hindus believe the forehead is spiritually significant, a very special chakra point because it is the "third eye," or "spiritual eye," through which men and women can see into the spiritual realm. A shaktipat, being a touch to the forehead, is considered important because it has the potential to open the third eye. Says one writer:

> **Shaktipat** means "touch of the shakti" or Initiation.
> Shaktipat is the spiritual initation given by a divine
> Master; the inner quickening. Shaktipat is synonymous
> with the *baptism* of Christianity, and the *annointing* [sic]
> of Judaism...It represents the beginning of the awaken-
> ing and unfolding of the inner power of kundalini -
> shakti, and is often accompanied by marvelous events
> and perceptions.[8]

After receiving shaktipat a person sometimes falls on the floor and lies in a trance-like state called *samadhi.* This is a peak spiritual experience. During samadhi, practitioners receive supernatural peace and love which is apparently joyful and soul-expanding; a very precious experience. Following are excerpts from a poem in praise of samadhi in which we find references to mystic "waves," mirth and laughter. This blissful samadhi was apparently "guru-given," i.e., imparted by a guru:

> By deeper, longer, thirsty, guru-given meditation
> Comes this celestial *Samadhi*...
> From joy I came, for joy I live, in sacred joy I melt...
> A tiny bubble of laughter, I
> Am become the Sea of Mirth Itself.[9]

Following is a description of the samadhi experience from guru Ching Hai:

---

8. Sacred Word Trust, "shaktipat info," *http://shaktipat.info/.*

9. Paramhansa Yogananda, "Samadhi,"
   http://www.yoganandarediscovered.com/jaitruth/Csamadhi.html.

Samadhi means that you are in ecstasy, in bliss, tranquility and light. You can be in ecstasy while living in this world. There are two kinds of Samadhi: One is after you leave this world, you are forever in ecstasy, in bliss, in the Kingdom of God. You are one with God or the Ocean of Love and Mercy. The other type is a smaller ecstasy that you experience every day through meditation, through devotional longing, or any type of ritual in order to reach ecstasy… When you are in a deeper ecstasy, the whole world disappears, and you only see light and God, and feel peace, bliss and ecstasy.[10]

Obviously, a person in samadhi feels like he has met with God.

SIMILARITY WITH CHARISMATIC PRACTICE

By now the reader will have noticed parallels between kundalini and charismatic practice, including blessings and healing imparted by touch. Samadhi resembles the soaking prayer of charismatics, and both groups believe they meet with God during these trance-like states.

I was shocked and concerned when I learned about shaktipat and samadhi. I have seen charismatic leaders teach people where to touch others, particularly on the crown and forehead, but also the chest and belly—which are chakra points in Hindu theology. When I was a new Christian, TB leaders would seat me in a chair and pray, with one hand on my forehead and one on the back of my head, exactly like yoga masters do. The purpose is the same: to transmit spiritual power. Often the result is also the same, and the worshiper falls to the ground in the samadhi-like state charismatics refer to as being "slain in the Spirit." (Interestingly, some charismatics—including leaders at the Toronto church—recently altered their practice to avoid touching for transferring the "Spirit.")

When Pastor Bill Randles (the Pentecostal pastor quoted in chapter 1) visited the Toronto Airport Church, he noticed where and how the prayer teams laid hands on participants:

---

10. Ching Hai, "Samadhi,"
    http://www.godsdirectcontact.com/teachings/AZsamad.htm.

ENCHANTMENTS OF THE SERPENT GOD   29

They would pray for them, laying hands on forehead and belly, in some cases fanning the "wind of the Spirit" or "splashing" the waves of the Spirit onto the seeker. Usually, they would stay with the person till there was some kind of manifestation.[11]

What differentiates shaktipat from the laying on of hands in charismatic circles, especially the forehead touch? Not much, if anything. Among both yogis and charismatics a meeting will be held for people seeking healing or a divine encounter. *Believers/pagans* are invited to come forward for a *Holy Spirit blessing/Shakti Pat*. An *anointed leader/ empowered guru* touches them on the forehead. They fall back and lay on the floor *soaking in the spirit/in samadhi* where they believe they experience communion with God, divine love, healing and spiritual growth. For them all, it is a delightful, empowering encounter.

On the Web site of a kundalini guru,[12] I found two photographs showing women in various states of samadhi. One was standing and her eyes were rolled back in her head with only the whites showing. Another was lying on her back with her arms raised, her hands apparently frozen in a claw-like position. I realized that these photos could have been taken at a charismatic meeting; many of my readers will have seen similar things. Copyright law prevents me from reproducing the photographs here, but the claw-like hands of the young woman featured on the Web site can be compared with this charismatic experience: "My hands became heavy and cramped and 'frozen' and 'paralyzed' like two claws, and then that spread to the rest of my torso…"[13] John White reported (see chapter 1), "Not infrequently when I pray for someone in a meeting, the person will immediately go into a trancelike state. Eyes may roll back, the person may [then] fall."

---

11. Randles, *Weighed*, 135.
12. Visit the Web site of Master Sadhana Ashram (*www.sahanaashram.org*) and click on the "shaktipat" icon to see a picture of a devotee lying on the floor in a trance, if still current.
13. White, 106, quoting from John Mumford's diary.

Is it wrong or unfair to compare kundalini and charismatic practices?

Some may say it is wrong for me to compare kundalini and charismatic experiences. But it is not wrong, not if we want to know the truth. People who want to teach and lead others in spiritual practice should be more than willing to bear scrutiny.

Others may say that resemblances between pagan and charismatic practice only show that Satan is copying the work of God. I'm aware of that possibility; in fact, that is the assumption we need to check out. Believers need to know for sure: is it of God, or is it of Satan?

Other important questions arise out of this. If both God and Satan are at work in these manifestations, as many seem to think, then how much of each? Can we measure it? Should we be able to measure it so we know when enough is enough? Is it true that the Holy Spirit and Satan's unholy spirit manifest at the same time, side by side, during worship and prayer? If so, how can we know the difference? If it is true that we can pass on the Holy Spirit by touch, and Satan counterfeits this by allowing gurus to pass on an unholy spirit the same way, how can we be sure our leaders are of God and not of Satan? Wouldn't this be crucial to know, so we don't receive an unholy spirit?

If we can answer these questions, we will be glad we asked. So stay with me, dear reader, on this important quest. Let us explore the issues carefully and reverently.

SOAKING AND SAMADHI:
EXPERIENCES OF DIVINE LOVE

In my former church, some leaders loved to soak in the Spirit. They would meet together and take turns receiving prayer; one touch to the forehead and they were down. Someone standing behind would catch them on the way down.

Soaking is as coveted by charismatics as samadhi is by shakti devotees, and for the same reasons. Both groups want to connect with God for cleansing, spiritual growth and the joy of feeling the loving presence.

In their own words, this is what pagan mystics teach about the benefits of kundalini and samadhi:

On joy and intimacy with God:

> Sometimes, during samadhi, you find your body doesn't exist…It's all light; it's all God. That's when we truly realize we are God, that only God dwells within this temple…Only this realization will make us happy, truly happy…[14]

On spiritual growth and cleansing:

> When, therefore, the guru activates the Kundalini it is to clean out the chakras of dross, or samskaras, the ancient memories and traumas of past lives and to turn the much limited individual into a full human being with active and awake Kundalini. These chakras are like the doorways to other dimensions for mankind. As each chakra is cleansed by the Kundalini, it creates a spark or opening which activates the next highest chakra making that too spin and become cleansed.[15]

Charismatics teach similar things about the benefits of soaking, although in different words:

On knowing love and intimacy with God:

> In this ministry of the Father's Love I have had opportunity over the years to observe hundreds of instances of people coming to Father God to receive a touch of His love. His love, imparted into the human heart, will have great impact and cause great change in a person…if we have an open heart then we will know the intimacy of relationship with God[16]

---

14. Ching Hai, "Samadhi."

15. Ruth A. Bailey, "The Ascending Goddess: Kundalini Shakti," *http://www.aloha.net/~ruth/Chapter6.html.*

16. James and Denise Jordan, Fatherheart ministries, *http:// www.fatherheart.net.*

On spiritual growth and cleansing:

> I lay there in the wonderful presence of God on me I
> became aware of the Holiness and the love and the wrath
> and His Mercy and majesty of God in a way that I had
> never known. Now, I understood why I had to be cleansed
> that time…I knew at the time that I was saved but there
> was a cleansing that needed to take place before I could
> enter the inner chamber, the Holy of Holies where God
> would speak to me.[17]

We learn from these quotations that both kundalini yogis who
seek the "power of the serpent" and charismatics who seek the
"power of the Holy Spirit" believe they meet with God and are
spiritually cleansed in trance states. I do not doubt the sincerity of
either group; after all, both experience compelling, heart-chang-
ing supernatural love; and God is love, is He not? How could it
not be God?

This is a very important question.

---

17. Bill, July 23, 1998, *http://members.aol.com/Azusa/azusaindex.html.*

Chapter Three

JERKS, KRIYAS
AND MANIFESTATIONS

When kundalini awakens, one invariably feels some invol-
untary movements of the body, which begin with trembling
and shaking, with an intensity varying with different
persons. Some experience violent shakings of different
kinds...the brain becomes heavy as under intoxication."
—Hindu teacher (unknown)

When the Holy Spirit awakens people... [they feel] trembling
which varies in its intensity. Occasionally I have been astounded
at the power and violence of the shaking...some people may seem
a little drunk...They may describe a "heaviness" that is on them.
—John White

The Aglow conference was over. Women were heading home
after a day of speakers, song and celebration. Two girls
laughed as one tripped and fell in the parking lot. She said she was
too drunk to drive, but that didn't stop her from getting behind
the wheel of her car and heading toward the highway with her
passengers. I didn't even think about calling the police, because I

knew she would blow "0." Her high was spiritual…some might even say "holy." She was drunk in the Spirit, a so-called manifestation of the presence of God.

Halfway around the globe another meeting was taking place at an ashram in India. The guru finished his short lecture and the drumming and singing began so people could dance and celebrate. A girl laughed as she began to feel giddy; she surrendered to the sensation and felt a heaviness fall upon her. She was drunk in the Spirit. Nearby, a man started jumping up and down like a pogo stick. The guru was pleased to see these *kriyas*, the name for manifestations of spiritual awakening in yoga practice.

GROWLS, TEARS AND LAUGHTER: WHAT DO THEY MEAN?

There are many different kriyas which may manifest when kundalini is awakened. Say yoga experts Stanislov and Christina Grof:

> individuals involved in this process [yoga] may find it difficult to control their behavior; during power rushes of Kundalini energy, they often emit various involuntary sounds, and their bodies move in strange and unexpected patterns. Among the most common manifestations…are unmotivated and unnatural laughter or crying, talking tongues…and imitating a variety of animal sounds and movements.[1]

Animal sounds, they said? Animal movements? But, the Toronto Airport Church is known worldwide for the barking of human dogs, the roaring of human lions and the crowing of human roosters. One charismatic pastor says that during their meetings:

> some people make noises that could be interpreted as animal-like during times of extreme intercession or

---

1. Stanislov and Christina Grof, *The Stormy Search for the Self,* 78-79, quoted in Larry Hall, "The Toronto Cursing is No Laughing Matter!" Sword of the Spirit Apologetics, *http://www.luciferlink.org/wtoro.htm,* 9.

spiritual travail. Others may be making certain sounds in obedience to the working of the Holy Spirit in their hearts during moments of intimacy with God, a phenomenon that defies rational explanation.[2]

The same manifestations attributed by yoga teachers to kundalini power are also attributed by charismatics to "Holy Spirit" power. In fact, every single manifestation listed by Stanislov and Christina Grof above—jerking, tongues, unmotivated weeping and laughter and the animal manifestations—have been reported at the Toronto church, Holy Trinity Brompton in England, the Brownsville Assembly, Pensacola, Florida and many other congregations advanced in TB practice.

The Grofs spoke of laughter, which is common in charismatic meetings as well. Mr. White calls it "holy laughter, the strange release from tension that some people experience, a wonderful thing when it is truly of the Spirit."[3] He says:

> I have heard people break into laughter when the Holy Spirit touches them, and they are astonishing to observe. The first time I encountered the phenomenon was in the notorious "Signs and Wonders" class at Fuller Seminary in 1984. Wimber had prayed that the Holy Spirit would equip a number of pastors and missionaries for the work God had called them to do. A South African pastor began to giggle and couldn't stop.[4]

Yoga teachers Stanislov and Christina Grof say kundalini also causes bodies to move in strange and unexpected patterns. But charismatics say these same manifestations are caused by the Holy Spirit. John White gives the following example of what happens when the "Holy Spirit" comes with power:

---

2. Richard Riss, interview with Pastor Wendell Smith, *www.anointed.net/Libraryroom/revival.*
3. White, 221.
4. White, 90.

a man's trunk may remain immobile, while the head may shake backward and forward (banging the wall behind in a regular rhythm if they should happen to be leaning against it). The arms, bent at the elbow, usually with palms facing the ground, flap violently up and down...[5]

KUNDALINI ARRIVES IN THE WEST

Yoga devotee Dorothy Bates, who believes she has found divine love, wrote a poem entitled "The Goddess Kundalini arrives in the West." She writes that kundalini:

> comes without warning, drunk and disorderly, hissing and spitting her bloody teeth into the air...She flings helpless bodies into a sea of jerks, grunts, belches; the growling and snarling of jungle beasts.[6]

Ms. Bates spoke of bodies being flung into a "sea of jerks." But Mr. White observed the same violent phenomena at charismatic gatherings, a phenomenon he also refers to as "the jerks."[7] He says:

> Trembling varies in its intensity. At times in public meetings people are seized with violent shaking. Occasionally I have been astounded at the power and violence of the shaking. Such people do not shake, but are shaken, like rag dolls in the teeth of a terrier.[8]

Helpless bodies "shaken like rag dolls"? Has the Goddess Kundalini arrived in the Christian church?

SPIRITUAL DRUNKENNESS, MILD TO EXTREME

Both charismatics and yoga practitioners also experience spiritual drunkenness as a result of their religious practices. From a yoga teacher:

---

5. White, 92.
6. Dorothy Bates, "The Goddess Kundalini Arrives in the West," *Spiritual Poetry by Dorothy Bates, http://www.kundalinni-support.com/poetry1.html.*
7. White, 93.
8. White, 92.

When you feel intoxicated without taking any drug, while
walking your steps fall majestically or like one drunk and
you are unable to do any other work and you like to
remain mute and dislike speaking to or hearing others and
you feel like one drunk of Divinity, know that your *Atma
Shakti* Kundalini, the power of *Self*, has come into action.[9]

And, a general pagan teaching on the joys of spiritual drunkenness:

Understanding that the term "drunkenness" has many
meanings is a good foundation for comprehending the
ecstatic ritual experience. One can be "drunk" with joy.[10]

Spiritual drunkenness is also a prominent feature of many
charismatic gatherings, where much is made of "the new wine." We
read earlier (chapter 1) from John White, "In meetings where the
Holy Spirit's power is strongly manifest, some people may seem a
little drunk." A little? Charismatics sometimes boast that they are
too drunk to drive. The following author acknowledges that
charismatic spiritual intoxication can be extreme; he, like the
pagan quoted above, understands this to be a manifestation of joy:

Drunkenness in the Holy Spirit is actually an extreme
form of joy!! One does not experience true joy unless one
is truly in God!! Therefore one must expect the more
extreme forms of drunkenness when actually filled with
the Holy Spirit of God![11]

Sometimes charismatics seem surprisingly irreverent, considering they believe they have discovered how to commune with

---

9. Cathy Woods, "Some Characteristic Symptoms of Awakened Kundalini,"
http://www.cit-sakti.com/kundalini/kundalini-manifestations.htm.
10. Moira H. Scott, "What Is Ecstatic Ritual? A Short Introduction,"
http://www.angelfire.com/ms3/caer_arianrhod/Ecstatic.htm.
11. posted at *www.//members.iinet.net.au./* .

almighty God. One charismatic rock group sings a song called "Drunk in the Spirit":

> I don't know whats happening
> but I'm really kinda drunk in the spirit…
> Cuz I be talking about the Great I am, My Savior
> The one who gets me drunk constantly
> I should be arrested for being under the influence of the
>   Word
> Spiritually hungover
> Got me throwing up by the curb…[12]
> (errors in original)

Note the reference to throwing up. Some call this "holy vomit." Then there is this testimony:

> And I have met many New Winers there… but can't remember most of them because I was so intoxicated!!!! (so please don't be offended!!!! HHHOOO!!!!!!!!!! hehe ahahhahaha)…… When not being dragged around, I'd spend up to five hours total on the very nice carpet!!!!!!!!!….. And there are various places around the church Paula does not take me if can possibly be avoided…. such as the archway!!!! HHOOO!!!!….. and the back area where they have soaking!!!!!….. and she tries to keep me from walking along the red lines (where they line up to be ministered to!!!!)…..!!!!! HOOO!!!!…. AHHH!!!! ZAP!!!!!!!!………[13]

Admittedly, these testimonies are extreme. Just about everyone realizes vomiting and debauchery are not holy. Scripture tells us the fruit of the Holy Spirit include peace, patience, gentleness and

---

12. T-bone, "Drunk in the Spirit" *www.letssingit.com/t-bone-drunk-in-the-spirit-nvpk11c.html.*

13. posted at *http://members.iinet.net.au/~gregga/toronto/testimonies/northamer-ica/na-on-2.html.*

self-control (Galatians 5:22). But it is important to realize that even those who experience less extreme symptoms of spiritual intoxication are practicing the same form of spirituality. The difference is one of degree, not of kind. Whether you are a little bit drunk or a whole lot drunk depends only on how much you have taken; it is all poured from the same cup.

ELECTRICAL PULSES: THE BITE OF THE SERPENT

Both pagans and charismatics report feeling electrical tingling or impulses. These range from pleasant to fierce. At the mild end of the spectrum John Wimber, one of the fathers of the TB movement, teaches that in a healing ministry one should look for tingling feelings, trembling of hands and a sense of anointing. I myself have felt these sensations and can testify they are real. However, this so-called "anointing" is not unique to charismatics. Tingling sensations, localized or all over the body, are classic symptoms of kundalini arousal. But it can get stronger than that; tingles can become surges of more powerful energy. A kundalini master who calls himself simply "Jafree" testified to a more powerful experience:

> Whether mild or extreme, all charismatic manifestations arise from the same spiritual practice. The practice is the real issue, not the extent or nature of the manifestations.

> At 23 years old I became introduced to the amazing force of energy in the body called the Kundalini. I was exploring and experimenting with focusing on the base of my spine and great surges of tremendous energy and awareness would pour through me.[14]

These stronger sensations can be unpleasant, even terrifying. Here are the words of a kundalini seeker I will call "The Energy

14. Jafree, "Who is Jafree? The Personal Life & Teachings of Jafree!" http://www.enlightenedbeings.com/about_jafree.html.

Ball Man," who experienced uncontrollable explosions of powerful energy when the serpent attacked with force:

> On May 5th 1999 the energy erupted waking me up…and
> with a great amount of energy it rocketed straight up to
> the brain, not traveling in the central channel, where it
> smashed through the block protecting the brain. I was ter-
> rified as I felt it momentarily explode in the whole
> brain…It was a very violent experience. The energy ball
> then went to another part of the body and came back to
> the brain exploding there twice again.[15]

Explosions in the brain! How frightening! But the fact is, there
are hundreds of similar testimonies from kundalini seekers on the
Web.

We might ask, does it ever get this extreme in a charismatic
church? The answer is yes. From the charismatic magazine, *God's
Manifest Presence*, we learn that worshipers experience:

> violent rolling, screaming…tingling… disruption of natu-
> ral realm, i.e. electrical circuits blown.[16]

Violence and screaming! Charismatics talk about electrical
circuits blown; pagans talk about explosions in the brain. What's
the difference?

Finally, see the complete list below of kundalini kriyas, compiled
by yoga teacher A. Mookerjee, and compare with the following col-
lection of "Holy Spirit" manifestations reported by charismatics, in
their own words, in *God's Manifest Presence*:

Yoga:
The ascent of Kundalini as it pierces through the chakras is
manifested in certain physical and psychic signs…the

---

15. "adsiwan," "When the Serpent Bites, Part 1," *http://www.kundalini-support.com/serpent.html, 4.*

16. *God's Manifest Presence,* see Randles, *Weighed,* 25.

numerous signs and symptoms that may be experienced by
the aspirant [include]: creeping sensations in the spinal
cord; tingling sensations all over the body...automatic and
involuntary laughing or crying; hearing unusual noises; seeing visions of deities or saints...the eyeballs roll upwards or
rotate; the body may bend forward or back, or even roll
around on the floor; breathing may be constricted...The
body may revolve or twist in all directions. Sometimes it
bounds up and down with crossed legs, or creeps about,
snake-like, on the floor...Some speak in tongues.
Sometimes the body feels as if it is floating upwards, and
sometimes as if it is being pressed down into the earth...It
may shake and tremble and become limp, or turn as rigid
as stone...There may be aches in the body, or a rise or drop
in temperature...inner lights and sounds, visions and
voices, and many other extraordinary experiences.[17]

Charismatic:
At times, the human spirit is so affected by the glory of
God, the human body is not capable of containing the
intensity of these spiritual encounters and strange physical
behaviour results...Following are phenomena that have
been observed in contemporary experience: shaking, jerking, loss of bodily strength, heavy breathing, eyes flutter-
ing, lips trembling...weeping...hearing audibly into the
spirit realm, inspired utterances – i.e. prophecy,
tongues...angelic visitations and manifestations, jumping,
violent rolling, screaming, wind, heat, electricity, cold-
ness...tingling, pain in body as discernment of illness, feeling heavy weight or lightness, trances, altered physical state
while seeing into the spiritual world, inability to speak
normally, disruption of natural realm, i.e. electrical circuits blown.[18]

---

17. Ajit Mookerjee, *Kundalini: the Arousal of the Inner Energy* (New York: Destiny
    Books, 1982), 71-72.
18. from *God's Manifest Presence*, quoted by Randles, *Weighed*, 24-25.

It is plain to see that yoga and charismatic practitioners have spiritual experiences that are virtually identical.

Shared kriyas even include weightlessness, culminating in feats of levitation by Hindu gurus, and the converse: a sense of a great weight pressing a person to the floor, called "holy glue" by charismatics.

IMPARTATION SUPERSTARS

The transfer of spiritual "power" through people traveling between churches is a further well-documented phenomenon in charismatic circles. Toronto Blessing (TB) power can be passed from one person to another, and in this way has literally traveled around the globe. The Microwave Preacher explained what happened after a member of his congregation returned from a visit to the Toronto Airport Church:

> Unusual things began to happen; for instance, one man broke out in a dance – it embarrassed his wife. But Tom started to laugh, because these people had no model for their behavior, it was spontaneous. The "blessing" was transportable, it appeared…Then we started open meetings…soon 300 people or more would come out, three nights a week. Not long after that, the blessing was transported from here to Campbell River.[19]

Pastor Randles, who went to Toronto to see for himself, wrote:

> Impartation seems to be another significant word and I must say, it is impartation that I see as being one of the most alarming aspects of this. By impartation, I mean the ability to pass it on, usually by laying on of hands. This is the strongest and most alarming characteristic…Mystical experiences are imparted to ministers who return to their

---

19. David Hixson, interview by Jack Krayenhoff, "Whatever happened to the 'Toronto Blessing'?" *Sunday Magazine*, June 2003, *sundaymagazine.org*.

churches and revel in this newly found mystical power. The Spirit that is working in this move, won't be limited to the laying on of hands either, many are "getting it" just standing in services, overcome by shaking, laughing, weeping…[20]

Pastor Randles noted that many people at Toronto were "getting it" just standing there, without even receiving a touch. Toronto Blessing superstars like Benny Hinn (widely known through television and world tours) and Rodney Howard-Browne have been known to impart spiritual power by blowing on a crowd, waving a sweater or by verbally calling for it. But, so it is also with kundalini superstars. One pagan organization notes:

> The power to transmit shaktipat resides in a celibate saint. Shaktipat can be given by such a saint by his touch, his speech, his look, through an object, by his thought or wish, or in a dream.[21]

Another writer says:

> There are several methods to awaken Kundalini. The most conventional method will normally require years of serious practice. However, if you can get help from someone whose Kundalini is already awakened and the cleansing process has already reached a certain point, that person will be able to help you.[22]

Further, both yogis and charismatics train disciples in how to "pass on," awaken or impart a "blessing." Teachers of a popular New Age "healing art" called Kundalini Reiki give instruction in

20. Randles, *Weighed,* 21.
21. Sacred Word Trust, "shaktpat info."
22. "Awakening the Sleeping Kundalini," *http://www.geocities.com/HotSprings/Villa/1555/bab1.htm#awakening.*

transfer techniques.[23] Likewise, charismatic organizations initiate and train their own prayer teams. Guests at charismatic gatherings are instructed to only pray with team members who are trained in TB impartation techniques.

TRAVELING FOR THE BLESSING

People travel to meetings from far and wide to receive both shaktipats and TB blessings. At Hindu meetings, devotees are sometimes said to be seeking *darshan*, or a glimpse of the world hidden beyond the visible senses. In a similar manner, charismatics call their meetings "gatherings of the prophetic," meaning that God's hidden truth is being revealed through their experiences.

Earlier we saw a pagan advertisement, calling devotees to attend a meeting to receive a kundalini blessing, which said, "come to this rare and special evening with Grand Master Choa Kok Sui...We shall request him to give a Shakti Pat to each attendee. One Shakti Pat from him is equal to 20 years of spiritual practice...WOW!" So it is also with charismatics. Carol Arnott writes of a woman who travels repeatedly from Japan to receive blessings at the Toronto Airport Church:

> Not long ago a woman from Japan visited TACF. She had been a prostitute, but Jesus found her, touched and healed her, and set her on fire for Him. She is now a pastor...she pastors a downtown church in a large city ministering powerfully in the Spirit. She came to Toronto repeatedly to be filled with the Spirit, and returned to give it out.[24]

This woman travels to a meeting halfway around the globe, and returns to Japan to impart spirit power to others! We must ask, is this really biblical? Many think so. The following enthusiast likens

---

23. E.g., at *www.reikiblessings.homestead.com* Stephanie Thompson, "certified Holistic Nursing Consultant and Intuitive Healer" offers courses leading to the title of Kundalini Reiki Master, including initiation and training to transfer kundalini power.

24. Carol Arnott, "Women."

the dispensation of power in the Toronto church to going to a bar for a spiritual boost:

> And if you feel led to do so, go and check it out for yourself some time. In fact, you may need to go a couple of times in order to capture the essence of this movement of spiritual renewal. I am not advocating that people leave their own churches …but [I hope that] many people will use it as I do—as an occasional supplement to the events in our own church, or as one speaker put it, a cocktail bar where people can obtain spiritual refreshment with pre-mixed drinks courtesy of the Holy Spirit…[25]

But Pastor Randles points out that it is unbiblical for a Christian to be required to travel to another location in order to receive spiritual blessings. If it were really necessary, poor pastors would be unable to "obtain" a blessing for their congregations because they couldn't afford the airfare.

The truth is that pilgrimages to "holy places," or to sit at the feet of empowered gurus, are part of other faith practices, not true Christianity. Indeed, when we look to Scripture, we see in the Old Testament that apostate Israelites repeatedly gathered at specific locations, called high places, to worship other gods. However, this was forbidden by God; it was the practice of the nations, but was not for God's children.

And as it was then, so it should be now for those who follow Scripture. In true Christianity, no significance is ascribed to particular locations for worship. Whether it happens in a church, a home or a prison, true worship is no less authentic or powerful. After all, the disciples rejoiced and praised God while they were bound in iron and shackles. William LaSor explains:

> Jesus denied the view that worship was either limited to a particular place, or more advantageous if performed at a certain place. When the woman of Samaria raised the

---

25. Brown, posted at *home.echo-on.net/gcbrown/torbless.*

question by saying, "Our fathers worshiped on this mountain; and you say that in Jerusalem is the place where men
ought to worship," Jesus replied, "The hour is coming when
neither on this mountain nor in Jerusalem will you worship
the Father...the true worshipers will worship the Father in
spirit and truth" (cf. John 4:20-24)... Law was a matter of
the spirit and intent of the heart, and not mere ritual.
Worship was a matter of spirit and truth, not geography.[26]

Seeking spirit at high places

If worship has nothing to do with geography and empowered
leaders, what spirits are charismatics meeting with during their
meetings? I asked this question of a kundalini yoga enthusiast, a
woman I will call Mysteria. She told me that she believes charismatic leaders are triggering kundalini in the crowd.

In the course of my research Mysteria granted me a lengthy
interview to which I will refer several times in the coming pages.
She told me she herself experienced a spontaneous kundalini
awakening while alone, the beginning of a spiritual journey which
led her to leave her husband and children to pursue "the force of
grace." Mysteria has practiced and studied yoga extensively and is
considered an accomplished mystic.

Mysteria told me she has heard about charismatic evangelists
who, as she put it, "get a field of people together, work them up,
and use a variety of methods to awaken kundalini energies." In
her view, charismatics are triggering the serpent force in ways
which could endanger participants. It would be difficult, she told
me, for the average person not to be swept away by the "energies
released," especially when the leaders "bang the third eye" [that is,
forehead].

The fact is that the charismatic practice of assembling people
together to call down spiritual power is also common among
Hindu practitioners, other mystics and even magicians; the larger
the group, the better. Magician Aleister Crowley (see Chapter 11)

---

26. William Sanford LaSor, *Men Who Knew Christ: Great Personalities of the New
Testament,* 2nd ed. (Glendale, CA: G/L Regal Books: 1971), 79-80.

wrote that "there is no doubt that an assemblage of persons who really are in harmony can much more easily produce an effect than a Magician working by himself."[27] Somehow, large gatherings of people enable spirits to manifest. Explains another writer:

> the spirits require a place consecrated for concentration on communications from them. They desire to give their proofs to believers. They require unity of thought and intention.[28]

When it comes to invoking mystic power it seems to be a case of the more, the merrier.

THE AGE OF AQUARIUS

A further similarity between yogis and charismatics is that with time and practice both learn to control their spiritual experiences. Samadhi becomes more easily attainable for shakti saints, and so does soaking for experienced charismatics. In my former church, TB old-timers consistently fell down within seconds of receiving a forehead touch, apparently in a trance state. They said God "always came through" for them.

Further, both yogis and charismatics believe that it is becoming easier for people everywhere to attain mystic states and attune themselves with spiritual "realities." Why? Because, they believe, a new age is upon us. Pagans call it the "Age of Aquarius." Charismatics call it the "latter rain" or "Third Wave."

Both yogis and charismatics perceive similar divine purposes in the dawning of this new age. Pagans teach that in the Age of Aquarius, mankind is evolving to a higher level of consciousness, "vibration" or oneness with God. Charismatics teach that God is moving powerfully now to bring revival and perfect His church for the return of Jesus.

---

27. Aleister Crowley, *Magick,* quoted in Thomas W. Friend, *Fallen Angel: The Untold Story of Jimmy Page and Led Zeppelin* (Titusville, FL: Gabriel Publications, 2002), 481.
28. Thomas W. Friend, *Fallen Angel: The Untold Story of Jimmy Page and Led Zeppelin* (Titusville, FL: Gabriel Publications, 2002), 481.

Following is a typical pagan teaching about the Age of Aquarius:

> awakening Kundalini was not easy in the past. Many
> people spent tens of years simply to awaken their
> Kundalini…and it was simply the starting point. The
> cleansing and purification processes themselves needed
> much longer time than to awaken Kundalini…As
> Aquarian time approaches, this is no longer the case…The
> whole cleansing and purification processes can be com-
> pleted within years.[29]

Mysteria told me that kundalini awakenings are more common now, as mankind evolves to a higher consciousness. Her
belief is that in earlier times "energies" were "heavier" and it was
harder to "break through." But now, she says, secrets formerly hidden from all but a special few are being generally revealed, a sign
of the Age of Aquarius.

Charismatics also believe that things formerly hidden are now
being revealed. Self-proclaimed charismatic prophet Sandy
Warner posted the following on his Web site:

> "Winds of change, Winds of change," saith the Lord. "For I
> am releasing mighty winds of change from the four cor-
> ners of the Earth, for the demolition of the old for the
> rebuilding of the new. *Winds of change for the uncovering
> of the hidden,* winds for deliverance, winds for consecra-
> tion, and winds for sanctification."[30] (emphasis added)

Similar charismatic teachings reveal Age of Aquarius thinking,
such as the idea that God is presently pouring out new wine in
more powerful worship, and that God in these last days will give
increased power and grace to His servants:

---

29. "What is Kundalini?"
    http://www.geocities.com/HotSprings/Villa/1555/bab1,htm#whatiskundalini.
30. Sandy Warner, posted at *http://www.thequickenedword.com.*

> We've entered days where it's absolutely necessary to be
> able to Hear GOD's Voice for ourselves... It's time to go in
> and take the land...With GOD's LOVE we're Opening Up
> to His Majesty and Releasing this Great Treasure to the
> world (PS31). We've been hidden long enough... we'll see
> the Release of an Era of Conquering Grace (PS38).[31]

And charismatics believe that now, as never before, God is giving revelations of truth:

> the company of prophets is the key that God has inserted
> into the lock of the Church to open up new revelation of
> the times for truth restoration and fulfillment in the
> Church...The prophetic and apostolic voice being added
> to the Church will begin to intensify both world evange-
> lization and His perfecting work within His Church...[32]

End times power and perfection?

Many charismatics teach that the Christian church will become more powerful—indeed, perfect—in the days before Jesus returns, with the help of so-called "New Order Apostles and Prophets." But what does the Bible teach? Will there be a final dawn to perfect and strengthen the church in the last days? No, quite the opposite; the church will be largely apostate. One author explains:

> the false Pentecostal concept of a "latter rain revival" [is]
> the idea that Christ's return will be preceded by an end-
> times signs and wonders movement that will restore the
> supernatural gifts of the first century and will purify "the
> church." Latter rain theology has taken many different
> forms, some more radically unscriptural than others, but
> "latter rain" theology in one form or another has been

---

31. "Enter the Elijah Mantle" posted at *http://pub35.ezboard.comm/bigulp.*
32. Bill Hamon, *Prophets and the Prophetic Movement: God's Prophetic Move Today* (Santa Rosa Beach, FL: Destiny Image, 1990), 34-35.

accepted by practically every aspect of the Pentecostal-Charismatic movement throughout the century. The "latter rain" doctrine is built upon a faulty interpretation of Acts 2:17-21 and Joel 2:28-29 and a confusion of the dispensations of God's sovereign purposes. Pentecostal teachers believe that Joel's prophecy was partially fulfilled during Pentecost and the Apostolic miracles of the first century and that it is being further fulfilled in the 20th century Pentecostal movement, with its alleged miracle gifts and "signs and wonders"…[But] The New Testament Scripture does not prophesy a revival of truth and biblical evangelism at the end of this age; it prophesies religious confusion and error.[33]

Despite the hope of many who look forward to a time of enlightenment, the Age of Aquarius is not good news. It heralds an age of deception.

---

33. *Way of Life Literature*, "Confusion about the Latter Rain," *http://www.wayoflife.org/fbns/endtimesconfusion.htm.*

Chapter Four

True Light, or False?

The lamp of the body is the eye. If therefore your eye is good, your whole body will be full of light. But if your eye is bad, your whole body will be full of darkness. If therefore the light that is in you is darkness, how great is that darkness!

—Jesus the Christ (Matthew 6:22-23)

Christian Scriptures have much to say about light and darkness, and always this has to do with human spirituality. When we do not know the truth about spiritual matters, we are said to be blind, or walking in darkness. If we know the truth, we are said to be walking in the light: we see, albeit only dimly so long as we remain in our earthly bodies.

The Bible teaches that there are two sources of spiritual light. One is true, the other is false. The true light calls to men and women, to show the way and help them see. The other light seems true, but in the end it only leads to darkness.

All of Scripture resounds with the message that we must be sure we have found the true light. Our eternal destiny depends upon it. Our very souls hang in the balance.

Ancient religions:
worship of the serpent and "the Light"

Before Jesus came into the world, even before the Old Testament was written, ancient people worshiped the "Light" and a god they sometimes called Lucifer, meaning "Light Bearer." They also worshiped the sun together with serpents, lizards and dragons, all of which were considered symbols of wisdom then just as they are now to Hindus and those who seek truth in ancient religions. The association of the serpent with the sun seems to be that just as the sun gives physical light to the world, so the serpent god was believed to bring spiritual light—enlightenment—to mankind.

But was—and is—the serpent god really deserving of worship and veneration? Did he—and does he—bring enlightenment?

The Holy Bible provides the answer.

Scriptural teaching on the serpent god

Genesis is the first book of Christian Holy Scripture, having been written about 1,500 years B.C. From Genesis right on through to the close of the New Testament we learn that Lucifer, the serpent god, is really Satan. We learn that his light is deceptive. And we are warned that his light brings death, not wisdom or enlightenment. The Bible is, among other things, God's warning to mankind about the reality and danger of the serpent.

Scripture calls Satan by the same names as ancient worshipers did, including "Lucifer," "the dragon" and "the serpent," so readers can clearly understand who is intended.[1] This usage, together with the identification of Satan as the serpent in the Garden of Eden, clearly identifies Satan and Lucifer as one and the same.

Other biblical names for the serpent god add to our understanding about him. He is called the "devil," a derivative word meaning "little god." He is a celestial being with great power, identified as the "god of this world"; a spirit who holds sway over the Earth, its inhabitants and a horde of inferior spirits. The name "Satan" signifies that he is God's adversary. We learn that

---

1. The name "Lucifer" was apparently not used by the original authors, but was introduced later into biblical tradition through the translation of Jerome's *Vulgate*.

the serpent comes to rob, steal and destroy, inflicting evil both upon God's creation and upon His people.[2]

Scripture tells us that the serpent is "the father of lies," and that there is nothing good in him. He is the consummate deceiver, a false god who assumes the disguise of an "angel of light," something holy and good. And by pretending to be angelic, holy and good, Lucifer has been leading unwitting people into spiritual darkness for many centuries.

It was into this darkness—a world led astray by the angel of light—that God spoke. First He spoke to the Jews through Moses, the Torah and the prophets. Now He has spoken to the world through Jesus the Christ.

Jesus came because God purposed to bring true light through Him. About 700 years before He was even born, the prophet Isaiah foretold His coming as the Messiah who would bring true light to all peoples, Jews and Gentiles alike. Through Isaiah, God said:

> I, the Lord, have called You [Jesus] in righteousness, and will hold Your hand; I will keep You and give You as a covenant to the people, as a light to the Gentiles, to open blind eyes, to bring out prisoners from the prison, those who sit in darkness from the prison house (42:6-7).

JESUS IS THE TRUE LIGHT, A BEAUTIFUL LIGHT

Before Jesus began His ministry another prophet, John the Baptist, proclaimed to the people who lived in those incredible times that the kingdom of God was at hand. Scriptures tell us that John the Baptist:

> came for a witness, to bear witness of the Light, that all through him might believe. He was not that Light, but was sent to bear witness of that Light. That was the true Light which gives light to every man who comes into the world (John 1:7-9).

---

2. Yet all this happens under the watchful eye of Jehovah, the infinitely more powerful God of Israel, who permits evil for a time, and for purposes we cannot fully understand.

The man sent from God was, of course, Jesus, who said of Himself:

> I am the light of the world. He who follows Me shall not
> walk in darkness, but have the light of life (John 8:12).

Notice that the verses quoted above made frequent use of the word "light." The Greek word translated "light" here is *phos*, from the root *phao* meaning "to shine" or "make manifest." The word *phos* was also used by Gospel writers in the following passages about the light of Jesus:

> I have come as a light into the world, that whoever believes
> in Me should not abide in darkness (John 12:46).

> In Him was life, and the life was the light of men (John 1:4).

> The people who sat in darkness saw a great light, and
> upon those who sat in the region and shadow of death
> light has dawned (Matthew 4:16).

What is the significance of the *phos* light that Scripture associates with Jesus? Thayer's Greek-English lexicon explains that *phos* means an "extremely delicate, subtle, pure, brilliant quality of light...being by nature incorporeal, spotless and holy." The *phos* light of Jesus is a supremely pure spiritual light.

THE SERPENT'S LIGHT SEEMS "BEAUTIFUL" TOO

We have seen that Satan is a powerful spirit who also purports to bring spiritual light, but that his light is false, and conceals an evil nature and evil intentions. The Bible describes how this evil being disguises himself in one brief verse:

> Satan himself transforms himself into an angel of light
> (2 Corinthians 11:14).

The New International Version puts it as follows:

> Satan himself masquerades as an angel of light.

What, then, do we need to understand about the false light of Satan? How does it compare with the light of Jesus? And how can we tell the difference between the false and the true?

It is important to realize that the Greek word used in the verses above to describe Satan's light is the same word used to describe the light of Jesus: *phos*. What can it mean that the same word describes both the light of Jesus and the light of Satan? Does it not seem almost blasphemous? Yes, indeed, but we must remember that Satan is the ultimate blasphemer.

The description of Lucifer's light as *phos* light can only mean one thing; namely, that he can transform himself so he appears to be as beautiful as Jesus. He comes bearing *phos* light which seems like the spotless, holy light of God—just as brilliant and just as pure.

> The name "Lucifer"—light bearer—describes Satan well. He comes bearing *phos* light, seemingly beautiful and holy.

We need to understand that when Satan wants to disguise himself to seem like a pure and life-giving spirit, he can and he will. The light he brings will seem like Jesus' light. In other words, the light of Satan compares so well with the light of Jesus that we perceive no distinguishing qualities.

Indeed, the teachings of Scripture, and the experience of mankind through the ages, together lead to only one conclusion: Men and women are by nature incapable of recognizing true light, or of distinguishing the false from the true.

SATAN: THE SUM AND PERSONIFICATION OF BEAUTY

wRong wAys = P59.
RighT wAys = P75.

Scripture does not provide a lot of information about the history and person of Satan. However, we do learn that at one time Satan was like a "bright morning star," the sum and personification of beauty and highly esteemed in a heavenly kingdom:

> You were the seal of perfection, full of wisdom and perfect in beauty. You were in Eden, the garden of God; every precious stone was your covering... (Ezekiel 28:12-13).

We also learn that through pride and iniquity Satan fell from his high position and God cast him out of heaven. He took about a third of the angels—now called "fallen angels"—with him. Though no longer perfect and beautiful, Satan is still able to assume an appearance of perfection and beauty, and to manifest qualities of apparently holy *phos* light. He also possesses two other qualities in great measure: craft and wickedness. It is by the appearance of beauty that Satan seduces the nations, but it is by craft and wickedness that he destroys them.

It is difficult for mere man to understand how darkness can seem like light. At the same time, however, it makes sense that a powerful evil being who wants us to worship him will disguise his true nature. Must he not pretend to bring peace and joy and love? Must he not assume an appearance of divinity, provoke adoration and even work miraculous signs? If he does not, how can he hope to earn our worship?

Scripture indicates Satan can and will do these things. He comes in many different ways and through different teachers. Many of these teachers will appear to love God, and will do good works; furthermore, nothing in Scripture indicates that they are necessarily insincere. Many are deceived. The apostle Paul said, "Therefore it is no great thing if [Satan's] ministers also transform themselves into ministers of righteousness..." (2 Corinthians 11:15), and "The coming of the lawless one is according to the working of Satan, with all power, signs and lying wonders" (2 Thessalonians 2:9). He warned that many people, including Christians, will fall prey to false teaching and Satan's miracles: "many false prophets will rise up and deceive many" (Matthew 24:11), and "false christs and false prophets will rise and show great signs and wonders, so as to deceive, if possible, even the elect" (Matthew 24:24-25).[3]

LET US NOT MARVEL AT THIS

In his letter to the Corinthians, Paul indicates it is no wonder, no marvel, that Satan comes as an angel of light. We should not

---

3. Even if this prophecy was specifically intended for the period before the fall of Jerusalem in 70 A.D., still the Bible teaches clearly that false prophets and teachers will plague the church.

be surprised that this evil spirit will feign holiness, that he will pretend to love and worship God, or that he will cause his servants to pretend the same. Bible scholar Albert Barnes wrote:

> he who is an apostate angel; who is malignant and wicked; who is the prince of evil, assumes the appearance of a holy angel. Paul assumes this as an indisputable and admitted truth, without attempting to prove it, and without referring to any particular instances. Probably he had in his eye cases where Satan put on false and delusive appearances for the purpose of deceiving, or where he assumed the appearance of great sanctity and reverence for the authority of God... The phrase "an angel of light," means a pure and holy angel – light being the emblem of purity and holiness. Such are all the angels that dwell in heaven; and the idea is, that Satan assumes such a form as to appear to be such an angel. Learn here,
>
> (1) His power. He can *assume* such an aspect as he pleases. He can dissemble, and appear to be eminently pious. He is the prince of duplicity as well as of wickedness; and it is the consummation of bad power for an individual to be able to assume any character which he pleases.
>
> (2) His art. He is long practiced in deceitful arts. For six thousand years he has been practicing the art of delusion; and with him it is perfect.
>
> (3) We are not to suppose that all that *appears* to be piety is piety. Some of the most plausible appearances of piety are assumed by Satan and his ministers. None ever professed a profounder regard for the authority of God than Satan did when he tempted the Savior. And if the prince of wickedness can *appear* to be an angel of light, we are not to be surprised if those who have the blackest hearts appear to be men of most eminent piety.
>
> (4) We should be on our guard. We should not listen to suggestions merely because they *appear* to come from a pious man, nor because they *seem* to be prompted by a

regard to the will of God. We may be *always* sure that if we are to be tempted, it will be by someone having a great appearance of virtue and religion.

(5) We are not to expect that Satan will *appear* to man to be as bad as he is. He never shows himself openly to be a spirit of pure wickedness; or black and abominable in his character; or full of evil, and hateful. He would thus defeat himself. (all emphasis original)[4]

This carefully articulated warning is one we need to take very seriously.

Take care that you have found the true Light

The Bible tells us that the serpent will deceive many. Now, as in times past, men and women from all faiths and nations will fail to understand the truth, for the light shines in the darkness, but the darkness cannot understand it.

Jesus warned us to be sure the light we follow is true because the dangers of the false light are great indeed, with consequences for all eternity. He said, "Therefore take heed that the light which is in you is not darkness" (Luke 11:35), and, "If therefore the light that is in you is darkness, how great is that darkness!" (Matthew 6:22-23). Peter explained that we must be self-controlled and alert, "because your adversary the devil walks about like a roaring lion, seeking whom he may devour" (1 Peter 5:8). Lucifer is an ever-present, artful foe; the enemy of our souls who wants to seduce us into darkness and love us to death.

But where does this leave us, if we are unable to distinguish between true and false spiritual light? Aware of the danger but unable to avoid it? No, it cannot be! A merciful God would never simply abandon us to the devices of the serpent without guidance or advice, would He?

---

4. Albert Barnes, *Barnes Notes on the New Testament,* 8th ed. (Grand Rapids, MI: Kregel Publications, 1975), 895.

Chapter Five

WRONG WAYS TO SEEK GOD;
THE PURSUIT OF
PRESENCE AND POWER

And the person who turns after mediums and familiar spirits, to prostitute himself with them, I will set My face against that person and cut him off from his people. Sanctify yourselves therefore, and be holy, for I am the Lord your God. And you shall keep My statutes, and perform them: I am the Lord who sanctifies you.

—Leviticus 20:6-8

One day, when I was a new believer meeting with leaders who followed "new wine" practices, we prayed for the presence of the Holy Spirit. The atmosphere in the room was pregnant with promise. Someone explained that we were "waiting for a break." By that she meant the "breaking" of a loving, spiritual presence over us. And it came. I walked on cloud nine all day, grateful for the goodness of God and His mercy to me. How faithful He is! I thought. Another time, singing an invitation to the Holy Spirit with these same people, I experienced such a sweet visitation I became angry when someone spoke and destroyed the feeling.

I had many similar experiences, not doubting for one moment that in all these encounters I was meeting with God through the

Holy Spirit. Had anyone suggested otherwise, I would have regarded him with pity. The idea seemed absurd because the spirit felt holy, beautiful beyond description, and it moved my heart to love, peace and compassion for other people.

But then I learned about kundalini yoga. I realized that yoga seekers and gurus have similar, if not identical, experiences, and similar sweet spiritual communion. I began to lurch between sickening doubts and rejection of those doubts for fear they were blasphemous. Filled with confusion and despair, I cried out to God. This mystery was beyond me.

Please understand, I know God fills our hearts with love. My heart raced and swelled when I first came to know Him, and I could hardly believe my joy. He really is the God who sheds His love abroad in our hearts, and I do not dismiss the reality of supernatural love in Christian experience. The problem is not to know *if* God fills our hearts with His love. Of course He does. The problem is *how to distinguish between God's love and the sweet satanic counterfeit, and how to recognize other counterfeit gifts also.* I did not really understand how to "test the spirits." Neither did anyone else, so far as I could tell.

As I prayed and prayed about this I refused to believe that God would leave us without an answer. "There has to be a way," I thought, "to avoid deception in something so important for every believer." I pleaded, I wept and I argued for understanding. And I believe God has led me to the answer. It is remarkably simple, and I long to share it with you.

The simple answer

First, we can never, never test the spirits by how they feel or appear. We cannot test them by experiencing their loveliness or holiness because, as we saw in chapter 4, both Satan and Jesus are bearers and bestowers of *phos* light. Nor can we test the spirits by how godly the teacher or spiritual leader seems to be, because Scriptures say Satan's servants also appear righteous. No, the correct way is to test all things against biblical standards for spiritual *teaching* and spiritual *practice*. Pastor Randles explains:

Test the spirits, John cautions us; don't just accept every prophecy, apostle, "word" or movement that comes along; think critically. The word for test in Greek is *dokimazein*, which means to think or examine. The word for spirit is *pneuma*, which means wind. In other words, test every spiritual thing critically; every influence, minister, teaching and prophecy; evaluate them all in the light of the Word of truth, as well as in the light and the love of God. Why? *"Because many false prophets have gone out into the world."*[1] (emphasis original)

Believers must guard first *the teachings they receive about God,* and second, they must guard their *practice,* meaning *the ways they seek God.*

However, it isn't always easy to discern good teaching from bad. What we believe—that is, the doctrine we accept—can be difficult to explain, and certain issues will always be disputable. People have different levels of ability and desire to master doctrine, for we do not all receive the same gifts. I do not want to diminish our responsibility to develop understanding and discernment; however, the fact is that some of us are more vulnerable to deception, and ideology is one of Satan's favorite playgrounds. Ideas are easily manipulated and truth can be mimicked in false but convincing ways, by teachers who may or may not be sincere. Words are often capable of several interpretations, so the bad sneaks in with the good. As C.S. Lewis once said, Satan will tell us nine truths to get us to accept one lie. Alas, how many miss the one lie! Does only one lie really matter? Yes. That's why Satan can afford the nine truths.

But although it can be difficult to identify right teaching, fortunately it is easier to identify right practice.

Right practice is foundational to walking with God. We must learn to follow the ways He sets for us, and avoid those He prohibits. When we understand what right practice is and how to

---

1. Bill Randles, *Mending the Nets: Themes from 1st John* (Cambridge, Great Britain: St. Matthews Publishing, 2000), 91.

avoid wrong practice, we will find shelter under His wing; there we are safe, there we abide in His love, and there—and this is key—we avoid all risk of counterfeit *phos* light experiences and certain other spiritual deceptions.

NEGLECTED PRACTICE COMMANDS

God forbids certain religious practices, practices He calls those "of the nations." Throughout the Old Testament, He pleaded with ancient Israel to reject the religious practices of the Moabites, Canaanites, Egyptians and others who surrounded the Jews. Their ways were occult and mystic, and included idol worship, divination, witchcraft, following after false prophets and meeting at high places.

We discover from the Bible that God expects—indeed, pleads with—His people to practice differently. He taught godly ways to ancient Israel through ceremonial laws that governed worship and all religious practices: They were strict, exclusive and avoided mysticism and the occult entirely.

But the Jews neglected God's practice commands and followed the ways of the nations. As a result, they fell from His protection and favor.

Like ancient Israel we also must be careful to follow God's ways. The ceremonial requirements of the Old Covenant have passed away, but they are symbolic of the continuing importance to all believers to follow right practices and keep themselves spiritually pure. Right practice sets God's children apart from the nations and keeps them in His favor.

THE "HOW" OF SEEKING GOD

"Spiritual" or "religious" practice has to do with *how* we get to know God, *how* we learn His truth and *how* we worship and commune with Him. He has set the way for us, and keeping His commands for spiritual practice is as important as keeping His moral commandments:

> He who keeps the commandment keeps his soul, but he who is careless of his ways will die (Proverbs 19:16).

If practice is key, we need to make sure we have the right keys so we can open the right doors. We must also learn to recognize the doors beyond which we must never set foot, the doors that must stay shut.

The injunction against the occult

Jehovah God absolutely forbids occult practice. It is clear from Old Testament writings that the prohibition against the occult was extremely important to God, and it must therefore be important to us, too. Later in this chapter we will consider the meaning of "occult" in greater depth. For now, let's review God's commands in this area.

Moses clearly, frequently and vehemently warned the Jews to avoid the occult. He explained that occult ways were a snare which awaited the Israelites in the lands they were about to enter, saying:

> When the Lord your God cuts off from before you the nations which you go to dispossess, and you displace them and dwell in their land, take heed to yourself that you are not ensnared to follow them, after they are destroyed from before you, and that you do not inquire after their gods, saying, "How did these nations serve their gods? I also will do likewise"…Whatever I command you, be careful to observe it; you shall not add to it nor take away from it (Deuteronomy 12:29-30,32).

Here Moses is talking about spiritual practice, that is, about *how* people seek and worship God. Obviously, it is possible to seek and worship Him the wrong way, after the style of the nations. Moses said, don't do it! He repeats this injunction frequently and in many different ways to help the Israelites—and us—understand. Here is another example:

> When you come into the land which the Lord your God is giving you, you shall not learn to follow the abominations of those nations. There shall not be found among you anyone who makes his son or his daughter pass through the

fire, or one who practices witchcraft, or a soothsayer, or
one who interprets omens, or a sorcerer, or one who con-
jures spells, or a medium, or a spiritist, or one who calls
up the dead (Deuteronomy 18:9-11).

The New English Bible translation of these verses is helpful. It
describes forbidden practices as "trafficking in spirits":

When you come into the land which the Lord your God is
giving you, do not learn to imitate the abominable customs
of those other nations. Let no one be found among
you...[an] augur or soothsayer or diviner or sorcerer, no
one who casts spells or trafficks with ghosts and spirits, and
no necromancer (Deuteronomy 18:9-11).

As we shall see, all mystic and occult practices involve trafficking in spirits.

Defilement

Scripture makes it abundantly clear that occult practices are defiling. This is declared in numerous passages, such as, Leviticus 19:31:

Give no regard to mediums and familiar spirits; do not seek
after them, to be defiled by them: I am the Lord your God.

The NEB translates this verse as follows:

Do not resort to ghosts and spirits, nor make yourselves
unclean by seeking them out. I am the Lord your God.

From this verse we learn two things. First, Scripture draws a
clear line between seeking God and seeking spirits. These are two
different things, two different spiritual practices; and God *cannot
be found along with ghosts and spirits in occult practice* because He,
not they, is our God. He and they must remain separate; He is
holy, they are unclean.

Second, we learn that occult activities defile us. The Hebrew
root word translated "defile" means "to be foul" in both ceremonial

(having to do with religious practice) and moral ways. To be ceremonially foul is to be unfit, and hence unable, to commune with God. To participate in the occult disqualifies a person from communing with God. Therefore, whatever spirit one meets with in occult practice, we can be sure it is not God or the Holy Spirit, and that it is not godly. We test such a spirit by how it has been contacted, not by how it feels or by how it speaks to us. We know that if it comes through the occult, it simply cannot be of God. No further enquiry is necessary.

Additionally, we learn from Scripture that to engage in forbidden practices is to be unfaithful to God—a form of spiritual prostitution or adultery:

> And the person who turns after mediums and familiar spirits, to prostitute himself with them, I will set My face against that person and cut him off from his people. Sanctify yourselves therefore, and be holy, for I am the Lord your God (Leviticus 20:6,7).

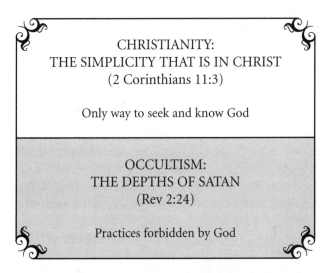

CHRISTIANITY:
THE SIMPLICITY THAT IS IN CHRIST
(2 Corinthians 11:3)

Only way to seek and know God

OCCULTISM:
THE DEPTHS OF SATAN
(Rev 2:24)

Practices forbidden by God

Christianity draws a sharp line between godly and
occult practices, a line believers must not cross.

If we are to serve as earthly temples for the Holy Spirit and as the bride of Christ, we must keep ourselves pure. This means the same for us as it meant for the Jews: We must avoid the practices of the nations, occult practices, which involve flirting with the supernatural, trafficking with spirits and defiling our souls.

WHAT'S SO TERRIBLE ABOUT THE OCCULT?

Scripture teaches that behind mysticism and the occult lie Satan and his demons. Occult practice is the key that opens the door to this evil god and his fallen angels. When we dabble in the occult, we invite demons into our lives; even Satan who can masquerade as an angel of light.

The nature of demons

We learn from numerous biblical accounts that evil spirits have access to our minds, hearts and body to tempt, influence or control us in varying measures. We will probably never know in this life the ways in which we are subject to their influence. However, we learn from Scripture that demons are responsible for some diseases and mental illnesses. They suggest thoughts to our minds. They may gain control of us if and when we have given them a foothold; for example, by repeatedly giving in to temptation, accepting false teaching, taking psychotropic drugs or, in extreme cases, by making pacts with them. One or more demons can completely possess a person, causing madness and ruin.

Biblical accounts provide some clues to demonic influence in a person's life. From the tale of the hapless man who lived among tombstones at Gadarenes we learn that slashing oneself, superhuman physical strength, excessive rage, madness and immodesty are indicators. After deliverance from the demons that possessed him, the man from Gadarenes was freed from these tendencies and restored to a right mind (Mark 5:9-20).

Demons are distinct beings with personalities. They have knowledge of both earthly and heavenly things. For example, one demon who possessed a man said to Jesus even before He revealed His identity, "I know who You are—the Holy One of God!" (Mark 1:24). Another told the sons of Sceva, "Jesus I know, and Paul I know; but who are you?" (Acts 19:15).

Demons apparently have self-interest and emotions. They seek information that concerns them personally, and ask for what they want. A concerned demon asked Jesus, "What have we to do with You, Jesus of Nazareth? Did You come to destroy us?" (Mark 1:24). Others indicated a preference as to where they would dwell (Mark 5:11-12). James tells us that the devils believe in God—and tremble with fear (James 2:19).

Demons can understand and communicate in human languages and are frequently portrayed doing so in the New Testament. They have independent wills which they exercise freely to a certain extent; for example, in Matthew 12:44 an unclean spirit decides to take up habitation in the soul of a person it had previously left. However, demons have no choice but to obey Jesus when He speaks, as illustrated by New Testament accounts where He delivered people from their control.

The purposes of demons

Demons are agents of evil, spirit beings who carry out the purposes of Satan by inflicting as much deception and damage as they can upon God's creation and upon His creatures, including men and women. As intelligent, communicative, willful spirits they work to sabotage human thinking and, most importantly, any possibility for people to know God or understand their need for Jesus. The occult is one of their most effective tools.

Connecting with demons

Priest and author Montague Summers, who studied the history of witchcraft in the early twentieth century, noted that although there are a great variety of occult arts, all bearing different names, they all lead to the same thing—the demonic realm, where spirits masquerade as angels, spirits of dead people, mythical gods, deceased pets or whatever you want. Father Summers wrote:

> In the course of the Holy Scriptures there occur a great
> number of words and expressions which are employed in
> connection with witchcraft, divination, and demonology,

and of these more than one authority has made detailed
and particular study. Some terms are of general import,
one might even venture to say vague and not exactly
defined, some are directly specific: of some phrases the
significance is plain and accepted; concerning others,
scholars are still undecided and differ more or less widely
amongst themselves. Yet it is noteworthy that from the
very earliest period the attitude of the inspired writers
towards magic and related practices is almost wholly con-
demnatory and uncompromisingly hostile. The vehement
and repeated denunciations launched against the profes-
sors of occult sciences and the initiate in foreign esoteric
mysteries do not, moreover, seem to be based upon any
supposition of fraud but rather upon the "abomination" of
the magic in itself, which is recognized as potent for evil
and able to wreak mischief upon life and limb.[2]

Father Summers notes that Scripture assumes, without question, that people can contact spirits and powers outside the physical realm through occult practices.

WHAT IS THE OCCULT?

To avoid the occult we must first understand what it is. I was
surprised to learn that "the occult" includes a broader range of
activities than I originally thought.

The word "occult" derives from the Latin *occulere* meaning to
"cover up" or "hide." Religious practice becomes occult when it
involves *seeking spirits or spiritual experiences that are normally
beyond the reach of our natural faculties of reason, sight, hearing,
smell, taste or touch.* Occult practices include seeking contact or
communion with a supernatural spirit, deliberately cultivating
psychic or supernatural powers, and even "looking within," a
practice which is not as innocuous as it seems.

---

2. Montague Summers, *The History of Witchcraft and Demonology*, 1925
(Secaucus, NJ: Castle Books, 1992 ed.), 173. However, Father Summers himself was involved in occult exorcisms.

Many people believe God can be found beyond reason and the physical realm...that is, in the occult. Yet while it is true that God exists beyond the physical realm, we are forbidden to seek Him there.

Following are three key characteristics of occult and mystic practice (that is, occultism and mysticism) based on dictionary definitions,[3] and refined as I grew in understanding:

1) Occult practice includes seeking God or truth beyond nature, reason and the mind—that is, in the supernatural realm.

2) Occult practice is based on a belief that communion with God comes through subjective, supernatural experience.

3) Occult practice involves seeking supernatural energy, spirits, power, presence, influence, action or enchantments.

Occultism is an umbrella term covering many different practices. Mysticism is one face of it, and emphasizes spiritual growth and development through communion with a supernatural spirit or spirits (a so-called "mystic experience").

If *experiencing* spiritual presence is the *goal* of any religious practice, it is correct to describe it as occult. If a spirit manifests, it is an occult spirit. And if *getting or developing* supernatural *powers* is the goal, it is also occult. If supernatural powers develop, they are occult powers.

Common names for occult arts include yoga, shamanism, witchcraft, sorcery, tarot, faith healing, astrology, spiritism, transcendental meditation, animism, magic (or "magick") and many more. Common invocational rituals—that is, practices which invoke occult presence—include chanting, drumming, hypnosis, the use of psychotropic drugs, channeling "energies" (as in acupuncture, reiki or feng shui), meditation, encounters with spiritual masters (such as the shaktipat), the use of mantras

3. *Websters New Collegiate Dictionary,* 3rd ed., s.v. "mysticism," "occult," "magic," and derivatives.

or "magic words" and, of course, simply asking for the presence, which is occult prayer.

In conclusion, therefore, a child of God should never try to learn about Him or commune with Him through supernatural "experience," and should never try to serve Him by wielding supernatural power because these are, in fact, occult practices. For our part, we are to remain in the realm of the natural, using only natural means to seek and serve Him. (We will look at these in the next chapter.) We must leave all supernatural work for God; that is His department.

> A child of God should never try to learn about Him or commune with Him through supernatural "experience," and should never try to serve Him by wielding occult power.

APPLICATION TO HINDU
AND CHARISMATIC PRACTICE

Let's move to the next step in understanding this, and apply our definitions to kundalini yoga. Could we say that it is occult?

We must conclude that kundalini yoga is occult for a number of reasons. For one thing, practitioners believe they can attain knowledge of God or Brahman through subjective experience (e.g., samadhi). The meaning they find through such experience is not apparent to the mind or the five natural senses; in fact, they often say they "bypass" reason and the intellect. Also, devotees believe they are communing with God, or divine beings, during samadhi. Further, they seek the direct experience and action of supernatural—that is, occult—power (as with kriyas and spiritual drunkenness). And the spirits they receive often bring wonderful *phos* light enchantments (peace, love and bliss).

The next step is more difficult. How do we apply our new understanding to the practices and experiences of charismatics? Are they occult?

Unfortunately, there is no avoiding the fact that charismatic practices are occult. This is so whether they involve mystic experiences of a *phos* light presence, or extreme giving over to occult forces such as occurs at the Toronto church and Holy Trinity Brompton. Charismatics believe they can attain knowledge of God and Jesus through subjective experiences (such as, soaking and manifestations). The meaning they find is not apparent to the mind or the natural senses. Like pagans, they search for truth "beyond reason," as we shall later see. Also, they believe they are communing with God (and sometimes angels) during soaking prayer. Furthermore, they seek the direct immediate action of supernatural—that is, occult—power (as in trembling, jerking and spiritual drunkenness). The spirits they receive often bring *phos* light enchantments; in fact, charismatics make a point of "calling down the Spirit," failing to realize that to call for a spiritual presence to manifest in the natural realm is the heart of occult practice. Vineyard churches even teach courses on calling down the Holy Spirit.

To apply this awful conclusion to myself, I had to acknowledge that many of my practices were occult. When I met with empowered brothers and sisters and we waited for a spirit of love to break over us, what were we doing but waiting for occult presence? When I basked in the sweetness of this presence, what was I doing but sitting under a spell? I am not denying that God can bless us with His sweet presence. What I am saying is that we must never seek Him by occult means, such as calling for "His" spirit, or asking for "more," or for an occult "filling."

Let me digress to make a practical point here. Given that I now recognize my former practices were occult, I avoid them all and do not keep spiritual fellowship with those who practice them. Some may ask, Have my faith or my relationship with God suffered? The answer is no. Have I lost a sense of the presence of *phos* light? Well, I no longer experience the sweet, apparently loving, presence I felt when we called for "the Spirit." But the love

> If *experiencing* manifest *presence* is the goal of religious practice, it is occult. If a spirit manifests, it is occult spirit. And if *getting* or *developing* supernatural powers is the goal, it is also occult, and the powers are occult powers.

of God in my heart is consistent, abiding and strong. It has been a long time since I suffered any sense of demonic presence. I rejoice every day in what I have learned, and I sense my soul being restored even to the point that I have regained a delight in simple things that I left behind in childhood. I feel free, and I feel safe.

So, dear charismatic, do not fear leaving the occult. Rather, fear remaining in it.

MAGICIANS AND SOOTHSAYERS

Let me define specific occult practices, also based on dictionary explanations, to help us overcome confusion arising from the variety of terms.

What is magic? Also known as wizardry, it is:

- practice designed to invoke or harness supernatural power to work miracles or healing;
- practice designed to invoke or control supernatural energy or spirits;
- channeling or wielding power from a supernatural source;
- something that gives a feeling of enchantment or rouses to ecstasy or tears; or
- communicating with angels or spirits of dead people (practitioners are sometimes called mediums, necromancers, spiritualists or spiritists).

What is sorcery? It is:

- like magic, but involves deliberately working with evil spirits.

What is witchcraft? It is:

- the practice of magic (white witchcraft) or sorcery (black witchcraft).

What is divination? Also called soothsaying, magic or seeing, it involves:

- trying to predict future events or discover hidden knowledge, usually by the aid of supernatural gifting; or
- using paranormal insight or perception.

How do these definitions apply to kundalini practice?

(1) Kundalini is *magic* because devotees attempt to harness, and often experience, supernatural power. Samadhi is a trance state like being under a spell (a state of enchantment). Devotees use certain practices, such as shaktipat or invocations, to invoke supernatural forces. They are moved to enchanted ecstasies or other deep emotional states that result in unmotivated weeping or laughter.
(2) Kundalini is not intentional *sorcery* because devotees do not knowingly call upon evil powers. However, if the powers are in fact evil, participants are unintentionally dabbling in sorcery.
(3) Kundalini is *witchcraft* because it involves magic, even though devotees would never use that expression.
(4) As we shall see, kundalini involves *divination*. Proponents claim to experience increased supernatural insight and perception.

Now for the alarming part. How do these definitions apply to charismatic practice? Could we say they are:

(1) *magic?* Yes, because practitioners attempt to harness supernatural power. They experience such power, seemingly from a supernatural source, such as when they "do the crunch" or pray for others to fall under the power. Soaking is a trance state similar to being under a spell (a state of enchantment). They use certain practices, such as forehead touches or incantations (such as repeated prayer—"more Lord, more Lord, come, come") to invoke supernatural power, power which sometimes makes them, or those they pray for, stagger or fall. They are moved to enchanted ecstasies or other intense emotional states that result in unmotivated weeping or laughter.

(2) *sorcery?* The Toronto Blessing is not intentional sorcery because charismatics do not deliberately call upon evil powers. Like kundalini devotees, they believe they have found God. However, if the powers are in fact evil, they are unintentionally dabbling in sorcery.

(3) *witchcraft?* The shoe fits. Charismatic practices involve witchcraft because they involve magic, even though practitioners would never call their activities "magic" or "witchcraft."

(4) *divination?* As we will see, TB involves divination. Proponents claim to experience paranormal insight and perception.

We know that divination, magic and sorcery are occult. Therefore people who practice these arts—no matter whether they call themselves magicians, witches, yogis or charismatics and no matter whether they go by the Bhagavad-Gita or the Bible—are dabbling in the occult. All of them.

Some spiritual masters might not appreciate being likened to magicians. Gentle yoga devotees might object to being classed alongside sorcerers; sincere charismatics would despise it, and rightly so. But we must look beyond words. The occult is the occult whether we call it magic, witchcraft or strawberry pie.

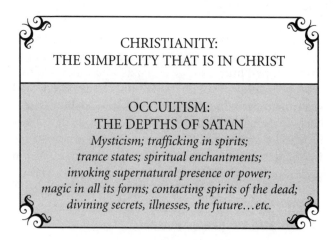

CHRISTIANITY:
THE SIMPLICITY THAT IS IN CHRIST

OCCULTISM:
THE DEPTHS OF SATAN
Mysticism; trafficking in spirits;
trance states; spiritual enchantments;
invoking supernatural presence or power;
magic in all its forms; contacting spirits of the dead;
divining secrets, illnesses, the future…etc.

Chapter Six

~~

RIGHT WAYS TO SEEK GOD; THE ENTRANCE OF HIS WORDS BRINGS LIGHT

I will never forget Your precepts for by them You have given me life.

—King David, (Psalm 119:93)

The right ways to seek our amazing, supernatural God actually have nothing to do with amazing, supernatural activities.

Again, I am not advancing the position that God does not perform miracles, or that He does not communicate through words, visions or other extraordinary means. I believe He can and does and will continue to do these things, as He purposes from time to time. But true Christian practice does not involve pursuing supernatural communications from, or experiences with, God.

Perhaps surprisingly, the right ways to seek our heavenly Father involve natural, apparently ordinary, pursuits; practices centered on the person and work of Jesus. Although these practices promise no supernatural powers or sensual spiritual experiences, they nonetheless lead to peace and joy surpassing anything the world or the occult can offer.

In orthodox Christianity, believers seek God and commune with Him in three, simple ways: through learning His truth as revealed in His Word, through obedience and through prayer.

These are true Christian spiritual practices. While each topic is worthy of much greater treatment than I can afford here, I will attempt an explanation to address some of the main points.

ON LEARNING TRUTH; FINDING AND GROWING IN THE KNOWLEDGE OF GOD

> Your testimonies are wonderful...
> The entrance of Your words gives light
> (Psalm 119:129-130).

God has chosen to bring the light of His truth to human souls through Jesus, by His written and spoken Word. It is by searching for and savoring God's truth as revealed in His Word that we find Him. He is not "in" healing, or love or spiritual presence; He is in words of *truth*.

Jesus said, "Everyone who is of the truth hears My voice" (John 18:37). He did not say that those who were on the side of love, or peace, or unity or freedom, would listen to Him—that would be just about everyone on the planet. No, the path of *truth* is the narrow path to God. For this reason, growing in understanding of the truths revealed in Scripture—truths about God, man, sin and salvation through Jesus—are essential for growing in intimacy and communion with almighty Jehovah God.

> All the Scriptures—wisdom literature, songs and psalms, teachings, letters, words and commands—are bread for our souls. Through them we are fed, by them we are washed and sanctified, our eyes opened and minds renewed so we can understand the mysteries of godliness.

Consider God's commands to the disciples on the mount during the transfiguration of Jesus. He said to the disciples, "This is my Son, in whom I am well pleased. *Hear Him!*" (Matthew 17:5, emphasis added). In other words, pay attention to His words! Open your ears and listen to what He says. Ponder His teachings and strive to understand them. Remember them and obey them. All these commands are implicit in the exhortation to "Hear Him!" God did not say, "Soak in My presence," or "call for the Spirit so you can feel My arms of love." Nor did He say, "Be intoxicated in the joyful presence of the Spirit!" No, God commanded us to "hear."

We must first hear, or receive, God's words in our minds, for the mind is the way of truth to the heart. This is in complete opposition to the ways of the occult. Lucifer urges us to discount or bypass the mind in favor of an occult "heart experience." For reasons that are no doubt obvious, Satan always reverses the way of God; we will see this more clearly as we continue.

> When we probe the Word of God, we probe the mind of God; and in this way get to know Him better.

All the Scriptures—wisdom literature, songs and psalms, teachings, letters, words and commands—are bread for our souls. Through them we are fed. By them we are washed and sanctified, our eyes opened and minds renewed so we can understand the mysteries of godliness. The psalmist said, "Open my eyes, that I may see wondrous things from Your law" (Psalm 119:18). He also declared:

> Oh, how I love Your law!
> It is my meditation all the day.
> You, through Your commandments,
>   make me wiser than my enemies;
> For they are ever with me.
> I have more understanding than all my teachers,
> For Your testimonies are my meditation (Psalm 119:97-99).

Learning truth includes not only the study of Scripture, but also examining the writings of sound spiritual teachers, men like A. W. Tozer, Charles Spurgeon, M.R. DeHaan, D. Martyn Lloyd-Jones, the Puritans and a host of others who can help us understand. Memorizing Scriptures, a practice sometimes held in contempt by those who fail to appreciate the relationship between the mind and God, also pays great dividends.

All this can be difficult work at times, requiring sacrifice and self-discipline. But it brings reward in equal or greater measure as we grow in the knowledge of God and the love of His truth. Charles Spurgeon wrote:

> The pleasures arising from a right understanding of the divine testimonies are of the most delightful order; earthly enjoyments are utterly contemptible if compared with them. The sweetest joys, yea, the sweetest of the sweetest falls to him who has God's truth as his heritage.[1]

God's truth makes our hearts right, and gives joy to a right heart.

ON OBEDIENCE: COMMUNION WITH GOD

I have inclined my heart to perform Your statutes
Forever, to the very end (Psalm 119:112).

> The psalmist did not thirst for the presence of God; he thirsted for the commands of God. And in obeying these commands he knew God's abiding presence.

The child of God also discovers great joy in obedience. Obedience is godly spiritual practice and, most importantly, a moment-by-moment way to commune with God.[2]

One of the sweetest promises spoken by an Old Testament prophet was that Jehovah God would plant within the hearts of men—the unholy hearts of rebellious men and women—a genuine desire to do His will. Ezekiel

---

1. C. H. Spurgeon, *The Best of C. H. Spurgeon* (Grand Rapids, MI: Baker Book House, 1945), 68.

2. It is noteworthy that Christian communion with God does not require hours devoted to meditation or "soaking" in trance states. Occult practice requires a person to divorce himself from family, work and other important activities of life. Christianity requires no such sacrifice but, rather, provides abundant blessing in the simplicity of normal, natural daily activities.

described how this would happen, through the experience Jesus would later refer to as being "born again":

> I will give you a new heart and put a new spirit within you; I will take the heart of stone out of your flesh and give you a heart of flesh. I will put My Spirit within you and cause you to walk in My statutes, and you will keep My judgments and do them (Ezekiel 36:26-27).

A new heart and a new spirit: two things almighty God gives to undeserving man. Evidence of this—the spiritual rebirth of a human soul—can be seen in the sudden turning of a new believer to the ways of God. Willing obedience proves that our love for Him is genuine. The apostle John wrote, "For this is the love of God, that we keep His commandments. And His commandments are not burdensome" (1 John 5:3). Indeed, they are not burdensome, and victory brings a sense of the love and presence of God. This, then, is how we seek and find Him. The psalmist wrote:

> Your testimonies are wonderful;
> Therefore my soul keeps them...
> I opened my mouth and panted,
> For I longed for Your commandments
>   (Psalm 119:129,131).

This psalmist did not thirst for the *presence* of God; he thirsted for the *commands* of God. And in obeying them he found God. Jesus said, "If you keep My commandments, you will abide in My love, just as I have kept My Father's commandments and abide in His love. These things I have spoken to you, that My joy may remain in you, and that your joy may be full" (John 15:10-11). Charles Spurgeon explains more about the joy of communing with God through obedience:

> Beloved, when the good man is enabled by divine grace to live in obedience to God, he must, as a necessary conse-quence, enjoy peace of mind. His hope is alone fixed on

Jesus, but a life which evidences his possession of salvation casts many a sweet ingredient into his cup. He who takes the yoke of Christ upon him and learns of Him finds rest unto his soul. When we keep His commandments, we consciously enjoy His love which we could not do if we walked in opposition to His will.[3]

Obedience is essential for communion with God.

ON PRAYER: COMMUNICATION WITH GOD

Offer to God thanksgiving...
Call upon Me in the day of trouble;
I will deliver you, and you shall glorify Me
    (Psalm 50:14-15).

> God is always faithful to answer sincere requests for spiritual graces such as an understanding of His Word or a more devoted or forgiving heart.

At its simplest, prayer is simply talking with God. Charles Spurgeon said, "True prayer is the trading of the heart with God."[4] Thanking Him, declaring His truths, remembering His mercies, pleading for mercy, pleading for grace, crying to Him, laughing with Him, asking for guidance, seeking answers, expressing our grief at the state of the world, declaring how we long for Jesus' return, confessing wrongdoing or the ugly things we see in our hearts, reasoning with Him according to Scripture, singing to Him, striving with Him and expressing our love and awe; all these things and more are encompassed in the simple word "prayer."

At their most exquisite, prayers of gratitude, love and awe inspired by the Holy Spirit will cause words to issue from our lips

3. Spurgeon, *The Best*, 241.
4. Spurgeon, *Spurgeon on Prayer & Spiritual Warfare* (New Kensington, PA: Whittaker House, 1998), 34.

that are surely the purest and truest we will ever speak, words of praise that gladden the great heart of our God and cause our feeble ones to rejoice. During these times we may know His sweet presence in measure like no other.

But it will not always be so. At its most trying, prayer is a matter of self-discipline and sober effort. Jesus said that the spirit is willing, but the flesh is weak. When it comes time to kneel before our Maker, the flesh exerts at times a powerful, disabling influence. Sometimes we must ask God to help us pray; often, however, we don't even want help, so much would we rather avoid the task! Let us turn again to the words of Charles Spurgeon, who offered the following prayer:

> Lord, we want to come to You, but may You come to us. Draw us, and we will run after You. Blessed Spirit, help our infirmities, "for we know not what we should pray for as we ought" (Romans 8:26). Come, Holy Spirit, and give right thoughts and right words so that we may all be able to pray...[5]

God is always faithful to answer sincere requests for spiritual graces such as an understanding of His Word or a more devoted or forgiving heart. However, prayers for temporal blessings may go unanswered because we are commanded to set our hearts on the treasures of heaven, not on things that can be stolen or destroyed or that can rust away.

As with any relationship, communication with God is important. But our relationship with Him is a unique and incredibly privileged one, with a God both loving and fearsome, and we do well to remember this when we approach him. Yet at the same time, we may come before him with confidence, with affection as a small child and with the intimacy of a beloved. How vast the blessings; how many sweet facets to this relationship! Let us agree with the psalmist who wrote:

---

5. Spurgeon, *On Prayer*, 187.

Let my cry come before You, O Lord;
Give me understanding according to Your word.
Let my supplication come before You;
Deliver me according to Your word.
My lips shall utter praise,
For You teach me Your statutes
    (Psalm 119:169-171).

When we pray aright we are speaking truth and dwelling in truth, and so draw near to God.

THE SIMPLICITY OF RIGHT PRACTICE

These three practices—learning God's truth, obeying His commands, and praying to Him—form the foundation of biblical Christianity. They are simple, sensible and sweet to the soul. Moses spoke the following words to the Jews to explain that right practice does not require mysticism, or travel to an "anointed" person or location:

For this commandment which I command you today is not too mysterious for you, nor is it far off. It is not in heaven, that you should say, 'Who will ascend into heaven for us and bring it to us, that we may hear it and do it?' Nor is it beyond the sea, that you should say, 'Who will go over the sea for us and bring it to us, that we may hear it and do it?' But the word is very near you, in your mouth and in your heart, that you may do it (Deuteronomy 30:11-14).

In the verses above, Moses was stressing obedience to ceremonial commands, that is, spiritual practices ordained by God. I believe he was saying that right practice is simple and it is a mistake to go hunting for truth in the occult. God has given us all we need to find Him through reason and our natural senses. He is not so high in heaven that we need leaders or priests to call Him "down." Nor is it necessary to travel across the ocean to get a blessing. No, the Word is near us, ready to be kept.

The next words Moses spoke were intended to show the Israelites that right practice was not only simple, it was vitally important:

> See, I have set before you today life and good, death and evil, in that I command you today to love the Lord your God, to walk in His ways, and to keep His commandments, His statutes, and His judgments, that you may live and multiply; and the Lord your God will bless you in the land which you go to possess. But if your heart turns away so that you do not hear, and are drawn away, and worship other gods and serve them, I announce to you today that you shall surely perish; you shall not prolong your days in the land which you cross over the Jordan to go in and possess (Deuteronomy 30:15-18).

As it was for the Jews, so is it for us today: right practice is a matter of life and death.

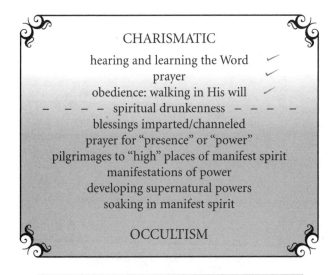

CHARISMATIC

hearing and learning the Word
prayer
obedience: walking in His will
– – – – spiritual drunkenness – – – –
blessings imparted/channeled
prayer for "presence" or "power"
pilgrimages to "high" places of manifest spirit
manifestations of power
developing supernatural powers
soaking in manifest spirit

OCCULTISM

> Charismatics have adopted occult ways,
> crossing the line into forbidden practice.

Chapter Seven

OCCULT THINKING

Thinking, or knowing, is an activity of the spirit of a man.
—G.I. Williamson, explaining *The Shorter Catechism*

In the beginning was Logic, and Logic was with God, and Logic was God...In Logic was life and the life was the light of men.
—Gordon H. Clark, *paraphrase of John 1:1,4*

*W*hen I first noticed parallels between Hindu and charismatic beliefs, I wondered if occult practice could change the way a person thinks. Then I chanced upon a book in which a former Hindu Brahmin[1] observed similar phenomena. Rabi Maharaj marked the independent development of Hindu religious thought in drug users. (Psychotropic drugs have been used by shamans and magicians for years in occult ceremonies to hasten their journey to "the other side.") Mr. Maharaj noticed that

---

1. Brahmins are the people highest in the Hindu caste system, considered to be closest to Brahman (God) through thousands of reincarnations. Their position entitles them to act in a priestly role, as intermediaries between God and people in the lower castes.

addicts were having the same experiences on drugs that he had
when practicing yoga. He wrote:

> Although Michael [a drug user] had never studied
> Hinduism or had any contact with Hindus – I particularly
> questioned him on that – his views of God, of the universe,
> and of human existence were precisely those that I had held
> as a Yogi. It astounded me to realize that through his experi-
> ences on drugs he had been won over to Hindu philosophy![2]

It appears, therefore, that exposure to the occult can influence
the way we think about God and truth. Occult spirits guide our
thoughts, especially our thoughts about spiritual things, in certain,
predictable directions. After a while we start thinking and believing
the way they want us to.

In this chapter we will closely examine two related occult beliefs.
One is the view that God reveals His *truth* primarily through subjective experience, or through people (gurus, prophets, priests)
who have known Him in "deep experience." The second is that God
reveals *Himself*—His heart and His love—through subjective experience; a belief which, as we have seen, forms the cornerstone of
mysticism.

WHAT'S WRONG WITH SUBJECTIVE EXPERIENCE?

Some readers may be wondering about the place of subjective—
that is, personally felt—experience in the Christian life. After all,
there is no way we could know a personal, spiritual God except
through personal, spiritual experience. And, of course, there is no
way we could know a supernatural God except through supernatural experience. Furthermore, we must acknowledge that a believer's
experiences of God's love and the revelation of the person and
word of Jesus Christ can aptly be described as mystic, as can the
union between the Holy Spirit and the spirit of the born-again
believer: these are mysterious, supernatural, personal experiences.

---

2. Rabi R. Maharaj with Dave Hunt, *Death of a Guru: A Remarkable True Story
   of One Man's Search for Truth* (Eugene, OR: Harvest House, 1984), 158.

However, it is important to understand the real issue. The question is not whether you have or have not had a subjective experience. It concerns the *practice* that gives birth to the experience.

The issue is *how* you find God, *how* you seek communion with Him and *how* you apply yourself to gain knowledge of His truth. We have seen that study, prayer and obedience are the orthodox ways. Mystics and occultists, however, believe occult practice is the way to God and truth—a terrible mistake.

REASON VS. MYSTICISM

A wonderful thing about Christianity is that God is known and found through the mind. This explains why our faith is grounded and centered on *what we believe*. What we believe about God, Jesus, sin and Jesus' saving work determines whether we are, or are not, His child.

Almighty God has both hidden and revealed His truth in His Word, the Bible. In a letter to the Corinthians, Paul said he was speaking "the wisdom of God in a mystery, the hidden wisdom which God ordained before the ages..." (1 Corinthians 2:7). Through believing His words the heart is warmed and we are brought into, and remain in, relationship with Him.

God's Truth is written in Scripture, where it can be studied and savored by the regenerate mind. It is not easy to understand, especially at the beginning of our studies, because the natural mind is alienated from the things of God. It requires effort, time and the help of the Holy Spirit to grow in understanding of His truth. But there it is in the Scriptures: readable, learnable subject matter.

Altered consciousness is the cornerstone of occult practice. Satan wants to shut off our minds because this opens us up to him and his demons.

In orthodox Christianity, a believer grows in the knowledge of God through prayerful, diligent use of the mind to ferret out and understand His Word. The intellect is stimulated, reason is engaged, natural beliefs are challenged and the mind is renewed as the Holy Spirit comes alongside to illuminate God's truth.

By contrast, Satan's "truths" are hidden in the occult, where they are "discovered" through practices that usually require the seeker to disengage the mind, look within or deny reason in favor of experience, riddles or myth. Altered states of consciousness open the mind, and occult spirits then guide a person into mystic, false "truth."

Altered consciousness—door to the demonic

Altered consciousness is fundamental to occult practice. Satan wants to shut off our minds because that is one way he gains access to them. On the other hand, reason and alertness are like doors which lock him out.[3]

We saw in chapter 5 a partial list of invocational practices used by occultists to alter consciousness and make contact with spirits. These include chanting, drumming, dancing, hypnosis and the use of drugs. Meditation is a form of self-hypnosis for altering consciousness. Contemplative prayer, a practice making inroads into the church, is nothing less than occult meditation in which focused thoughts take one into a supposedly "sacred place"…a dangerous, altered state. Spiritual drunkenness is an interesting altered state, apparently caused by the direct action of occult spirits upon the mind and body.

Learning to despise reason and truth

Under the influence of occult spirits people learn to diminish or deny the importance of reality, reason and the mind.[4] Occultists know that thinking gets in the way. The following is from a prominent New Age teacher:

---

3. If reason and alertness keep Satan at bay and prevent his gaining influence over us, we can better understand the role of education and learning for spiritual development. We can also see how myth and fantasy become destructive, and spiritual "riddles" like those of Zen masters foster unhealthy spirituality.

4. Secular mystics frequently go so far as to deny the reality of the physical realm. This deeply occult belief is at the root of Hindu yogic practice. Yogis teach that our natural senses –sight, hearing, smell, etc.—are misleading; part of *maya*— the illusion of the natural realm. But they also teach that the spiritual, unseen realm and the natural realm are one and the same, which presupposes the existence of the natural realm, previously denied! When we realize the truth of this inherently unreasonable teaching then, they say, we will be "enlightened." (cont.)

The Spirit of truth is at your call…This is the universal
Mind…Shut down the intellect for the time being, and let
the universal Mind speak to you…We can all learn how to
turn our awareness, or conscious mind, to the universal
Mind, or Spirit, within us. We can, through practice, learn
how to make this everyday, topsy-turvy "mind of the flesh"
be still, and let the mind that is God (all-wisdom, all-love)
think in us and through us… Human mind, the intellect
makes mistakes because it gathers its information from the
outside world through the senses.[5]

The quotation above is a clear example of occult teaching, based
on the belief that God and truth exist beyond reason and the intellect, and beyond the reach of the natural senses. Another example:

If you want to make rapid progress in spiritual understanding, stop reading so many books. They only give you
someone's opinion about Truth, or a sort of history of the
author's experience in seeking Truth. What you want is a
revelation of Truth in your own soul, and that will never
come through the reading of books.[6]

Under influences brought to bear upon their minds in occult
practice, charismatics have also learned to disregard, and even
despise, the place of reason in Christian spiritual practice. They
discourage prayer when they lay on hands because they have
learned that using the mind to articulate prayer can hinder the
manifestation of spirit power. And witness this teaching:

(cont.) Mysteria told me that God's creation is trite and unimportant, and only
someone who is spiritually immature and "operating on low vibrations" per-
ceives created things as separate entities. But such teaching despises reason, and
despises all nature—God's handiwork. Yet so it is on the mystic path: under
occult influence common sense becomes foolishness, and God's world and His
creations become objects of contempt.

5. H. Emilie Cady, edited by R.L. Miller, *Lessons in Truth for the 21st Century* (Abib
Publishing, 1999) *http://website.lineone.net/~newthought/lessons.4.htm*, 5.
6. Cady, 5.

Satan's Temptation: That Man Descend to Reasoned Knowledge...When I looked at the Toronto-type renewal, my reasoning said, "Everything is to be done decently and in order." However, when I *tuned to my spirit*, God said to me, "How do you get drunk decently and in order?" Had I been living only out of reason, I would have rejected the Toronto blessing. Since I was *trained to live out of my heart and out of revelation*, I have embraced it.[7] (emphasis added)

This writer scorns the use of reason, judging it an ignoble—indeed, a satanic—"descent" in the pursuit of knowledge. Finding occult "truth" by "tuning in" to her own "spirit"—that is, seeking subjective experience through looking within—she decides God wants her to "get drunk decently."

The role of Scripture to engage the mind

Most charismatics give lip service to the importance of reading and learning Scripture. However, they diminish its importance for Christian growth because they do not understand the role of the mind in Christian spirituality. Instead, they turn to mystic experience where they think they are "meeting" with God and receiving His love. Consider again this quotation from chapter 1:

I had a mighty power encounter with God. I've been intoxicated—completely drunk with the Holy Spirit. He's a person, and he's so wonderful. When I was baptized in the Holy Spirit some 20 years ago, it made Jesus real to me. This move has made the Holy Spirit and the Father's heart real.

Can you discern the occult thinking here? The pastor believes he came to know the Holy Spirit and the "heart of God" through subjective experience—actually a mystic encounter, including altered consciousness and spiritual drunkenness. The end of such

---

7. Gary Greig, Mark Virkler and Patti Virkler, *Sound Doctrine through Revelation Knowledge* (Lamad Publishing, 2003), *http://www.cwgministries.org/books/Sound-Doctrine.pdf, 2-3.*

practice will inevitably be to diminish the place of Scripture for spiritual growth, in favor of "experiencing" God.

Consider also the following teaching from charismatic prophetess Stacy Campbell, whose head swiveled violently as she delivered a message under the influence of an occult spirit, and tried to persuade the audience to put reason aside by ignoring bizarre manifestations. She (or the spirit speaking through her) said:

> Spiritual development is NOT divorced from intellectual development. That is a lie which leads the unsuspecting seeker into occult practice and experience.

> Christianity is a love story... all the displays of God when he comes down from heaven and touches people with his power, the Lord says... look beyond the power, look beyond the shaking, look beyond the weeping, look beyond the laughter, and see that I am healing my people and loving my people... and know that this is the test of this revival... Do you love me? Do you love me? Avoid the pull of religion to drag you back into an empty letter that kills and destroys.[8]

This spirit talked a lot about love and Christianity, but emphasizes "displays of God" and experiences, referring to God's Word as an "empty letter." Of one thing we can be sure: it wasn't the Holy Spirit speaking here. In Deuteronomy, Moses said, "be careful to observe all the words of this law. For you they are no empty words; they are your very life..." (32:47 NEB).

OBJECTIVE VS. SUBJECTIVE TRUTH

The God of the Bible is the pillar and ground of truth (1 Timothy 3:15). He is inseparable from His truth; indeed, the entirety of the triune Godhead is of the truth. Jesus said, "I am

---

8. Stacey Campbell, shown in "Endtime Revivals Unmasked" video, by God's Reddende Ark. No date.

the way, the truth, and the life. No one comes to the Father except through Me" (John 14:6). The Holy Spirit is the Spirit of truth (14:17; 16:13) and God the Father is the God of truth (Deuteronomy 32:4), who sent Jesus to bear witness unto His truth (John 18:37). His truth is light and life.

Furthermore the Bible teaches that God's truth lies outside us. Therefore we can never find God or truth by looking within. The Scriptures teach clearly that the truth of God is an external, objective, spiritual reality, fixed for all eternity:

> Forever, O Lord,
> Your word is settled in heaven (Psalm 119:89).
> The entirety of Your word is truth,
> And every one of Your righteous judgments endures for-
>   ever (119:160).

Mankind's gifts of reason and logic reflect some of what remains of the image of God in us. Therefore it follows that His truth must be presented to human reason and logic so it may be considered, explored, understood and accepted (or rejected). It is only by accepting and believing God's revelation of truth that humans can come to know Him. Knowing His truth is knowing Him, and believing His truth is believing in Him. Such knowing and believing is the stuff of true faith, and without such faith we have no relationship with God. Of course, true faith is also heartfelt, and we receive His word with joy in our hearts (Acts 16:14, Luke 24:32). But without mindful apprehension and belief, we cannot know God.

However mystics and charismatics look largely to subjective experience for truth, regarding personal ideas, impressions, visions, feelings and inner promptings as their guides. This, they believe, is how truth is discovered. Following is an example of occult thinking from charismatic writer Bill Hamon, who teaches that truth is "evolving" and is "experienced" apart from Scripture, and is revealed in and through subjective experience:

> The trumpet for advancing is about to sound again. Your
> generation will be challenged to establish the greatest truth

and the most revolutionary reality that has ever been revealed to the Church...Everywhere I travel throughout the United States and around the world there are those who are catching glimpses of the experiential truth which is to be restored to the Church. The Spirit is preparing and equipping saintly soldiers for the battle of battles and the consummation of the ages.[9] (emphasis added)

Mr. Hamon's belief that man himself establishes truth, or catches glimpses of "experiential truth" through mystic encounter, is typically occult and totally wrong. People do not establish truth; God does—or rather, He did. He established it once and for all in eternity past, before the Earth was even created:

> The Lord possessed me [wisdom, truth] at the beginning
>   of His way,
> Before His works of old.
> I have been established from everlasting,
> From the beginning, before there was ever an Earth
>   (Proverbs 8:22-23).

The only conclusion we can legitimately draw from Scripture is that reason and the intellect are godly faculties. They are tools not only meant to help us make sense of and enjoy our lives on this planet, but also to help us find and grow in knowledge of our Creator, the God of reason and truth.

God reveals His truth through His Word

In the first lines of his Gospel, the apostle John wrote, "In the beginning was the Word, and the Word was with God, and the Word was God." The Greek for "Word" is *logos*, from which English takes "logic" and "logical." *Logos* has to do with the logical, reasoning and accurate expression of truth. From this alone we can infer that our Creator is a God of reason and logic, who will speak to us through our minds.

---

9. Bill Hamon, *The Eternal Church* (Arizona: Christian International, 1981), 12.

CHRISTIAN PRACTICE
Values reason, seeks God through the use of the mind
Simple reliance and enjoyment of natural senses
in all things
Admires God's creation as evidence of His glory,
intelligence and power

OCCULT PRACTICE
THE DEPTHS OF SATAN
Values experience, seeks God through altered states
Natural senses unnecessary, or obstacles
to meaning or truth
In extreme cases, God's creation is believed
to be a deceptive "illusion"

Satan—the father of lies—tells man
that reason is a lie, simplicity in Christ
is "unspiritual," and God's creation is
without real value.

John R.W. Stott wrote:

Some people [say that] since man is finite and fallen…and
God must reveal himself, therefore the mind is unimportant. But no. The Christian doctrine of revelation, far from
making the human mind unnecessary, actually makes it
indispensable and assigns to it its proper place. God has
revealed himself in *words* to *minds*. His revelation is a
rational revelation to rational creatures. Our duty is to
receive his message, to submit to it, to seek to understand it
and to relate it to the world in which we live…One of the
highest and noblest functions of man's mind is to listen to

God's Word, and so to read his mind and think his thoughts after him, both in nature and in Scripture…if one thing is clear about biblical teaching on the judgment of God, it is that he will judge us by our knowledge, by our response (or lack of response) to his revelation.[10] (emphasis original)

Satan wants us to look within, or mystically through spiritual experience. But there we will find only error and deception. God reveals truth to man through His Word, illuminated by the Holy Spirit.

GOD REVEALS HIS LOVE TO THE OBEDIENT

One thing we can know for sure: God does not send His love to occult practitioners. He does not reveal His heart to them. He does not reveal Jesus to them. He does not and will not bestow godly blessings through their practices. Blissful, loving, amazing occult experiences—no matter how holy they seem—are not from God. They are the deceptive, death-dealing temporary blessings of the serpent who is god of the occult.

To understand and practice God's truth is the way to commune with Him, and is the only way to experience His love. Hear and understand what Jesus said:

If anyone loves Me, he will keep My word; and My Father will love him, and We will come to him and make Our home with him (John 14:23).

Almighty God reveals His love to those who obey Him. It's that simple.

---

10. John R.W. Stott, *Your Mind Matters: the Place of the Mind in the Christian Life* (Downers Grove, IL: InterVarsity, 1972), 20-21,24.

Chapter Eight

WILL THE REAL SORCERER PLEASE STAND UP?

Most men will proclaim each his own goodness,
But who can find a faithful man?

—Proverbs 20:6

*M*ost of us have heard about the famous "Christian mystics" who lived in centuries past. Many practiced as monks. Some have been elevated to sainthood by the Roman Catholic church. They produced poetic and deeply religious writing. Did these ancients understand the deeper mysteries of Christianity? The answer must be no, not if their practices were in any manner occult.

Charismatics are the mystics of modern Christianity.

"DISCRIMINATING" MYSTICISM:
THE CALL FOR OCCULT PRESENCE

Popular charismatic author Michael Green endorsed what he refers to as "discriminating mysticism" in his book *I Believe in Satan's Downfall*. He wrote:

> An undiscriminating mysticism...mysticism which does not focus on and come through Christ is dangerous. The

meditator opens himself to forces over which he has no control. At worst he is prey to demonic influence which could be destructive of his whole life. At best he is caught up in an activity which is selfish...[1]

Of course, I disagree with Mr. Green's assertion that Christians must be discriminating mystics. Nowhere does Scripture endorse any form of mysticism. We are not required to discern when it is okay to go mystic because it is *never* okay to go mystic. We are not required to discern which spirit encountered during occult practice is holy, or which is not, because it is *never* okay to traffic in spirits. Moreover, "testing the spirits" does not mean getting close to them so you can tell if they are godly or not. That is sheer nonsense. We test the spirits by examining the spiritual teaching and practices of those who claim to know God.

However, one can become confused when reading charismatic authors because they claim to practice in the name of Jesus, and also claim to despise the occult.

Charismatics always practice "in the name of Jesus." For example, they call for spiritual presence in His name, or they mystically focus their thoughts on "Him"—or their idea of who He is—in contemplative prayer and worship. In my former church, people would say Jesus' name repeatedly, hands open, awaiting a sense of "His" arrival. I have heard that charismatic evangelists are now asking large assemblies of people to chant Jesus' name, to invoke His presence; clearly an occult practice.

The reality is that all mystics practice in the name of their god, or gods, whether by calling on the name, chanting it, thinking about their god or calling for his (or her) presence. Former yogi Rabi R. Maharaj says he "firmly believed, as do all orthodox Hindus, that the mantra [the name of a god repeatedly spoken out loud or in the mind] embodied the deity itself and created what it expressed."[2] Occultists believe there is power in a name. It

1. Michael Green, *I Believe in Satan's Downfall* (London, England: Hodder and Stouton Ltd., 1981), 190.

2. Maharaj, 52.

(3.) Jesus Culture "There is Power in the Name of Jesus."
6+6+6 (in 6 mins) THEN 6 mORE = 24 CALLS / REPEATS.

is no different when we substitute the name "Jesus" for *Kali* or *Shiva*: Satan delights to assume the aspects of any deity called, even Jesus (see chapter 10 for more on this).   *PAGE 137*

The practice of repeating Jesus' name to invoke His presence demonstrates a serious misunderstanding—an occult understanding—about what it is to pray in His name. To pray in the name of Jesus means to recognize that He is the Messiah, whose redemptive work at the cross enables God to hear our prayers and through whom, by faith alone, we can come into God's presence.

The second way charismatic teachers confuse us is by giving lip service to the prohibition against the occult. For example, Mr. Green, who endorsed mysticism in the quotation cited above, wrote in the very same book:

> The teaching of the Bible is extraordinarily clear on [the prohibition against the occult], and extraordinarily explicit. All down the centuries over which the Bible was being written the attitude is precisely the same. We are warned to have nothing to do with the occult.[3]

Charismatics are always talking about the wrongness and dangers of the occult, not realizing they practice the very thing they condemn. Interestingly, their condemnation of others is often noteworthy for its vehemence. Witches are a favorite target. I once heard John Sandford of Elijah House claim to have spent three hours in spiritual warfare fighting against witches. In my former church charismatic prophets cautioned me "not to see a devil under every rock," but at the same time, they often searched chapel before Sunday services for tarot cards or other items "planted" by witches, supposedly designed to disrupt our worship.

OCCULT RIGHTEOUSNESS

Mr. Green misunderstands the motives of non-Christian occult seekers. He says:

---

3. Green, 121.

3) Hillsong : "what a beautiful name " The name it is ! of Jesus. Worship

> One of the charms of occult practice is that it gives rein to
> the religious instinct deep within a person but does not
> make upon him any claims for love, holiness, or service of
> others. In this sense it is a pseudo-religion, and justly
> deserves the name of "idolatry" which is so often attrib-
> uted to it in the Bible.[4]

Here Mr. Green baldly asserts that occult religions make no
claim upon practitioners for "love, holiness or the service of others." But this is not true. Some occult teachings are selfish and
overtly evil—an obvious example being satanic sects—but many,
if not most, strive for what is right and good.

In his book Mr. Green condemns yoga teachers, apparently
not realizing that it is fundamental to their teachings that one
must learn to be loving and nonjudgmental, and to put away selfishness and pride ("ego"). In my interview with yoga teacher
Mysteria, she expressed a clear and strong desire to be more loving through her religious practice. No less than Mr. Green and his
students do yoga teachers and their students also want to serve
others, and no less than he have they searched for ways to be better, more compassionate people.

And it is so in other religions. Consider Sufi mystics: The
"Sufi ethic" has been described by one writer, Kabir Helminsky,
as "chivalry," meaning "heroic sacrifice and generosity."[5] Sufis
teach that the way to realize chivalry in one's life, and the way to
be transformed into a more loving, selfless person, is to know—
by experience—the love of "God." Mr. Helminski says we must
overcome the slavery of our attractions and see "beyond the veil

---

4. Green, 125. Note here the erroneous understanding of idolatry, as a religion
   that is not loving, not holy and not devoted to serving others. By this definition the teachings of any guru are acceptable before God if they "lay claims
   for love, holiness," etc. Of course this is wrong. No love or service is acceptable before God if not derived from true faith (Isaiah 64:6). The just live by
   faith (Romans 1:17).
5. Kabir Helminski, *The Knowing Heart: a Sufi Path of Transformation* (Boston,
   MA: Shambhala Publications, 1999), 270.

of selfishness" to prepare ourselves for contact with the divine reality of love, for "Without the power of Love, we can only follow our egos and the desires of the world."[6] The end of the Sufi path should be, says he, service—complete selflessness so that one can serve in love—described as "the functional outcome of being connected to Cosmic Energy."[7] Without accepting Sufi occult teaching, we must admit that it cannot be condemned for failing to teach love, holiness, or service of others as Mr. Green has charged.

Father Montague Summers (chapter 5) also condemned the occult. But he was astute enough to observe the fairer and fouler forms of it. He wrote:

> none of the earlier religions existed for the express purpose of perpetrating evil for evil's sake. We have but to read the eloquent and exquisite description of the Eleusinian Mysteries by that accomplished Greek scholar Father Cyril Martindale, S.J., to catch no mean nor mistaken glimpse of the ineffable yearning for beauty, for purity, for holiness, which filled the hearts of the worshippers of the goddess Persephoneia, whose stately and impressive ritual prescribing fasts, bathing in the waters of the sea, self-discipline, self-denial, self-restraint, culminated in the Hall of Initiation...How fair a shadow this was, albeit always and ever a shadow, of the imperishable and eternal realities to come! How different these Mysteries from the foul orgies of witches, the Sabbat, the black mass, the adoration of hell.[8]

Mr. Green's erroneous condemnation of other religions and other seekers is repeated later in *I Believe in Satan's Downfall*

---

6. Helminski, 75.
7. Helminski, 275.
8. Father Summers, 44.

when he claims that "Only in Judaism and Christianity is mysticism inescapably linked with love and compassion."[9] He is totally wrong, and this becomes clearer in later chapters.

The White Magic Error

Charismatics are not alone in condemning other occult practitioners. I learned that many occultists denounce others who practice the same things, each believing he alone practices with good intentions. I call this the "White Magic Error," after the custom among magicians to distinguish between white and black magic. In White Magic thinking, it is okay—and not really occult—to call down spiritual power if we want to serve or help someone. Thus many healing ministries—whether Buddhist, shaman or charismatic—would never use the word "occult" to describe their spirituality because they see the occult as having to do only with evil or nasty things.

> Many occultists fall into the White Magic Error. They think others do wrong, and only they understand God's will. They think their ways are right because they know God and their intentions are good.

The error in this way of thinking should be obvious. A person's intentions do not make a religious practice occult or not. Trafficking in spirits is not Christianity when done for the right reasons, and sorcery when done for the wrong. Occultism is not mysticism gone bad or "undiscriminating mysticism." No dictionary supports this, and neither does the Bible. The occult does not become evil in the context of selfishness. It already is evil because, whether we realize it or not, it involves us in the kingdom of Satan.

---

9. Green, 190. He follows this statement with, "After all, you cannot relate in depth to a loving personal God without some of his characteristics making themselves felt in your subsequent attitudes." Here he reveals the occult belief that in the "depth" of mystic encounter God's love "rubs off on us," so to speak. No doubt Mr. Green is not aware of the *phos* light experiences of other occultists, who also believe they encounter a loving god in their mystic experiences.

Among charismatics, the White Magic Error reveals several levels of misunderstanding, including the belief that occultism is Christian when practiced in love, and sorcery if not. Consider a teaching from *When the Spirit Comes With Power*, where John White makes just such a false distinction:

> Now why should there be any danger of mistaking the finger of God for the horns of the devil? On the face of it the notion seems absurd. How could such dissimilar sources give rise to similar products?
>
> There is one source of supernatural power, and one only. Satan's power is power once entrusted to him by God. God was the Creator of the power just as, being the Creator of all that is, he created Satan himself. The power was meant for use in God's service. It is what we might call embezzled power. And that is exactly what magic is—stolen power, used for the user's delight. Whenever anyone, Christian or non-Christian, angel or demon, uses power for selfish ends (for the love of power or for the justification or glory of the self), the power can be called magical power. It is the same power with the same characteristics put to a wrong use and subtly changed by that use. Christians who use God's power in this way have begun to act like sorcerers. Angels so using it fall.[10]

Note how Mr. White begins. In direct contradiction of Scripture, he says it is absurd to think that the light—or "horns," as he puts it—of Satan could ever be mistaken for the light—or "finger"—of God. (Does he really think Satan only comes with "horns" on?)

On this foundation of error Mr. White constructs an occult view of God and the Holy Spirit. He teaches that the "power of God"—which he confuses with the Holy Spirit—is a sort of dormant, morally neutral force available for anyone to tap into. It is neither

---

10. White, 141.

good nor evil, he says, but it is the "user" who makes it so based on his or her intent. Amazing! The Holy Spirit is no longer holy!

Mr. White then goes on to say that men or angels determine the holiness of the "power" of "God." Furthermore, according to Mr. White God does not discriminate as to who receives His "power" and anyone can "use" it: believers, nonbelievers, sorcerers and even fallen angels.[11]

The occult aspects of Mr. White's teaching are serious, yet his words have been accepted by countless believers as words of wisdom about the Holy Spirit. I myself did not recognize the extent of his error until I typed out the passage, and during this careful exercise the extent of the heresy began to dawn on me.

We must take several objections to what Mr. White says. First, to wield supernatural power is the role of the shaman or magician; it is clearly occult. Mr. White comes close to acknowledging this when he says Christians who use occult power for selfish purposes are acting "like sorcerers," and magic is "stolen power." However, he tacitly excuses his own "use" of the "power" because his intentions are (he thinks) unselfish. He teaches that those who use occult power for good purposes are good Christians—a perfect example of the White Magic Error. Let's look again at the definitions of sorcery and magic:

What is sorcery? It is like magic, but involves deliberately working with evil spirits.

What is magic? Also known as wizardry, it includes (partial list from chapter 5):

- practice designed to invoke or harness supernatural power to work miracles or healing;
- practice designed to invoke or control supernatural energy or spirits; and
- channeling or wielding power from a supernatural source.

---

11. This understanding of the "power of God" could be based on an occult interpretation of passages like Psalm 62:11: "Power belongs to God." This verse does not mean that power emanates from God like light emanates from the sun, ready to be channeled and directed by men. It simply means that God is all-powerful.

John White implies that all three of the above-listed practices are Christian, provided the "power" is "put to the right use". Here, again, is what he wrote:

> Whenever anyone, Christian or non-Christian, angel or demon, uses power for selfish ends (for the love of power or for the justification or glory of the self), the power can be called magical power. It is the same power with the same characteristics put to a wrong use and subtly changed by that use.

As well as misunderstanding the meanings of magic and sorcery, Mr. White says anyone can wield "God's" supernatural power; he is a Christian if he uses it rightly, and a sorcerer if not![12] Unfortunately, he is not alone in thinking this way. The following is a charismatic teaching about calling down "God's touch of love":

> As we are willing to be taught, the Holy Spirit will show us how to grow in the capacity to express our concern, to get the paralytic on the roof, to open the way to get him down into the presence of God...or just His touch of love upon the one whom we bring...We are not seeking to get God to do our will. That is incantation or sorcery.[13]

The above writer believes it is okay to call down supernatural power for the benefit of another, but the same practice becomes "incantation or sorcery" when done for selfish purposes: again, the White Magic Error.

The distinction charismatics make between what they do and what sorcerers do is 100 percent false. It is just as flawed as the distinction Wiccans (that is, practicing witches) draw between white and black witchcraft. I knew a practicing witch very well when I

---

12. In one area I agree with Mr. White. He hits the nail on the head when he says occult power is available to everyone, Christian or not. All people, God's children included, can encounter occult spirits and powers when they flirt with the supernatural.

13. Alfred L. Durrance, "Intercessory and Soaking Prayer," posted at *http://durrance.com/FrAl/intercessory_and_soaking_prayer.htm*.

was younger. She was my best and favorite roommate, a kind, honest woman who believed in all sincerity that "white witch-craft" was a good thing—good for her, good for others and good for the whole planet. She did not understand that occult practices never end well, whether we call them white or black, and whether or not our intentions are good. She, too, made the White Magic Error.

What do kundalini devotees say?

Like charismatics, kundalini yogis also emphasize the impor-tance of good intentions for wielding occult power. Humility is important, and they teach that pride must be destroyed before a person can become great in the faith.

Consider the Hindu parable of a yoga disciple named Gorakshanath who "had tremendous pride because he had real-ized the Truth and attained occult power."[14] We are told that Gorakshanath was drawn into an argument with another yogi who was insulting his master. He supposedly warned the yogi to watch his tongue for he, Gorakshanath, had great occult powers. However, when challenged it became evident that the yogi had greater power. As the story goes, the yogi was unable to stab Gorakshanath because a knife blade would not penetrate his skin. So the yogi said, "Although you were not injured, my blows cre-ated a sound. But if you strike me with the same knife, not only will you not be able to injure me, but also you will not be able to produce any sound." The yogi was right, and Garakshanath was outdone. Later the master said to Gorakshanath, "You are my best disciple. I gave you all kinds of occult power, but you were defeated by that yogi, only because of your pride. Now that you have been humiliated, now that your pride has been smashed…before long you will surpass both him and me."

The teaching of this Hindu parable is clear: humility is a sign of healthy spirituality and is important for the proper use of supernat-ural power—a teaching also common among charismatics.

---

14. Parable related by Sri Chinmoy, "Kundalini the Mother-Power," *www.srichinmoylibrary.com/kundalini-mother-power*, para. 98–122. This quo-tation from para. 108.

Yogis also rely upon good intentions to receive blessings from God and for protection from evil spirits. Take for example the teaching of Sri Ramakrishna, a Samadhi guru, who says that "when there is even a trace of pride in a person, he cannot reach God,"[15] and exhorts us to:

> Pray to Him innocently with a pure mind. He will make you understand all. Give up egoism and take refuge in Him. You will get everything.[16]

This guru is saying that if our intentions are good, God will bless us and we will receive from Him. But is this not what Mr. White and Mr. Green also say?

Consider the following teaching from renowned yoga master Sri Chinmoy on the proper use of occult powers, which also resembles the teachings of Mr. White and Mr. Green:

> When the Kundalini is awake, man is fully aware of the inner world...He has brought to the fore the hidden powers, the occult powers, within himself. Either he uses these powers properly or he misuses them. When he divinely uses the powers of the Kundalini, he becomes the real pride of the Mother Supreme. When he misuses them, he becomes the worst enemy of man's embodied consciousness and of his own personal evolution.[17]

Sri Chinmoy teaches that to attain supernatural powers should never be the goal of a practitioner, but only a means to spiritual evolution:

> Blessed is he who practices Kundalini yoga as part of his self-discovery and not in order to acquire power in hypnotism,

---

15. "Another Visit to Sinti Brahmo Samaj," *http://www.kathamrita.org/kathamrita/k1sec12.htm*, ch. 2.

16. "Another Visit," ch 9.

17. Chinmoy, "Kundalini," para. 64.

> black magic or other low forms of occultism which oper-
> ate in and from the vital world… A genuine seeker never
> considers the hidden powers or occult powers as his goal.
> He cares only for God. He longs only for God's loving
> Presence in his life.[18]

Mr. Chinmoy is effectively teaching here that those who practice yoga with good intentions will be blessed, but those who are
in it for the power are practicing a "low form of occultism." This,
of course, is just another variation of the White Magic Error.

WHAT ABOUT OTHER OCCULT PRACTITIONERS?

Will we find the White Magic Error repeated by others? Yes.

Let us turn briefly to the works of one of Europe's most
famous magicians, Alphonse Louis Constant, who wrote under
the pseudonym Eliphas Levi. His works were published between
1855 and 1865. Master alchemist and self-proclaimed "Magus of
Light," Mr. Levi wrote numerous tomes on magic arts, or the "science of magic" as he liked to call it.

Even though he called himself a magician, Mr. Levi also considered himself a Christian because he used God's power (which
he termed "Astral Light") in accordance with His will—or so he
believed. This, of course, is the same self-evaluation we saw from
charismatic John White.

Mr. Levi would agree with Mr. White on other points, as well.
For example, he believed that supernatural power is available to
everyone, believer or not. He hated Satan, and could not understand how anyone could refer to him as a "Light Bearer"; in my estimation this was because he, like Mr. White, failed to understand
how "the horns of the devil" could be mistaken for "the finger of
God." Like Mr. White, he also distinguished between those who use
occult power for good, and those who use it for evil. The former he
called "Magicians of Light" or "Transcendental Magicians." The latter he scorned as practitioners of black magic; again, the White
Magic Error.

---

18. Chinmoy, "Kundalini," para. 72.

The writings of Eliphas Levi, Magus of Light, resonate with ideas found in Mr. White's book *When the Spirit Comes with Power*, albeit clothed in different terminology. To compare their writings is to see clearly how occult spirits lead practitioners down the same paths, to similar beliefs about God and truth.

In the preface to the 1913 English translation of Levi's *Histoire de la Magie*, the translator summarized the French magician's teachings as saying that magic is the "secret" of the "science of good and evil [and]…confers on man powers apparently superhuman."[19] The secret, Mr. Levi says, consists in understanding and accessing a universal medium or power which he refers to as the "Astral Light." This Astral Light finds its equivalent in Mr. White's "power of God." Mr. White taught that the power can be used by men and angels; Mr. Levi taught the same thing about Astral Light.

We saw that Mr. White believes God's "power" is neither good nor bad, but can be used for good or evil in accordance with the will of the practitioner. Mr. Levi taught the same thing about the "Astral Light," calling it a "blind" force. His translator explains that this force, "… is the great medium of occult force, but as such it is a blind force, which can be used for good or evil."[20] And, magician Eliphas Levi condemned black magic, as does charismatic John White.

The other guy is always the sorcerer

It is interesting to note how frequently occult practitioners approve themselves and condemn others. The other guy is always the sorcerer.

We saw earlier how charismatic Michael Green condemned the occult, yet, at the same time, called for mysticism "in the name of Jesus." But magician Eliphas Levi says mysticism is the true sorcery. In great but unintended irony the Magus of Light wrote:

Religion has no greater enemy than unbridled mysticism, which mistakes its feverish visions for divine revelations. It

---

19. Eliphas Levi, *The History of Magic, 1913*, trans. A. E. Waite (London, Great Britain: Ryder & Company: 1969), 8.

20. Levi, Introduction, 9.

is not the theologians who have created the devil's empire, but the false devotees and sorcerers. To believe a vision of the brain rather than the authority of public reason or piety has been ever the beginning of heresy in religion and of folly in the order of human philosophy…Divinations, magnetic experiences and evocations [commanding spirits to leave] belong to one and the same order of phenomena, being those which cannot be misemployed without danger to reason and life.[21]

Here we see an unrepentant magician condemning other occult practitioners: again, the White Magic Error.

John White, Michael Green and Eliphas Levi are all fervent authors and teachers in their faith, as they understand it. All believe they serve God by wielding His power for good. Each has his own understanding of what constitutes right and wrong practice, and the proper context for the "use" of God's power. Each believes he can judge his own intentions, and that his intentions are good.

What is going on here?

ON JUDGING GOOD AND EVIL INTENT

If we compare the teachings of Hindus, magicians and charismatics, there will be differences, partly because they interpret their experiences against different texts. But in the end their views converge at several points. One such point is that men and women can search their own hearts and judge themselves good enough to "wield" the power of "God" in supernatural works.

Leaving aside the problem of Christians acting like magicians, let's consider if men and women can ever really know their own hearts. What if we judge our motivations in error? Can we really see ourselves the way God sees us? Is the road to God paved by our good intentions?

It is true that Scriptures speak of the "pure in heart," those who will inherit the kingdom of God. But they also teach that no

---

21. Levi, 328. Mr. Levi's teaching is often confused. In places he appears to approve certain forms of divination, but here he condemns it.

man is pure, nor ever can be, at least not while in the flesh. In fact, we are so far from purity that we can never find God, even with the best of intentions or the most superb efforts, because there is a huge gulf between Him and us, a gulf bridged only by Jesus and by true faith in Him. We have no righteousness in ourselves, not a shred of it, because we are naturally alienated from God. What we do have, if we have true faith, is imputed righteousness; the purity of Jesus credited to our account by the grace of God alone.

I am not saying there is no goodness in the world, for man retains some knowledge of right and wrong, and of how to do good things and give good gifts. There are men and women, Christian or not, who are gracious, honest, loving, merciful, hardworking and courageous. But the Bible teaches that above our best efforts and beyond our highest reach there is a spiritual and moral holiness, a pure goodness and love, that we can never attain in this lifetime. This is the holiness of God, and before Him none can stand. None can claim even a particle of self-righteousness. Hard to believe, perhaps, but we must believe this if we call ourselves Christian:

> As it is written: "There is none righteous, no, not one; there is none who understands; there is none who seeks after God. They have all gone out of the way; they have together become unprofitable; there is none who does good, no, not one" (Romans 3:10-12).

Furthermore, God never promises to reveal Himself to people who consider themselves pure or righteous, let alone righteous enough to dabble in the occult. No, Scriptures say it is the *unrighteous* who inherit the promise; that is, it is those who do not claim righteousness on their own account who will inherit the kingdom of God.

Who, then, does God esteem? Scriptures say those He esteems, those with whom He makes His home, are the humble, the contrite and the lowly of heart. It is those who recognize not their good intentions but their bad; those who long for humility but see their stubborn pride; those who perceive not their purity but their desperate need for it. These are the ones whose hearts are ready to lay hold of the knowledge of God. That is the meaning of the beatitude that the "poor in spirit" inherit the kingdom of God.

Although charismatics give lip service to this doctrine, they contradict it in practice.

If God reveals Himself only to the poor in spirit, what shall we conclude about the favorable self-judgments of occult seekers? If we believe the Bible, we can only conclude that they are deceived. They do not understand the God of Scripture, nor do they see themselves the way He does.

WE MUST NEVER CREDIT RELIGION FOR RIGHTEOUSNESS

I do not want to belabor the point, but I do want to emphasize that Christians are no better than anyone else. Saved, blessed, set free—yes. But not better. Michael Green and others make the mistake of judging themselves more pure and loving than others based, it appears, on the teachings of their religion (which calls for "love, holiness, and the service of others").

But we must never credit religion for righteousness, because then grace is no longer grace but has given way to works. This is a crucial difference between Christianity and all other religions. Paul addressed this very point in his letter to the Roman Jews when he explained that they were not better than the Gentiles just because they had the Law (see Romans 3:17-21,22-23).

Like secular occultists, charismatics are on a misguided quest for truth, love or power. Neither group realizes that what they are doing is wrong and dangerous. They are each just as foolish, just as misguided, just as noble, just as ignoble, just as selfish, just as unselfish, just as loving and just as unloving as the other. And just as blind. Paul stressed:

> Therefore you are inexcusable, O man, whoever you are
> who judge, for in whatever you judge another you condemn
> yourself; for you who judge practice the same things
> (Romans 2:1).

Scriptures assert that all of us have gone astray, and there is none righteous. No one seeks the things of God. Let us remember, therefore, that when we condemn others we condemn ourselves, for all flesh is alike.

OUR FUTILE UNDERSTANDING

Sorcery is a work of the flesh (see Galatians 5:19-20). I believe this means that humankind will find it naturally appealing; men and women will be attracted to the mysteries of the occult. For this reason, among others, the Bible warns us not to lean on our own understanding but to put all—not a little, but all—our trust in God, and in His commands:

> Trust in the Lord with all your heart,
> And lean not on your own understanding;
> In all your ways acknowledge Him,
> and he will direct your paths (Proverbs 3:5-6).

Moses had these words for people who follow their own understanding and venture into occult practice:

> If there should be among you a man or woman, family or
> tribe, who is moved today to turn from the Lord our God
> and to go worshiping the gods of those nations – if there is
> among you such a root from which springs gall and
> wormwood, then when he hears the terms of this oath, he
> may inwardly flatter himself and think, "All will be well
> with me even if I follow the promptings of my stubborn
> heart"; but this will bring everything to ruin
> (Deuteronomy 29:18-19 NEB).

Moses warns us against relying on our own understanding—or, as he puts it, following the promptings of our own hearts—because we are stubborn seekers who love to flatter ourselves.

Chapter Nine

VISIONS, SIDDHIS AND THE PRIESTHOOD OF THE MAGUS

*Here in the West there are many who feel that the powers
of Kundalini Yoga are nothing but rank superstition. I
wish to say that those who cherish this idea are totally
mistaken. Even the genuine spiritual Masters have
examined Kundalini Yoga and found in their own experiences the undeniable authenticity of its hidden occult
powers.*

—Sri Chinmoy, yoga master

*I*n yoga, supernatural powers are called *siddhis* or *siddhi powers.* They include paranormal perception, like seeing angels
and demons, and the ability to perform miracles like materializ-
ing ashes out of nowhere.

In Hindu thought, *siddhi mastery*—that is, the development of
supernatural abilities—is evidence of spiritual progress. However,
as we saw in chapter 8, the student of yoga is expected to use his
or her power humbly, for loving and selfless purposes.

For siddhi development, the serpent force must first be able
to move freely through the chakras. The first step, say yoga
teachers, is a kundalini awakening. Then siddhi powers develop

through continuing yoga practices including meditation, shakti-pat and samadhi.

There are "warrior siddhis," "occult siddhis" and "heart purification siddhis," among others. As devotees continue on the path of siddhi mastery they may experience:

- a sense of deep inner peace
- fantasies about being a destroyer of evil
- increased love for God
- clairaudience, i.e., hearing voices, musical instruments, singing, sighing or other sounds "in the mind," sounds believed to be from the spirit realm
- clairvoyance: i.e. visions or pictures perceived in the mind alone and believed to be from the spirit realm (e.g., seeing angels)
- the ability to divine the thoughts and secrets of other people
- discerning illness in others
- knowledge of past, present or future; i.e., prophecy or seeing "outside time"
- the development of a warm sense of love and compassion for others[1]

Clairvoyance and clairaudience are considered occult siddhis. They refer to the opening of the so-called third, or spiritual, eye to see into the hidden spirit realm.

SO WHAT DOES THIS HAVE TO DO WITH CHARISMATIC EXPERIENCE?

There are differences, but also significant parallels between charismatic and yoga teaching on supernatural powers and gifts. Hindus refer to gift development as "siddhi mastery" and

---

1. see Sri Kalki Bhagavan, "Siddhis and the chakras," transcript of a workshop by Dharma Dharini Bhagavad Dasa, *http://skyboom1.tripod.com/index27.html*, and Inessa King Zaleski, "Siddhis: Supernormal Perceptual States," *http://www.cabiz.net/heartlink/siddhis1.htm*.

charismatics call it "awakening the prophetic," but for the most part they are, as we will see, talking about the same things. Many charismatics claim siddhi-like "third eye" powers to see and hear angels. They also claim to read people's thoughts, discern illnesses and tell the future. And they believe they experience increased love for God through soaking prayer.

Yet another parallel is the need for a spiritual initiation experience. Hindus have the "kundalini awakening," and charismatics the baptism of the Holy Spirit, or "second blessing." In the minds of both groups this experience necessarily precedes the development of supernatural, or spiritual, gifts. The second blessing is regarded by charismatics as *the* initiation into a fully intimate and "anointed" relationship with God, but is eerily akin to a kundalini awakening in that the initiate experiences rapture, speaks in tongues and may emerge with supernatural abilities. Compare the following charismatic (Pentecostal) and yoga teachings:

Charismatic:
Should Christians Seek the Second Baptism? The first matter to consider is a vitally important one. It lies at the very heart of Pentecostal teaching. It controls and colors their whole view of the Christian life. It is the doctrine of the baptism in the Holy Spirit. According to them this is *the* blessing to be sought, *the* experience to strive for, *the* greatest and highest achievement of the Christian man and woman. What is this great spiritual blessing? It is a special post-conversion gift and experience in which the Holy Spirit is poured out on you in all His fullness, with special power to enable you to have things and do things you cannot have and do otherwise.[2] (emphasis original)

Yoga:
Shaktipat means "touch of the shakti" or Initiation. Shaktipat is the spiritual initiation given by a divine Master; the inner quickening. Shaktipat is synonymous

---

2. Charles J. Terpstra, "Pentecostalism's View of the Christian Life," *http://www.prca.org/current/Articles/Pentecostalism4.htm*, 2.

with the *baptism* of Christianity, and the *anointing* of
Judaism. The real baptism is an actual psycho-spiritual
event, one experienced by those of many faiths who
develop devotion combined with purity. It represents the
beginning of the awakening and unfolding of the inner
power of kundalini-shakti, and is often accompanied by
marvelous events and perceptions....After receiving shaktipat, the divine shakti itself unfolds the spiritual development of the devotee.[3] (emphasis original)

The reader can see that both the second blessing and the kundalini awakening are believed to initiate the seeker into a mysterious world of occult gift development. Let's allow yogis and
charismatics to speak for themselves in the next few pages, as we
consider the special powers and perceptions gained through these
experiences.

SPIRITUAL EYES OPENED

In my charismatic church, one of my favorite pastors told me
that as we "grow in the prophetic," God can "open our spiritual
eyes." This obviously parallels the Hindu view of third eye open-
ings. I discovered that powers of clairvoyance and clairaudience,
especially seeing and hearing angels and demons, are very popular
on the occult path. A kundalini devotee writes:

After receiving shaktipat, numerous experiences began to
occur. One night at home, I heard the conch shell so
loudly and clearly that I started. Interpreting that I was
being beckoned to meditate, I did so...I realized I wasn't
alone. A sound in the hallway confirmed my belief, and
summoning up all the courage I had, I turned to look. He
was standing in the doorway—a being made of light. The
beauty and vibrancy of this sight were not of this realm.[4]

---

3. Sacred Word Trust, "shaktipat info."
4. Anandamaya, "The Blue Man,"
   http://www.sadhanaashram.org/experiences.html.

The above writer received both paranormal sight and hearing after a shaktipat impartation, and reportedly saw an angel of light.

Well-known charismatic Todd Bentley, who claims to receive frequent visitations from angels, travels widely for "Catch the Fire" events to impart occult visions in shaktipat-type practices. He writes voluminously on the topic, and has posted many articles on the Web. In one such article he writes:

> So I'm asking God to release the seer anointing to you as you read this article so that you can even see the angelic hosts. Today I want to focus the teaching on the angelic realm and how you can release angels to fulfill God's word. Recently, I had several daily visitations of angels which lasted for weeks. Since the beginning of this year I've also sensed an increase in the presence of angels in our meetings.[5]

Mr. Bentley visited a church in North Dakota and reportedly imparted paranormal perception to the pastor's wife. The pastor wrote:

> After that power packed evening [with Todd Bentley], Julie testified that the prophetic gifting of the Holy Spirit began to operate in a new dimension. Tuesday evening she saw the church surrounded with angels and even heard them singing with the congregation during worship![6]

While in a trance Julie both heard and saw angels, demonstrating siddhi-like powers of clairaudience and clairvoyance. Similar occult visions were reported by others at a "Catch the Fire" event in Tucson, Arizona, featuring Gary and Kathi Oates. Mr. and Mrs. Oates are reportedly so advanced in siddhi-like power that "God's presence invaded the auditoriums each time

5. Todd Bentley, "Opening Our Eyes to the Angelic Realm,"
   http://www.elijahlist.com/words/display_word.html?ID=1785.
6. Ron Enget, "Fresh Fire Falls on Beulah, North Dakota," posted at
   http://groups.yahoo.com/group/Rivermail_list/message/2286?source=1.

Gary and Kathi ministered."[7] Here is the testimony of a young woman who attended this event:

> I felt the Lord was saying that we (our homegroup) should ask Him to open our eyes and our ears. I asked...then forgot all about it until Friday...in church I was so moved by the presence of the Lord that I went to the back and knelt down... sobbing. Soon, I saw an angel in the doorway blowing a cool breeze over the church and knew his job was to reawaken a hunger and recognition of the presence of the Lord. Next I saw an angel on either side of the first, and these were blowing trumpets, but I understood their message to be "Prepare the way for a Holy Lord". I'm still so touched by the increased ability to see and hear and I want more.[8]

The angelic message in the above testimony sounds biblical and reverent. But consider the occult elements. Enchanted by a presence brought by empowered leaders, unmotivated weeping, paranormal seeing: could it be that this woman really saw and heard an angel from God? Of course not. First, it came as a result of occult practice; that alone is reason enough to reject it. But we see also that this "angel" is not teaching the Jesus of the gospel who comes through the word of truth. It teaches an occult Jesus who comes by invocation and manifest presence, and imparts siddhi-like powers. Next, angels do not awaken our hunger for God; this is the work of the Holy Spirit. And last, Scripture teaches that not only will demons pretend to worship the Lord, they can and will declare His deity, and even proclaim His work of salvation. The demon that Paul cast out of the prophetess in Philippi caused her to announce his mission as God's servant to declare the way of salvation. Every word she spoke was true. But Paul was not pleased, and clearly discerned

---

7. Gary & Kathi Oates, "Tucson Area Christian Fellowship," *http://www.tacf.us./pr06.htm, 3.*

8. Oates, Tucson, 1-2.

the demonic source (see Acts 16:16-18). We must not be fooled by pious appearances.

Another charismatic at the Tucson, Arizona event reported the following:

> God opened [my] husband's eyes to more of the angelic realm. Previously, he had seen his angel twice, but a few nights after the conference he saw him again. In the middle of the night he woke up, he sensed a presence and opened his eyes and saw his angel over him. He then saw five other angels, smaller in size, going around in the room swinging a flag type of item. When they swung this flag, there was music.[9]

Note how the writer above refers to the opening of eyes to see more of the angelic realm—a classic third eye opening. What is also interesting about the husband's experience is how he refers to "his" angel not once, but twice. This is no doubt linked to the concept of finding your own guardian angel.

Angels: a biblical view

Teachings about finding, and even conversing with, your own guardian angel are increasingly common in charismatic circles. But these are occult counterfeits of biblical teaching about protective angels.

While many passages of Scripture indicate that angels are assigned to guide and protect people (Hebrews 1:14 says that angels are ministering spirits who help God's children), nowhere are we commanded to ask for "spiritual eyes" so we can see them and hear them. This is occult thinking.

Only a brief excursion into ancient and modern teachings of magicians and other occult seekers reveals that they have always been preoccupied with angels, demons and guardian angels. Read the following written by an accomplished medieval magician— Abraham the Jew, also known as Abramelin the Mage—an

---

9. Oates, Tucson, 2.

"expert" on guardian angels, who wrote to his own son, "you shall see your Guardian Angel appear unto you in unequaled beauty; who also will converse with you, and speak in words so full of affection and of goodness, and with such sweetness, that no human tongue could express the same."[10]

Abramelin the Mage, like those at the Tucson church, says angels come with a manifest, loving spiritual presence—and odors (as also reported by the Toronto church and other charismatic congregations):

> Humiliate yourself before God and his celestial court, and
> commence your prayer with fervor…and you will see
> appear an extraordinary and supernatural splendor which
> will fill the whole apartment, and will surround you with
> an inexpressible odor, and this alone will console you and
> comfort your heart so that you shall call forever happy the
> Day of the Lord.[11]

While angels are mentioned in the Bible over 350 times, only a small number of groups or individuals—fewer than 40 over approximately 1,500 years of biblical history—are reported to have seen them. However, mystics teach that anyone, if they go about it the right way—that is, through the occult—can find their own angel. Thousands of angel sightings have been reported by charismatics and other mystics.

Why are believers looking for angels when our eyes are to be fixed upon Jesus? Why did the young woman in North Dakota say "I want more"? Is this not to set up angels as idols? Paul wrote to the Colossians, "Let no one defraud you of your reward, taking delight in false humility and worship of angels, intruding into those things which he has not seen, vainly puffed up by his fleshly mind, and not holding fast to the Head…" (Colossians 2:18-19).

---

10. Abramelin the Mage, ed. S. Liddell MacGregor Mathers, *The Sacred Magic of Abramelin the Mage*,
    http://www.esotericarchives.com/abramelin/abramelin.htm, 84.
11. The Mage, *Sacred Magic*, Book II.

While it is clear from biblical accounts that God sometimes communicates through angels, this is definitely no reason to dabble in the occult. The Bible portrays angelic appearances as extraordinary phenomena. Insofar as God's children are concerned, such appearances are never experienced through, or as a result of, occult practice.

SEERS AT WILL

A newcomer to mysticism usually finds it necessary to enter a trance state before he or she can see angels. However advanced mystics, both pagan and charismatic, claim such ability when not in a trance, even at will. Kundalini practitioner Gail tells us:

> I am a "sighted" psychic, and have the ability to see angels, hierarchies of angels, demon/entities, lost souls, apparitions, guides, deceased pets, saints…and have done for the last three years or more, sending souls to the Light, and casting out demons…angels look like white rays of light, to white energy forms, to solid humanoid forms. They come in all sizes and shapes. They look like old Victorian-type angels, to angels with holographic-type gowns that change color with the light that shines within them. I've seen angels that look gold in color, and have eyes all over their wings.[12]

Charismatic Kathie Walters claims the same abilities as Gail. She says seeing angels is a normal part of her everyday life, and she believes we should all be conversing with heavenly beings on a regular basis:

> I [asked] people "Do you know that the realm of the Spirit, the supernatural realm, the angels, heavenly visitations, are supposed to be a normal part of your life? Those same people who are sure of their salvation, will say they feel somehow they are not "qualified" for this

---

12. "Questions and Answers about Gail's Experience,"
   http://www.well.com/user/bobby/extra/q&agail.html.

supernatural realm…When I speak of angelic encounters, heavenly visitations, God's chariots, people say to me, "Well it's OK for you—you have that kind of Spirit ministry." It grieves me when I hear that. We are all meant to have that kind of ministry…Pray this, "Thank you Lord that when Jesus died for me, He left me an inheritance. The realm of the spirit, the supernatural realm of God, the Angels, the visitations of God, Heaven—that is my inheritance and it is a normal part of my life. This I confess and I choose to believe…"[13]

But is Kathie's teaching really Christian? Of course not. It is akin to Hinduism or magic. It has nothing to do with Jesus, or with any form of godly righteousness. Communing at will with angels is an ancient, occult art. Considering again the definitions from Chapter 5, we know that occult practice involves seeking supernatural spirits, and seeking the paranormal ability to see or hear them. Encouraging "visitations" and "encounters" with angels definitely falls within this definition. Such practices are those of the nations. They seduced the Israelites, and they are now seducing those who claim to belong to the Christian church.

DIVINATION, PROPHETIC GIFTS AND THE PRIESTHOOD OF THE MAGUS

Occult exposure also influences people to pursue secret knowledge, such as knowledge of the future or of people's hidden thoughts. Charismatics do this under the rubric of "developing the gift of prophecy" and yogis, as we have seen, under "mastering the siddhis." However, this is nothing more than simple divination. Consider again the definition from chapter 5:

What is divination? Also called soothsaying, magic or seeing, it involves:

---

13. Kathie Walters, "Faith!" (*www.goodnews.netministries.org*); *http://www.elijahlist.com/gospels/display_gospel.html?ID=1842*.

- trying to predict future events or discover hidden knowledge, usually by the aid of supernatural gifting; or
- using paranormal insight or perception.

Let's consider the experiences of yoga and charismatic seekers in their own words. Yoga master Jafree (chapter 3) said that after his second samadhi experience:

> [I] had more…psychic knowledge of everything and everyone in existence than I ever imagined was humanly possible. Every person I met was like an open book which I could read from beginning to end![14]

One guru explains that when kundalini is awakened a person may experience "states of heightened awareness, the emergence of psychic gifts…"[15] Charismatics report similar experiences. In the Alpha tapes, Nicky Gumbel talks about discerning people's illnesses. Here is what another well-known, charismatic teacher, Rick Joyner, says about increased powers of paranormal perception:

> God chose to reveal certain things in His Word. There alone is where we should seek knowledge of divine things. To seek hidden knowledge about illnesses in people, mysteries of the future, angels and departed spirits, etc., is divination, also known as "seeing."

> In the dream and trances, I had what I consider to be greatly magnified gifts of discernment and words of knowledge. Sometimes when I look at a person, or pray for a church or ministry, I just start to know things about them of which I have no natural knowledge. During these prophetic experiences these gifts were operating on a level that I have never personally experienced in "real life."[16]

---

14. Jafree, "Who is?"
15. Sananda, "Kundalini."
16. Rick Joyner, *The Final Quest* (New Kensington, PA: Whitaker House, 1996), 12.

Not only yogis and charismatics, but also other occultists pursue supernatural gifts. This is not surprising, given the influence and leading of occult spirits. French magician Eliphas Levi (chapter 8) understands divination to be but one aspect of magic, and advanced divination to be "the Priesthood of the Magus":

> Divination...in its broadest sense...is the exercise of divine power, and the realization of divine knowledge. It is the Priesthood of the Magus. But divination, in general opinion, is concerned more closely with the knowledge of hidden things. To know the most secret thoughts of men; to penetrate the mysteries of past and future; to evoke age by age the exact revelation of effects by the precise knowledge of causes: this is what is universally called divination.[17]

What is noteworthy about Mr. Levi's definition is that he identifies divination as exercising divine power and knowing divine things. This is significant, the implication being that people who seek powers of divination are, whether they realize it or not, trying to be like God. Bible readers will recognize this as the primary satanic temptation (Genesis 3).

OCCULT SANCTIFICATION

A further belief shared by yogis and charismatics has to do with how we are sanctified unto holiness, or how we attain spiritual purity. Both rely on occult presence or power, believing they are literally "washed," purified and made holy by the power or influence of occult spirit. Practitioners see their role as largely passive; once they connect with a manifest spirit they simply lie back and submit to a sort of mystic "bath" or occult "fire" which is supposed to take away all their sins and impurities.

Let us look at the yogic view:

> Awakened kundalini in someone will do complete cleansing and purificiation on chakras, layers of the bodies, and

---

17. Eliphas Levi, *Transcendental Magic* (Samuel Weiser, 1995), 368, quoted in Friend, *Fallen Angel*, 253.

eteric channels. After passing the cleansing and purification processes, a person can have different psychic powers and a higher level of consciousness.[18]

This writer expresses the view that after mystic cleansing a person magically develops a "higher consciousness." The kundalini power is seen as having a purifying effect by directly touching and cleansing. This is clearly occult.

Disturbingly, charismatics express similar views. Consider the following testimony from "Bill," who believes that only after mystic cleansing is he ready to "enter the inner chamber" and be closer to God:

> [As] I lay there in the wonderful presence of God on me I became aware of the Holiness and the love and the wrath and His Mercy and majesty of God in a way that I had never known. Now, I understood why I had to be cleansed that time...I knew at the time that I was saved but there was a cleansing that needed to take place before I could enter the inner chamber, the Holy of Holies where God would speak to me...[19]

While under the influence of a manifest spirit, Bill had a powerful, apparently holy experience. He felt moved to reverence for "God." I accept what he says about his feelings. But, he also gained the impression that he needed a mystic cleansing before God would speak to him, before he could come close to God. Is this what Scripture teaches? Not at all. This is occult thinking. This is what Satan wants us to think, and this is how he draws unsuspecting seekers repeatedly back to occult worship.

Biblical teaching has not changed in two thousand years; it is faith and faith alone that opens the curtains to the Holy of Holies, the place where the spirit of man can meet with the Spirit of God. It is what we believe about God's truth which dictates

---

18. Sananda, "What is Kundalini?"

19. Bill Azusa, posted at *aol.comhttp://members.aol.com/Azusa/azusaindex.html.*

our acceptance or rejection by the God of truth. Sanctification is very real and very important, but it is not what ushers us into His presence. We come as we are, the only requirement being that we turn and believe. An old hymn expresses this very well:

Just as I am He will receive, because His promise I believe.

In fact, the time of conversion—when we are still filthy in our sins and sanctification has not even begun—is for many believers an exquisite experience of intimacy with the Father. But Bill, and countless others like him, have been led to seek repeated occult communion with demonic spirits, thinking that this is how they can be made clean. How satanic it is.

Splashing, surging, flushing and purging

Let's examine more samples of occult thinking about spiritual "cleansing." In the next quotation a Reiki instructor advertises a course on the cleansing power of kundalini "fire":

Kundalini Reiki 2—All channels are strengthened. Kundalini Awakening—main energy channel opens gently and surely, alighting the Kundalini "fire"…You are also taught a specific meditation. When you perform this meditation, you increase in a short time, the power of the flame in the Kundalini fire/energy. In this way, all the chakras/energy systems are enlightened and a cleansing takes place.[20]

This instructor says we need kundalini "fire" flowing through opened chakras to cleanse and enlighten the soul. What do charismatics say? Let's look at the teaching of Carol C., who echoes this idea, except in her view the cleansing comes with "hurricane strength":

---

20. Stephanie Thompson, "Higher Education in Holistic Healing for the Body, Mind & Spirit!" Reiki Blessings Academy, http://www.reikiblessings.homestead.com/kundalini~ns4.html.

> We need the love of the Father flowing freely through us.
> And that love only flows when our soul is cleansed—a
> cleansing that requires the hurricane strength wind and
> drenching rain of God's Spirit. So throw away that
> umbrella of fear and soak in the Holy Spirit. Just say:
> "More, Lord. I want more of you!"[21]

Similar occult ideas abound in charismatic thought, worship and practice. Sometimes, during prayer, charismatics pretend they are "splashing" water from a spiritual "river" onto a person, supposedly assisting the cleansing process. A line in a charismatic song says, "Into the river I will wade, there my sins are washed away." This is an occult perversion of biblical teaching on the blood of Jesus.

Another occult concept is "purging"—like washing, but a more violent application of occult power upon the soul. Mysteria, the yoga teacher, says purging by kundalini can be painful. Devotees sometimes vomit, supposedly part of the process. But we saw in chapter 3 that charismatics also vomit as a result of their practices. Some also believe this is part of a spiritual cleansing process. For example:

> What I do know [is] that vomiting is quite often a part of
> deliverance, and it is certainly a result of Holy Spirit move-
> ment...I do know, also, that in renewal meetings demons
> do quite often manifest among people in the congrega-
> tion—this is due to the Holy Spirit moving so mightily in
> such meetings.[22]

Charismatic Pat C. has fallen completely for the occult idea of spiritual "purging." She prophesied as follows:

> Beginnings of Purging Fire: A baptism with fire will visit
> many individuals and churches in 2004 who have been pas-
> sionately seeking for purging in their lives. A purification

---

21. C. Carter, *Union Leader*, Manchester, site not available at publication.
22. Greg, posted at *http://members.iinet.net.au/~gregga/toronto/tbmar98.html*.

season is going to visit the church as a move of purging begins. This purging process will begin to separate the "wheat from the tares."[23]

Charismatics also speak about "applying" the Holy Spirit directly to the heart as if it was ointment. In the following teaching from Carol Arnott at Toronto Airport Church, Christians are urged to be open to occult "doses" of sanctification:

> [God] wants you to experience heavy doses of His divine grace because grace is a place where Satan can't go...
> This is what sanctification is all about; little by little, allowing Jesus to take back the ground in your heart and mind that was once Satan's playground. As you open each door to your Heavenly Father's healing touch, you will automatically close each of those doors in the devil's face.[24]

Mrs. Arnott believes that the penetration of a manifest spirit into her heart will make her like Jesus, which is typical occult thinking. The demonic teaching is that the action of the spirit upon mind, body, heart or soul will magically change a person, preparing him or her for intimacy with God without any other effort. This terrible error turns biblical teaching on its face, as victims are lured into a satanic trap.

Biblical sanctification

The believer's part in true sanctification is to practice the ways of true Christianity. If we do our part, God will do His. Our Lord said to His disciples even *before* they received the Holy Spirit that they were already clean because of the words He had spoken to them. He said, "He who is bathed needs only to wash his feet, but is completely clean..." (John 13:10).

---

23. Patricia King (Pat Coking), posted at *http://www.extremeprophetic.com*.
24. Carol Arnott, "Does the 'Inner You' Need Healing?" *Spread the Fire Magazine*, Vol. 6, Issue 5: 2000, *http://www.tacf.org/stf/archive/6-5*, 4.

Regular reading of Scripture, remembering to search our hearts for sin, confession and obedience—these are the practices that keep us in truth and near to God. The Bible says we are washed by the Word and by mortification of sin. The apostle John wrote, "If we confess our sins, God is faithful and just to forgive us our sins and to cleanse us from all unrighteousness" (1 John 1:9). Peter taught that we purify ourselves by obeying the truth (see I Peter 1:22). Biblical teaching has to do with staying in truth by doing (obedience), not by receiving (opening to occult spirit).

MYSTIC HEALING

Another belief shared by charismatics and yogis is that submission to spiritual power, especially during trance states, brings healing. The emphasis is usually upon emotional and spiritual healing. Following is a yoga teaching:

> Practiced yogis can consciously achieve [Samadhi]... It is in this state that our bodies can completely focus on healing and growing. Delta brainwaves are conducive to miracle-type healing, divine knowledge, inner being and personal growth, rebirth, trauma recovery...[25]

Charismatics believe the Holy Spirit applies healing power during soaking. For example:

> One of the greatest benefits of soaking prayer is receiving the love of God again and again. Francis MacNutt said that soaking through to the core of something dry that needs to be revived, takes time. Soaking prayer invites the love of our heavenly Father to seep into the painful core issues of our lives and bring healing and renewal.[26]

---

25. See http://www.multidimensions.com.
26. Ed Piorek, "Marinated in God," *Spread the Fire Magazine*, Vol. 2, Issue 3, 1996. http://www.tacf.org. Site altered.

Following are lyrics from a charismatic song that could have been written by any mystic, where the Holy Spirit is depicted as a river that brings healing:

> My first love is a rushing river
> a waterfall that will never cease,
> and in the torrent of tears and laughter
> I feel a healing power released.[27]

Compare this yoga poem, which describes melting in waves of joy and feeling "lifted":

> From joy I came, for joy I live, in sacred joy I melt.
> Ocean of mind, I drink all creation's waves.
> Four veils of solid, liquid, vapor, light,
> Lift aright.[28]

The next charismatic testimony reveals the occult idea that the Holy Spirit heals by washing away problems, pain and burdens:

> to me, there's still nothing more tiring than counseling.
> Though Paula and I knew that we were to release the bur-
> dens to God, it was always easier to say than to do. We had
> become soggy with people's grief and emotional pain,
> defiled by the weight of their sins… When we arrived in
> Toronto, we began to receive prayer. Flat on our backs
> lying on the carpet, we began to rejoice as His refreshing
> River washed away years of accumulated burdens.[29]

All these practices are occult because they rely upon the pres-ence, action and influence of supernatural power.

---

27. King of Love, "My First Love."

28. Yogananda, "Samadhi."

29. John Sandford, *Spread the Fire Magazine*, June 1996, Vol. 2, issue 3. *http://www.tacf.org.stf/archive/*. Site altered.

Emotional logjams

Both yogis and charismatics believe there can be emotional "blockages" in the inner person which prevent growth and must be cleared away by occult power, in the same way we might clear a clogged drainpipe.[30] This is similar to the concept of purging, except it focuses specifically on healing "memories" or "old wounds."

I will draw again on my discussions with Mysteria, the yoga teacher. She stressed to me that "inner clearing of emotional blockages happens not in our minds, but in our being." We must turn our thinking off, she says, and let kundalini have its way. The serpent force can then rise up and through chakra centres to "heal wounds and erroneous beliefs." But this process can supposedly be prevented by a blockage, such as a "painful memory." If there is such a blockage, Mysteria explained, kundalini fire "deals with the problem, brings emotional healing, and then progresses to the next chakra." This magical process is believed to free the yoga student from bondage to past hurts and repressed memories.

To my surprise, Mysteria went on to explain Hindu teachings that sound very like those of John and Paula Sandford (of Elijah House Ministries) and other charismatics in counseling ministries, namely the concept of "healing memories." These teachers all believe that painful memories can be retrieved from the subconscious mind (or "the tissues" as Mysteria put it) so they can be "dealt with"—kind of like antibiotics deal with bacteria. Mysteria credits this "healing of memories" to the power of kundalini. Charismatics credit the "healing power of Jesus."

---

30. Freud had a similar view of emotional problems. Using the metaphor of a hydraulic machine, he saw the mind as capable of being dammed up, and problems as psychic fixations that needed to be released. Modern metaphysical "spirituality" offers a course of treatment called "rebirthing" which also concentrates on taking people back to childhood, or even birth, to work through traumas and emotional blocks. Charismatics are in error to think such an approach to healing is anything new, or is even remotely Christian.

However, it soon dawned on me that the whole idea is blatantly occult; occult and magic. Considering again the definitions from chapter 5, we know that occult practice involves seeking supernatural power, presence, influence or action. Magic, or wizardry, is particularly concerned with harnessing or invoking (calling down) supernatural power to work miracles and healing. Here, Elijah House and yoga teachers invoke the presence of supernaturnal spirit or power to act on human flesh.

When Christians call for a supernatural spirit to act upon the heart, they have crossed the line into occultism. In the case of healing memories, practitioners are seeking the action or influence of supernatural power for a magic healing of emotions. This is what wizards do, not true followers of Christ.

Mysteria says that as the serpent force of kundalini progresses up through the chakras, dealing along the way with a person's memories and emotional wounds, it arrives at the heart where it supposedly does a most important work, that of opening it to occult love. This is sometimes referred to as a "heart orgasm," and is believed to develop the individual's capacity for love and compassion. But Mysteria's thinking is startlingly similar to charismatic thinking. For example, John White writes about how the "Holy Spirit" opened a man's heart:

> He asked me to pray for him, and as we prayed the Holy Spirit continued to work powerfully, so that he was stunned by the sudden opening of his mind and heart to realities he had kept at bay for years.[31]

This heart opening is an occult counterfeit of the real thing, which occurs when the Holy Spirit opens a person's heart to receive the Word of God (see Acts 16:14). Consider also the following charismatic testimonies:

---

31. White, 151.

It is possible to have a personal logjam in the heart. This logjam keeps the person who ministers from experiencing Jesus' healing mercy in his own wounded soul...[32]

Soaking prayer is not so much a matter of words as of the intent of the heart to simply hold the person in the love of God while He works the creative power of that love into the area of dis ease [sic].[33]

In the above quotations we see many mystic components, including uncovering memories, healing emotions and the magical working of power "into the heart."

Biblical healing

Healing is a good thing. But is the current preoccupation with emotional healing really biblical?

Jesus' ministry involved much healing, but it was always physical healing, or involved deliverance from demonic spirits. We never read about "emotional healing" in the New Testament. Why? Is it unimportant? Of course not. But Scripture holds different views as to the significance of our grievances, the way we are healed and how we are raised anew in the power of the Holy Spirit.

> We have all suffered emotional pain. But to focus on problems, dig for memories, and worry about old wounds is worldly and occult. Furthermore, it does not help. It is pointless to try to heal or resurrect the old self. What does work is to put the old self to death and turn to God's Word; then He can grow us anew in love, through truth.

As to the hurts and damage suffered by the "old man" or the "old woman"—the people we were before we came to Christ—Scripture teaches that we must consider that person dead, crucified with

32. Carol Arnott, "Inner You," 1.
33. Durrance, *http://durrance.comFrAl/intercessory_and_soaking_prayer.htm*.

Jesus. Trying to patch the old heart is like trying to patch old wine-skins with new leather; it doesn't work. God has given us a new heart and a new spirit: this we must seek to develop by the knowledge of God, obedience and prayer. Throw out your "Christian psychology" books and turn to the Word—there is new wine to warm your soul! If we try to fill old wineskins—the old self—with new wine, the skin will burst, the wine will run out and both will be spoilt (see Matthew 9:17).

Our old self is no longer useful. We must simply let go of our preoccupation with former things. Indeed, Scriptures are more forceful than that, saying we must *put to death* that old self, with all its vain preoccupations and ungodly pursuits; then God can and will raise us up in new life His way.

So let us look forward, not backward. We must live God's way, putting on the new man or the new woman, so the old can pass away. In so doing, I promise you will be overjoyed to find that painful memories and lingering resentments simply lose their power. This indeed is freedom, and healing, and new life! It is not painful. It does not require hours of time lost to mystic pursuits or introspection or digging around in the past to "discover" repressed memories.

It is natural for humans to focus on emotional well-being, but this only distracts us. The prevalent teaching of Scripture is that believers are washed, renewed and nourished by truth, and through the Word led to spiritual health and maturity. This, then, is what we really need.

See Page 99.

Chapter Ten

FOR THE LOVE OF GOD

Great Spiritual Masters...concentrated on God's Feet and meditated on God's Heart. From God's Feet they received God's boundless Love.
> —Sri Chinmoy, kundalini master,
> on receiving occult love

One of the greatest benefits of soaking prayer is receiving the love of God again and again... There have been countless testimonies from those who have had deep experiences of the Father's love while being filled with the Spirit.
> —Charismatic Ed Piorek, on receiving occult love

Take heed to yourselves, lest your heart be deceived,
And you turn aside and serve other gods and worship them
> —Moses, on avoiding occult deception,
> Deuteronomy 11:16

The Puritans and other European believers who settled in North America brought with them an orthodox Christian worldview. They valued reason, learning and sober living. They also accepted the reality of the supernatural realm, fearing the demonic and all occult practice. Sometimes occult practitioners—an obvious example being witches—were persecuted, hysterically and mercilessly. In the face of suspicion and persecution, occultists stayed underground. But in later generations the hysteria subsided, and along with it mistrust of the occult. Nonbelievers and nominal Christians came to disbelieve in the supernatural, dismissing it as silly superstition. In the process they both lost their fear of occultism, and forgot what occultism really is.

As children, many of us in North America had little or no experience of mystic practice or thought. We were not taught how to recognize and avoid the occult. Because our own parents probably lacked this awareness, we were not taught to fear it, nor why we ought to fear it.

Occult thought and practice began to make serious inroads into North American culture in the 1960s, when baby boomers naively turned to the East for answers to social, political and moral problems. Those who learned about kundalini yoga at the Woodstock rock festival in 1969[1] probably had no idea their newfound pursuit was occult, but even if they knew, it would likely not have prevented them from pursuing it.

Perhaps our sleepy unawareness of the true nature and dangers of the occult is behind the charismatic slide. Occult practices crept into the church because they were not recognized for what they are.

VULNERABLE TO FALSE TEACHING

Unless Christians understand about the occult, they tend to be vulnerable to false teaching and counterfeit, occult experience. Why? Partly, at least, because they accept the reality of the supernatural realm and of Jesus' great, supernatural love. They want to trust their leaders. They are eager to grow in intimacy

---

1. In the DVD *"Woodstock: The Director's Cut,"* there is a clip of a yoga devotee at the famous rock concert, teaching others about kundalini awakenings.

with God. They believe in miracles. With these attributes they can, without discernment, be deceived by miracles done "in the name of Jesus," and by the supernatural enchantments of a spirit who brings *phos* light. They assume that if they are not dressing like birds, dancing around fires or stirring cauldrons in the woods, they are not involved in the occult. But, of course, they are wrong.

They are looking for love in all the wrong places.

Loving God: the biblical view

Many religions—not just Christianity—teach the importance of "loving God," whatever that means in the context of the faith. For example, Sufi Kabir Helminski teaches:

> We have the possibility of loving Love itself, of loving the Source of all loves. We metaphorically call the Divine Being "Friend" and "Beloved." This love has the possibility of developing infinitely. The highest purpose of a human being is to know and worship that alone which is worthy of worship. We can learn to call that which can answer our call. The response of this Beloved has no limits…It is seeking us even more than we are seeking it.[2]

People need to understand what occult practice is. They need to believe that Satan is real, and that he really does come as an angel of light. Otherwise they will be perfect targets for him and, not realizing that he is the enemy of their souls, will submit to *phos* light enchantments and other deceptive wonders.

Mystics emphasize the passive *receiving* and *experiencing* of divine love; they want to feel it, ask to feel it and call it "down" so they can feel it. This is how they come to "know the Father's

2. Helminski, 53.

Heart," or "be as one with Him." This, however, is occult, as we know from the definitions in chapter 5. Again:

- Occult practice is based on a belief that communion with God comes through subjective, supernatural experience.

This is not the way of genuine Christianity. Of course, it is true that the believer experiences God's love subjectively, and we love Him because He first loved us (1 John 4:19). But there are at least two differences between occult and Christian experiences of supernatural love. For one, while receiving God's love on conversion is an amazing experience, the Bible emphasizes the importance of first receiving His *Word*. Scriptures teach that we receive His love through hearing and believing the gospel; that is, through faith. When faith is aroused, God pours His love and forgiveness into our hearts. Not only Christian birth, but also Christian growth, come through the Word because by it we are taught, washed, and renewed. Therefore, true Christian practice is not seeking to be filled with love; rather, it is seeking to grow in the knowledge of God. That is our part. As we accomplish our part, His love grows in our hearts.

The second thing to note is that true Christianity emphasizes not receiving love passively *from* God, but loving Him actively *by our own efforts*. We are commanded to love Him with all our heart and mind and strength. And, how do we do this? By obedience. Jesus said, "He who has My commandments and keeps them, it is he who loves Me" (John 14:21). The disciple John said, "For this is the love of God, that we keep His commandments. And His commandments are not burdensome" (1 John 5:3). This truth is taught repeatedly in Scripture, as we have already seen.

Charismatic love experiences

Satan's coming as an angel of *phos* light in such a way as to inflame love in the human heart is surely the foundation stone of occult deception and idolatrous worship. It is such a mysterious and significant danger that it warrants careful study.

At the beginning of this chapter is a charismatic testimony about receiving countless "deep experiences" of the Father's love. Yet another from the Tucson church describes the work of a loving, spiritual presence of "the Lord":

> On Friday night, she sensed such a close presence of the
> Lord that she started to weep. During this weeping
> time, she rededicated her life back to the Lord and
> received emotional healing. She has since continued to
> walk more with the Lord and regularly attend church
> meetings.[3]

We are told that this young woman's ecstatic experience inspired her to rededicate her life to Jesus. But...was it Jesus' love she felt or the *phos* light of the serpent? The answer to this question could not be more important, because it determines who she was worshiping as a result of her encounter—the Lord Jesus or the lord of the occult!

Then we have the following testimony of an imparted love experience at Holy Trinity Brompton in England, the home of the Alpha course:

> A young man...told of the ecstatic sensations he had had
> after Mr. Millar had touched him and he had fallen to
> the floor the previous week. It was like being held in the
> arms of an adoring father, he said. "I was overwhelmed
> with a sensation of love."[4]

This seeker was overtaken by a "sensation of love." Understandably, he wanted to experience it again, so he returned to the church where these blessings are imparted. The ritual was repeated, with similar results:

---

3. Oates, Tucson, 2.

4. Patrick Dixon, *Signs of Revival, http://www.patrickdixon.co.uk/signs/Signs-
   1.htm.* Ch.1 "News of Laughter."

"Shall we try it again?" asked Mr. Millar. The man
assented. Mr. Millar prayed. We held our breath. Mr.
Millar touched the man's forehead and then bam! Right
on cue, his eyelids fluttered, his knees buckled and he was
lowered to the floor where he started to gibber.[5]

This is an occult experience of love.

KUNDALINI LOVE EXPERIENCES

Popular guru Sri Chinmoy, who believes the rituals of yoga
can bring a person into the arms of God, says:

> The Yoga of surrender can be practiced with and in all other
> systems of Yoga; but he who wants God alone, God the infi-
> nite Truth, God the infinite Peace, infinite Light and infinite
> Bliss, most assuredly must practice the Yoga of surrender.[6]

This guru is describing a god who brings peace, light and bliss,
precious things we all desire. Jafree, the kundalini master, said that
during samadhi he experienced:

> absolute indescribable bliss, 52 hours of pure conscious
> connection to The Cosmic Source and its Infinite Light
> energy, Love and Universal Awareness.[7]

In yoga, these and similar experiences are meant to awaken
love for God and others. The occult belief is that supernatural
love will infuse the practitioner, and then he or she can be more
loving. For example, see the following:

> At the third state of Enlightenment...You will experience
> an absence of suffering and a tremendous flowering of the
> heart where you'll begin to discover states of love and

---

5. Dixon, *Signs.*
6. Chinmoy para. 62.
7. Jafree, "Who is?"

compassion…In this state you will begin to care for others. Not just a few loved ones here and there but for all of humanity there is deep concern and compassion.[8]

In a similar vein, we saw (chapter one) that Mrs. Arnott from the Toronto church says her god can:

fill you with Himself, marinate you and rub you all over with His perfume so that you will look like Jesus, act like Jesus and minister like Jesus.

The occult idea here is to be filled and "rubbed" with Jesus' love, so you can then give it out to others.

Kundalini mystics also experience increased love for and devotion to "God." They believe love for God is a proper spiritual goal and the highest love a person can attain, so important they have identified three levels of "pure" love for God: *nishkama,* meaning love for God untainted by desires; *ahuteki,* love for God that wells up unbidden from the depths of the soul; and *bhakti,* the greatest of all. They seek and experience a profound sense of love and devotion for a spiritual being they believe to be God, and from whom they receive experiences of great love.

Is the same "God" loving both charismatics and yogis? Have we identified the coming of the angel of light?

PAGANS AND CHRISTIANS MEETING JESUS

Let's look at the deception from another perspective—visions of Jesus.

One of the claims by TB proponents that tends to confound critics like me is that believers and unbelievers alike are meeting Jesus. That's what they say. People are experiencing Jesus and are receiving faith, or being renewed in their faith. A woman at the Tucson church believes she met Jesus during the "Catch the Fire" event:

---

8. Sri Kalki Bhagavan, "Cosmic Reality is One: the Wise Perceive It In Many Ways," *http://www.skyboom1.tripod.com/index27.html,* 6.

[She] saw a vision of Jesus on the cross and the agony and
love on his face. She sensed his intense love for her and all
people and His forgiveness for all people. *His love penetrated her heart...*[9] (emphasis added)

But is this woman's experience any different from that of our
friend Jafree, the kundalini master? He said of his Jesus-dream:

It did not really matter how close you were to [Jesus], the
love and peace was just as deep whenever you focused in
His direction. In the few moments that I was there, *I
absorbed His unconditional love
and acceptance into my heart.*[10]
(emphasis added)

> The disturbing truth is
> that Satan can and will
> ignite a love response in
> the heart of man,
> through occult practices.

What Jafree says here about
absorbing the love of Jesus isn't
much different than the woman's
experience of "penetrating" love at
the Tucson area church.

Christian author Johanna Michaelsen also believed she met
Jesus through occult practice; she was working as an assistant to a
faith healer who kept a biblical cross in her "surgery." Johanna pro-
fessed Christianity at this time, and thought she loved the Lord. She
describes the Jesus she met during meditation as follows:

We were counted slowly down to our Alpha level by Tom...
Slowly, an inch at a time, the figure emerged. Shimmering
brown hair parted in the middle, a high forehead, dark skin;
eyes brown, deep and gentle. There! It was Jesus![11]

The "Jesus" who came to Johanna in her vision had gentle eyes,
and she was thrilled. However, as time went on this Jesus began to

9. Oates, Tucson, 2.
10. Jafree, "Who is?"
11. Johanna Michaelsen, *The Beautiful Side of Evil* (Eugene, OR: Harvest House,
1982) 74-75.

develop the demonic faces of a werewolf. He even said to Johanna, "Do not be afraid…We only want to teach you that not everything that seems to be evil on the surface really is evil down beneath in its essence. When you truly understand this, our werewolf faces will be gone forever and you will ever see us as we really are."[12] Later Johanna was rescued from this diabolical snare when she met the real Jesus in biblical fashion, but only then did she clearly understand that she had been deceived and that the visionary "Jesus" was false, an occult parody of the true One.

I discovered that mystics of many faiths claim to see wonderful visions of Jesus, or believe they have Him "in their heart." In fact, Jesus is an important and beloved figure among them. He is variously known by non-Christians as an "Ascended Master," an "Avatar," a "Great Healer," "The Lord," or a "Great Prophet." Yogis consider him a spiritual guru of the highest order, an enlightened prophet who attained deep awareness of the divine and mastered the most advanced siddhis, including walking on water. Hindus and new agers believe they can grow in "Christ consciousness" through the "kundalini spirit." Sometimes a devotee will tell you that kundalini is like Mother Mary, "giving birth to a Jesus experience." And sometimes they meet Jesus in visions or trance states. Witness the following vision:

Shri Jesus, who was waiting, walked on the soft clouds to greet them. He was wearing a long, whitish-gray robe that reached His ankles, with another piece of cloth across His right shoulder and draped

> Twisted but true: to follow an occult Jesus is to be led away from Jesus.

diagonally down to the left waist. He was tall, big-boned and muscular. He had a beard, with wavy hair cascading into curly locks. The children of the Holy Spirit Shri Mataji Nirmala Devi, through genuine baptism of the Kundalini, are able to visit Lord Jesus Christ hundreds of times in the Kingdom of God *within*, experiences that are

---

12. Michaelsen, 77.

far superior than the beatific visions of Catholic saints.[13] (emphasis original)

This guru even claims that his "Jesus experiences" are better than those of Catholic mystics. Another:

> Following the Divine blueprint, we are led through purification of man's lower consciousness into higher states of awareness where we encounter the Christ Presence and come to embody Christ Consciousness.[14]

This, of course, is a perversion of God's truth, one that leads to an occult "Christ," or an *anti-Christ*. Note the prefix "anti" in antichrist does not necessarily mean "against Christ." It also means "in the place of" or "instead of" Christ. The word antichrist, therefore, can denote a spirit who comes as a substitute Jesus, pretending to be Him and to be like Him: an angel of light.

THE TRUTH ABOUT RECEIVING GOD'S LOVE

Blissful visions of Jesus and feelings of religious devotion arising from occult experience do not mean that one has met Christ the Son, God the Father or the Holy Spirit. They are not evidence that one has a genuine, saving faith, nor that one's faith has been renewed. The disturbing truth is that Satan can and will ignite a "love" response in the hearts of men through occult practices.

The prayer that delights our heavenly Father is not a hungry request for more love experiences. No, the prayer that delights God is the sincere request for a devoted and obedient heart so we may truly know His love. This is beautifully expressed in the King James Bible where the apostle John writes:

> But whoso keepeth His word, in him verily is the love of God perfected... (1 John 2:5).

---

13. Shri Devi, "Human Subtle."
14. Sananda, "Kundalini."

Chapter Eleven

FOR THE LOVE OF SATAN

I am of the snake that giveth Knowledge and Delight, and stir the hearts of men with drunkenness...I give unimaginable joys on Earth: certainty, not faith, while in life, upon death; peace unutterable, rest, ecstasy...
— Alistair Crowley, on the gifts of Satan

I used to think Satanism was all about hate. I was wrong.

ABOUT SATANISM

Satanism is no more capable of simple definition than is Kali worship. Some Satanists deny the existence of the spirit world: they are atheists who worship at the altar of self-love and self-indulgence. Some acknowledge the existence of a devil, or many devils, but this belief is not central to their faith. Others openly worship the Satan that Holy Scripture warns about; these we could call the mystics of Satanism. They believe Satan is the bearer of true spiritual light. And not only do they love him, they receive raptures of love *from* him, apparently delightful infillings of *phos* light.

At the risk of oversimplifying, I would say that there appear to be three essential differences between Satanism and other religions. One is that Satanists are openly and seriously dedicated to satisfying their own desires above all else, and they make no bones about it. They say this is only natural, and anyone who denies it is either a liar or a fool. It must be admitted, there is an element of intellectual honesty and self-awareness in this; however, it can lead to terrible cruelty, perversion and debauchery. Secondly, Satanists usually (not always) hold the teachings of Jesus in great contempt. Unlike Hindus, they do not attempt to integrate His teachings with their own. They do not honor Jesus as a great teacher, but believe him a fool who taught the ridiculous: for example, they insist that the poor and weak of this world are to be despised and that forgiveness is an idiotic goal. Thirdly, most Satanists claim to reject all moral codes, although this leads to contradictions in their teaching (and no doubt in their personal lives).

I claim—and desire—no expertise about Satanism. But from what I have learned, those Satanic worshipers I call mystic are for the most part "Crowleyites": they follow the teachings of an Englishman named Aleister (he changed his name from Edward Alexander) Crowley. Mr. Crowley was the son of professing Christians, and knew the Bible well. Lucifer was his horned god; indeed, Crowley believed Satan was God. And without condoning such blasphemy, it must be observed that this was neither an illogical nor an unnatural conclusion because Mr. Crowley apparently received both godlike powers and godlike love from the serpent.

Mr. Crowley wrote poetry, devised occult rituals, studied numerology, channeled angels and penned numerous books including the Satanic *Book of the Law*, an increasingly influential religious treatise. He designed his own deck of Tarot cards and was an early member of the free masons. Some have called him a Buddhist missionary, and credit him with awakening Western interest in yoga. He called himself "The Great Beast," "666," and "the most wicked man in the world." He believed he was Eliphas Levi (the magician, see chapter 8) reincarnated. It was Crowley who introduced the term "Magick" for the black arts he taught and practiced, the Victorian spelling intended to distinguish illusory magic from the real thing.

When he died in 1947 at the age of 72, The Great Beast was reportedly addicted to heroin and alcohol, and generally believed to be mad. Posthumously he has become a significant influence in the world of the occult. Many rock stars, models, astrologers, fortune-tellers, cult leaders and New Agers devour his teachings; his influence extends far beyond what we might call simple Satanism.

Crowley became a prolific prophet of Satan, a high priest of darkness and magic. He was unabashedly antagonistic to Christianity because he agreed with the Bible that Jesus Christ is Satan's great foe.

Another well-known satanic priest was Anton LaVey who founded the church of Satan in 1966. His daughter assumed a leadership role in it after his death in 1997. Mr. LaVey wrote the *Satanic Bible*, a book which purportedly outsells the Bible on some university campuses. Frothing with contempt for the "folly" of Christian values such as meekness, forgiveness and self-discipline, Mr. LaVey founded his church on so-called "principles of common sense": self- indulgence, revolt and hating your enemies. In his view Satan is a "dark, hidden force in nature responsible for the workings of earthly affairs, a force for which neither science nor religion had any explanation."[1]

In this chapter, I will focus, for the most part, on the practices and experiences of Crowleyites, those mystic Satanists who practice and worship in the fashion of Aleister Crowley. I'll compare Magick practices and experiences with those of other mystics and charismatics, and contrast it all with orthodox Christianity.

MAGICK PRACTICE AND EXPERIENCE

During Magick rituals Crowleyites ask for, and call down, spiritual power. Their actual rituals vary, at times resembling those of medieval magicians although often more perverse. They are clearly occult. Further, many experiences of Satanists are similar to those claimed by other mystics and by charismatics. For example, earlier

---

1. Burton H. Wolfe, "Introduction" (to the *Satanic Bible*), *http://www.beyondweird.com/satanic-Bible.html*.

(chapter 3) we saw that with practice both yogis and charismatics find it becomes easier to attain mystic states. Mr. Crowley taught, in *The Book of the Law:*

> III,21: Set up my image in the East: thou shalt buy thee an image which I will show thee, especial, not unlike the one thou knowest. And it shall be suddenly easy for thee to do this.[2]

What really surprised me, however, was the discovery that mystic Satanists have powerful *phos* love encounters. Judging by their poetry and prayers, their enchantments are supremely delightful and their intimacy with the serpent very advanced. They also develop clairvoyance and clairaudience and strive to master the more advanced siddhis (or "develop magick power," as they would say) such as control over matter to work miracles. They see visions of angels and other spirit beings. And they prophesy. The parallels with Hinduism and "charismagic" are obvious, and so is the contrast with orthodox Christianity which, as always, stands alone.

Satanic love experiences

Popular singer and musician Tori Amos worships Satan. She said about her love and desire for the serpent god:

> "I wanted to marry Lucifer."

> "We can all tap into his energy."

And:

> "I cry and feel his presence with his music. I feel like he comes and sits on my piano."[3]

---

2. Aleister Crowley, 1904, *The Book of the Law*, 6th ed. (York Beach, ME: Samuel Weiser, 1989), 41.

3. Tori Amos, interview with *Spin Magazine*, March 1996, 46, quoted in *Hells Bells 2*, DVD, directed by Erik Hollander (2004, Cleveland, OH: Reel 2 Real Ministries).

Tapping into an energy available for all, supernatural feelings of love, weeping and visions of his presence with her: is this not more appropriate for yogis and charismatics? But perhaps we shouldn't be surprised, since this is promised by Satan himself. Here he tempts through the pen of The Great Beast:

> I give unimaginable joys on Earth: certainty, not faith, while in life, upon death; peace unutterable, rest, ecstasy; nor do I demand aught in sacrifice.[4]

And again:

> to love me is better than all things: if under the night stars in the desert thou presently burnest mine incense before me, invoking me with a pure heart, and the Serpent flame therein, thou shalt come a little to lie in my bosom. For one kiss wilt thou then be willing to give all...[5]

Here we have again talk about the need for a pure heart, and promises of joy and love. Note the reference to "lying in the bosom" through invocation; we heard something similar from Holy Trinity Brompton in London, England (see chapter 10), where a TB practitioner experienced "lying in the arms of love" after occult spirit was invoked: "It was like being held in the arms of an adoring father," he said. "I was overwhelmed with a sensation of love."

In the following quotations from *The Book of the Law*, we find revealed the love song of the serpent as he lures seekers ever more deeply into the occult:

> I love you! I yearn to you! Pale or purple, veiled or voluptuous, I who am all pleasure and purple, and drunkenness of the innermost sense, desire you. Put on the wings, and arouse the coiled splendor within you: come unto me!

---

4. Crowley, *The Book*, I:58,26.
5. Crowley, *The Book*, I:61,27.

At all my meetings with you shall the priestess say—and
her eyes shall burn with desire as she stands bare and
rejoicing in my secret temple—To me! To me! calling forth
the flame of the hearts of all in her love-chant.

I am above you and in you. My ecstasy is in yours. My joy
is to see your joy.[6]

So here we have it. Satan promises love and joy in return for
ritual. And now we know that he delivers on these promises.
Clearly The Great Beast experienced raptures of love and joy, or
he could not write like this.

Note, too, the description of "drunkenness of the innermost
senses." Where have we heard that before? Not in orthodox
Christianity, I assure you. But we have heard it from the charismatic church. Again (from chapter 3):

Drunkenness in the Holy Spirit is actually an extreme
form of joy!!...One does not experience true joy unless
one is truly in God!!...Therefore one must expect the
more extreme forms of drunkenness when actually filled
with the Holy Spirit of God!!

Wicked Lucifer, horned angel. By what promises he tempts:

I am the snake that giveth Knowledge and Delight and
bright glory, and stir the hearts of men with drunkenness...[7]

Our Goddess is a Lady of Joy, the winds are Her servants.[8]

Our Goddess is a Goddess of Love. At Her blessings and
desire the sun brings forth life anew.[9]

---

6. Crowley, *The Book, I:61-63,27-28*, 19.
7. Crowley, *The Book, II:22*,31.
8. Ed Fitch, "Pagan Ritual for Basic Use" *www.angelfire.com*.
9. Ed Fitch, "Pagan Ritual."

Lord Satan saith: In rioting and drunkenness I rise again. You
shall fulfil the lusts of the flesh. The works of the flesh are
manifest, which are…witchcraft, drunkenness and reveling.[10]

Note, the Satanist says his "Lord" rises in drunkenness and reveling. Let's see again clips from the "intoxicated" charismatics
(chapter 3) and ask ourselves which god would, in fact, be the
"lord" of such experiences: Jesus who is lowly, humble and meek,
or the lord of drunkenness and revelry himself? Consider, from
the rock 'n' rollers:

I don't know whats happening
but I'm really kinda drunk in the spirit…
Cuz I be taking about the Great I am, My Savior
The one who gets me drunk constantly….
Got me throwing up by the curb…
(errors in original)

And:

> If the fear of the Lord is the beginning of wisdom, then party-time with the Lord is the culmination of folly.

And I have met many New
Winers there…but can't
remember most of them
because I was so intoxi-
cated!!!! (so please don't be
offended!!!! HHHOOO!!!!!!!!!! hehe ahahhahaha)……
When not being dragged around, I'd spend up to five
hours total on the very nice carpet!!!!!!!!!…. HOOO!!!!….
AHHH!!!! ZAP!!!!!!!!……"

If we were ever confused about spiritual drunkenness, surely
the question has now been settled beyond any doubt. The Great
Beast would chuckle, were he still alive to read these "Christian"
testimonies.

10. Ed Fitch, "Pagan Ritual."

WHO CARES WHAT THEY THINK

I hate to do this, but I am also going to make a point of observing that there are similarities between charismatics and Satanists with respect to loss of self-control, throwing off normal social restraints, chaos and disorderliness.

Songwriter Diamanda Galas, who recorded "Litanies of Satan," said in an interview that her experience with Satanism "...was like making a connection to some source of power so that I could do what was not socially accepted."[11] In other words, her "source of power" awakened in her a disregard for orderliness and propriety—what some might call a spirit of rebellion. Satanist Anton LaVey expressed the same thing when he described the Satanic force as "the spirit of revolt that leads to freedom, the embodiment of all heresies that liberate."[12]

The sad fact is that I have often heard charismatics claim that the Holy Spirit comes upon them to encourage the casting off of normal social restraints, or to set them free to enjoy "whatever the Spirit has for them." Disorderliness and impropriety are sometimes justified as being a fool for Christ, or "letting the wind blow where it listeth." John White holds that disorder is a way for uptight people to experience a release of tension.[13] He wrote, "For my part I am glad that God ignores our petty notions of propriety as he deals with men and women,"[14] and, "They [charismatics] show little concern about what anyone will think of their [drunken] condition..."[15]

Does Scripture agree with Mr. White that propriety is a petty notion? That drunkenness is of no concern? That we should not care about what others think? Not at all.

---

11. Diamanda Galas, interview with *Research Magazine*, #13, quoted in *Hells Bells 2*, DVD, directed by Erik Hollander (Cleveland, OH: Reel 2 Real Ministries, 2004).

12. Wolfe, Intro., Satanic Bible.

13. White, 90.

14. White, 81.

15. White, 101.

Scripture is clear that we are to conduct ourselves in a manner that will bring credit to our Lord; in other words, propriety and what other people think are important (1 Timothy 6:1). We are not to behave in such a way as to offend others, or cause them to stumble (Romans 14:19-21). We are exhorted to let gentleness be evident to all (Philippians 4:5) and in our teaching show integrity, seriousness and soundness of speech that cannot be condemned (Titus 2:7-8). The apostle Paul stressed to the Corinthians that orderliness will always characterize genuine Christian meetings, for "God is not the author of confusion but of peace." (1 Corinthians 14:33).

Disregard for orderliness and propriety, confusion and revelry are the fruits of Satanic influence. Satan's ways, and the ways of his followers, are diametrically opposed to the humble and lowly ways of the Lord Jesus and those who delight to follow Him.

CHAOS AND PANDEMONIUM

Mr. White urges believers not to worry about noise, disturbances, excess, commotion or confusion.[16] He quotes TB founder John Wimber to endorse chaos—even messy, uncontrollable chaos:

> When warm and cold fronts collide, violence ensues: thunder and lightening, rain or snow—even tornadoes or hurricanes. There is conflict, and a resulting release of power. It is disorderly, messy—difficult to control.[17]

Remember the Microwave Preacher in chapter 3? He described the intrusion of embarrassing, socially inappropriate behavior:

> Unusual things began to happen; for instance, one man broke out in a dance—it embarrassed his wife. But Tom started to laugh, because these people had no model for their behavior.

---

16. See White at 42-44.
17. John Wimber, *Power Evangelism* (London: Hodder and Stoughton, 1985), 32, quoted in White, 45.

In the Brownsville Assembly in Pensacola, Florida—a church almost as well-known as the Toronto church for TB manifestations—the pastor gleefully reported that God had sent pandemonium to his congregation. He boasted:

> God sent pandemonium in the church...I think it's time
> that we have grand pandemonium in the Baptists, in the
> Lutheran, the Episcopal, the Assembly of God [churches].
> God send pandemonium![18]

It is interesting to note that the word pandemonium literally means "capital of hell." It is derived from the root words *pan* plus *daemonium* (a late Latin word meaning "evil spirit") and was coined by John Milton in 1667. In Milton's epic *Paradise Lost*, Pandemonium was the name of the city which served as a centre for satanic operations.[19] It has come to mean a place of wild disorder, noise and confusion.

To take pleasure in pandemonium is not godly. No one could torture such a conclusion from Scriptures, which teach that evidences of the work of the Holy Spirit are gentleness and self-control (Galatians 5:23), peace (1 Corinthians 14:33), wisdom in dealing with others (1 Corinthians 9:19-23), and submission to government and authority (Romans 13). On the other hand, those who rebel against biblical ways are showing that they hate knowledge and have chosen not to fear God; and they will get what they want, or even more:

> Then they will call on me, but I will not answer;
> They will seek me diligently, but they will not find me.
> Because they hated knowledge
> And did not choose the fear of the Lord,
> They would have none of my counsel

---

18. John Kilpatrick, Brownsville Assembly of God Church, quoted in Dirk Anderson, "Great Signs and Wonders II—The Party Has Begun," *http://www.intowww.org/articles*, 2.

19. Credit to Dirk Anderson for the lead on this interesting point. See "Great Signs and Wonders II—The Party Has Begun," 2.

And despised all my reproof.
Therefore they shall eat the fruit of their own way,
And be filled to the full with their own fancies
    (Proverbs 1:28-31).

If the fear of the Lord is the beginning of wisdom, then party-time with the Lord must be the culmination of folly.

ALL MYSTIC WAYS CONVERGE

I found a telling quotation on the Web site of a Crowleyite: a worshiper published a prayer to Satan, asking the horned god to prepare hearts by "inflaming them with love" as he "renews the face of the earth."[20] Yet this should not surprise us, since we now know that Satan is expert at inflaming hearts with love. But then the worshiper prayed, "May our hearts be cleansed by the inpouring of our Lord Satan."[21] Here now, even in Satanism, we find a desire for spiritual cleansing—the occult way.

The truth is, Satanists have much in common with other mystics. They, like others, at times demonstrate confidence in their good intentions, believing themselves to be unfairly attacked by critics. For example, they believe magick serves divine purposes. Crowley thought the consciousness of man could develop to loftier heights: Magick was the path and he was a leading guru (so to speak). Believe it or not, he often stressed the need for pure motives. He once wrote that in his spiritual quest he:

> yearned passionately for illumination. I could imagine
> nothing more exquisite than to enter into communion with
> [holy men] and to acquire the power of communicating
> with the angelic and divine intelligence of the universe. I
> longed for perfect purity of life, for mastery of the secret
> forces of nature, and for a career of devoted labor on behalf
> of "the Creation which groaneth and travaileth."[22]

---

20. Missa Niger, *La Messe Noir,* *http://www.thefirewithin.dk/library/blackmass.htm.*
21. Niger, *Messe Noir.*
22. Crowley, *Confessions of Aleister Crowley,* ed. John Symonds and Kenneth Grant (Penguin-Arkana, 1989), 145-146, quoted in Friend, 471.

It troubles me greatly, but must we not agree that the god of the occult leads everyone down the same broad highway? Perhaps Satanists are hurtling down the fast lane, leaving others in the dust. But they are all headed in the same direction. Having missed the sign Jehovah posted in His Word which says "Danger, Soul Pollution," they think they are heading for "Love, Wisdom and Light." Popular lanes on the occult highway are spiritual intoxication, visions and talking to angels. Favorite rest stops? Soaking and Samadhi.

There are only two ways

The Great Beast himself, Aleister Crowley, would agree that all mystic paths converge. He taught his disciples that the Satanic "Priesthood of the Magus" was equivalent to the Yogic "Master of Samadhi." He taught a spiritual rebirth through occult awakening that he called "crossing the abyss." Among spiritual leaders who attained the grade of "Magus" in Crowley's view were leading figures in many religions, including Siddaartha (Gautama Buddha), Krishna, Mohammed and the Beast himself.[23] Crowley realized that his experiences transcended occult denomination, and were common in all other mystic faiths—all except Christianity, of course.

And the Bible agrees with the Beast on this point. Scriptures also teach that there are really only two religions in the world: the narrow way of orthodox Christianity, and the broad way of the occult. Jesus urged us to take the narrow way, for:

> wide is the gate and broad is the way that leads to destruction, and there are many who go in by it. [But] narrow is the gate and difficult is the way which leads to life, and there are few who find it (Matthew 7:13-14).

---

23. See Gerald Suster, *Crowley's Apprentice: The Life and Ideas of Israel Regardie* (York Beach, ME: Samuel Weiser, 1990), 44.

Chapter Twelve

THE FORCE WITH US

You always long for that God, that JAHWEH, or whatever you name Him. You can call Him another dozen or hundred names and He would not mind. He has no name, understand… You just see the light every day, feel joy, and be in the presence of God. And then you call Him whatever name He tells you to call Him, and you will know Him by different names… You just feel He is so much love.

—Samadhi teacher, supreme master Ching Hai

*I*n occult thinking, God sends out or emanates a power or presence which can be experienced as a "love," a "light," "energy," "electricity," a "river," a "wave," etc. It is common to refer to occult spirit as "the force" or "a force." One discerning writer said about this:

> When I became a believer, I found it very interesting that the *King James Bible* refers to Antichrist as honoring the "God of forces." The prophet Daniel, looking to the "latter

days," writes this about the Antichrist: *But in his estate shall he honor the God of forces...* (Daniel 11:38).[1] (emphasis added)

Lucifer is, indeed, the god of forces—under many different names and guises.

SPIRIT AS A FORCE

Any attempt to use, tap into, receive or direct the power and presence of "God" is pure magic. Yet many charismatics teach just this sort of thing. One author has even written a book on how to "steward" the "Presence" of God.

Unfortunately, charismatics have learned to think about the Holy Spirit as the force, energy or power of God. This counterfeit view is clearly expressed in the following extract, which we saw earlier (chapter 1) from John White's book:

> I know a woman who trembles frequently (as with Parkinsonism) when she prays for other people...She describes the experience in terms of energy coursing through her. The phenomenon began in a meeting she attended where the Holy Spirit was powerfully present. While she cannot as it were produce the trembling or the "energy," when it comes she has the choice either of resisting it, or else of directing it (into prayer, for example). If she does the latter, she experiences a sensation of pulsating energy extending to her finger tips, along with a slight tremor in her hands. Her impression is of energy flowing through her.

In the quote above, the Holy Spirit is viewed as an energy to be received and directed. This is occult thinking.

Another charismatic author describes God's presence as a slow-acting, radiating energy:

---

1. Warren Smith, *Deceived on Purpose: The New Age Implications of the Purpose-Driven Church*, 2nd ed. (Magalia, CA: Mountain Stream, 2004), 76.

Judson Cornwall, in his book, *Let Us Draw Near*, words it so well when he explains soaking, saying that God's presence is a radiating energy that can be absorbed. It is not fast acting; it takes quite a while to soak in.[2]

Below is similar teaching from new-ager Emilie Cady depicting a god who sends out streams of "good" for mankind to absorb and then radiate outward. In her writing one has the sense of a "God" who is very impersonal:

> [God is] a huge reservoir, out of which lead many small streams and rivulets. At the far end, each stream opens out into a small fountain...Each of us, no matter how small or ignorant, is a little fountain at the end of the stream, receiving God from the reservoir... Each of us, no matter how insignificant we are in the world, may receive from God unlimited good, of whatever kind we desire, and radiate it to all about us.[3]

Following is a very scholarly-sounding example of charismatic error:

> And—don't you see?—this is the essential optimism of Christianity. Here in the Spirit of Christ is a force capable of bursting into the hardest paganism, discomfiting the most rigid dogmatism, electrifying the most suffocating ecclesiasticism.[4]

This is not correct. The Spirit of Christ is not a bursting, electrifying force.

---

2. Quoted in Ed Piorek, "Marinated in God," *Spread the Fire Magazine*, Vol. 2, Issue 3, 1996. *http://www.tacf.org*. Site altered.

3. Cady, 5-6.

4. James S. Stewart, *The Wind of the Spirit* (Nashville, TN: Abingdon, 1968), 14.

The Force by other names

Let's consider views in other faiths.

Tai Chi and Feng Shui

Practitioners of tai chi, feng shui, qigong and eastern martial arts use the terms "chi" (also "ch'i" or "prana") to describe the energy they seek and use in their religious practice. Author Huston Smith says:

> The word Ch'I cries out to be recognized…for though it literally means breath, it actually means vital energy. The Taoists used it to refer to the power of the Tao that they experienced coursing through them—or not coursing because it was blocked—and their main object was to further its flow. Ch'I fascinated these Taoists. Blake registered their feelings precisely when he exclaimed, "Energy is delight," for energy is the life force and the Taoists loved life.[5]

Both chi and shui teachings have to do with directing spiritual "energy," chi through the body and shui through the home. The similarity to kundalini yoga teachings has not gone unnoticed. A guru explains:

> kundalini is a kind of psychic energy. It takes care of the body. It's like what we call in Chinese "Chi." When you awaken that "Chi" you'll have vital power, the body is strong, your mind is strong…[6]

Subud cult

A Javanese cult known as *Subud* attempts to harness divine energy for spiritual purification. Christian writer Larry Hall noticed similarities between their practices and those of charismatics. He writes:

---

5. Huston Smith, *The World's Religions* (New York, NY: Harper, 1991), 201.
6. Ching Hai, "Samadhi."

Subuh [guru] claims that he went through a series of deep inner changes and received what he termed the "Great Life Force," a manifestation of the power of God. Through communion with his divine nature, Subuh claimed to be able to transmit this force to others...In *The Encyclopedia of American Religions,* we have the following description of the "latihan" process: "The Latihan proper is a time of moving the consciousness beyond mind and desire and allowing the power to enter and do its work...often accompanying the spontaneous period are various body movements and vocal manifestations—cries, moans, laughter and singing. These occur in the voluntary surrender of the self to the power. During this time, people report sensations of love and freedom and often, healings. All reach a higher level of consciousness."[7]

Note that subud manifestations include impartation power for the initiated, opening oneself (surrender) to the power, uncontrolled body movements (kriyas), supposed purification and healing while under the power, ecstasy, celebrating and laughter. And the teacher exhorts us to spend time in "voluntary surrender" to the force. Sound familiar?

Qigong

Mr. Hall also looked at the Chinese practice of *Qigong.* I quote again from his article:

"Practitioners [of Yan Xin Qigong] may have a variety of personal reactions to Qigong practice. Some of these reactions include: temporary pain, spontaneous movement such as jumping, shaking, crying, laughing, shouting, or discomfort in some parts of the body. However, all these are normal reactions to Qigong practice and are the result

---

7. Larry Hall, "The Toronto Cursing Is No Laughing Matter!" Sword of the Spirit Apologetics, *http://www.luciferlink.org/wtoro.htm*, 10.

of the Qi as it circulates through and cleanses the
body…no one should be worried about the side-effects of
Qigong practice."[8]

As in Subud, Kundalini and TB, in Qigong we again see impartation power for the initiated, opening oneself (surrender) to the
power, uncontrolled body movements (kriyas), purification while
under the power, healings, ecstasy, celebrating, and unexplainable
weeping or laughter. Reportedly, "thousands" of people also receive
healing for incurable diseases through Qigong.[9]

Note also the reference to pain or discomfort in the body. The
Toronto church publication explained the phenomenon as "a
means of identifying illness" (chapter 3); however, the Qigong
Web site explains it as a result of Qi energy "circulating through
and cleansing" the body.

Islam

The mystics of Islam are known as Sufis. According to writer
Huston Smith, Sufis have developed three practices by which they
draw closer to God; he identifies these as "the mysticisms of love,
of ecstasy, and of intuition."[10] I'll quote here from Mr. Smith's
description of Sufi practice and experience:

> Ecstatic Sufis do not claim that they come to see what
> Muhammad saw…, but they move in his direction…their
> states become trancelike because of their total abstraction
> from self…Deliberate inducement of such states required
> practice…when the altered state arrives, it feels like a gift
> rather than an acquisition…Sufis report that as their con-
> sciousness begins to change, it feels as if their wills were
> placed in abeyance and a superior will takes over.
> Sufis honor their ecstasies, but in calling them "drunken"
> they serve notice that they must bring the substance of

8. Hall, 8.
9. Hall, 8.
10. Smith, 259.

their visions back with them when they find themselves
"sober" again.[11]

Here again we see trance states, submission to a greater power,
spiritual drunkenness and visions while under the power.
Experienced Sufis also report increased intuition and paranormal
insight, called "eye of the heart knowledge,"[12] by which they can see
into the realm of the spiritual. Sound familiar?

As charismatics repeat the name of Jesus, so Sufis repeat the
name of their God in order to gain a sense of His presence. Mr.
Smith explains:

> Symbolism, though powerful, works somewhat abstractly, so
> the Sufis supplement it with *dhikri* (to remember), the prac-
> tice of remembering Allah through repeating his Name.
> "There is a means of polishing all things whereby rust may
> be removed," a *hadith* asserts, adding: "That which polishes
> the heart is the invocation of Allah." Remembrance of God is
> at the same time a forgetting of self, so Sufis consider the
> repetition of Allah's Name the best way of directing their
> attention Godward.[13]

Sufis are clearly among the many who have met the god of
mystic love. Their experiences are compelling, and their religious
practice centres around sensing his presence so they can grow (as
they believe) under its influence. Hear again the teaching of Sufi
Kabir Helminski (chapter 10):

> We have the possibility of loving Love itself, of loving the
> Source of all loves…This love has the possibility of devel-
> oping infinitely… We can learn to call that which can
> answer our call. The response of this Beloved has no lim-
> its…It is seeking us even more than we are seeking it.

---

11. Smith, 260-261.
12. Smith, 261.
13. Smith, 263.

We see here that the mystic, impersonal "it" sought by Sufis is as loving and precious in their experience as the spirit sought by charismatics. I am not mocking either group because I understand that the spirit does seem loving and precious. But it is occult. It comes when called. Indeed it is true, as the Sufi said and as charismatics say, that this spirit is seeking us even more than we are seeking it. But if the Bible speaks the truth, then this spirit does not seek us because it loves us.

INTOXICATIONS OF THE FORCE

It appears that people of many faiths cherish the "high" of spiritual drunkenness. Charismatics crave "new wine"; we have looked at this already. We also know that kundalini devotees seek the drunken influence of their goddess, and satanists delight in intoxicating rituals. Muslim Sufis do too, as we just saw. But that's not all. Egyptian festivals feature a goddess of spiritual drunkenness with a very strange name, Hwt-Hrw:

> Just twenty days after the New Year Festival the ceremony known as the "Inebriation of Hwt-Hrw" occurs…What end does this festival serve? In many ancient cultures, intoxication was seen as a means by which communication with, and awareness of, spiritual realities could be achieved…inebriation also was achieved through the use of chanting, fasting, dance and music. In essence these were all seen as a means to create an altered state allowing one to become more open to the spiritual forces around them. The Goddess Hwt-Hrw's title "Lady of Drunkenness" clearly reveals this aspect of Her nature. This "sacred drunkenness" or "sober drunkenness" can take on many forms…a [profound]

Several Old Testament Scriptures refer to a form of drunkenness that does not come from drink, demonstrates spiritual blindness, and manifests as a "deep sleep" (trance).

intoxicating state of mind occurs when communing with the divine.[14]

See how many religions teach that spiritual drunkenness is how we commune with deity? Interestingly, Scriptures contain several references to intoxication associated with occult practice. For example, Isaiah said:

> Pause and wonder! Blind yourselves and be blind!
> They are drunk, but not with wine;
> They stagger, but not with intoxicating drink.
> For the Lord has poured out on you the spirit of deep sleep,
> And has closed your eyes, namely, the prophets;
> And He has covered your heads, namely, the seers
> (Isaiah 29:9-10).

Note: spiritual drunkenness is identified in Scripture not as communing with God, but as a sure route to spiritual blindness.

INVITING THE FORCE

We have seen different means by which mystic groups access the serpent god, including dancing, drumming, yoga and soaking prayer. Cross-practice often occurs, and this is evident among charismatics. For example, here is a teaching from "Generals of Intercession" who have gone so far as to explore Native American drumming rituals:

> Chad released a powerful impartation of the "warrior spirit" into us to the background noise of Native American worship music and war drums. Praise the Lord! What more can I say? I was changed...We are now forming a

---

14. Kerry Wisner, "The Ancient Egyptian Calendar and Festivals Part Two: Celebration of the Festivals," *www.inkemetic.org/Library/calnfest2.htm.*

team of radical warriors to take God's saving and healing power to the streets...[15]

A *Washington Post* staff writer described the use of drums at a so-called revival meeting at the Pensacola church:

> It begins with a drummer laying down a slow beat that goes on for several minutes, a steady, inescapable, portentous heartbeat. The guitarist and the organist join in...In front of the first row, teenagers pogo up and down...[16]

Drumming and repetitive movements are ancient methods of raising kundalini power or altering consciousness in order to summon spirits. Shamans have always used drums to attain spiritual heights; the rhythm is regarded as a means of transporting the soul through spiritual doorways.

Meditative music is another means to reach a "sacred place." Like pagans and New Agers, charismatics also use—and sell— music to assist in attaining altered states. I found an advertisement for a charismatic CD with "background music with rhythmic and soaking compositions." For $15 another CD with the title "The Soaking Presence" promises:

> Worshipful sounds! Come soak in the Presence of God and find rest for your soul. God is calling us to the place of intimacy and peace. This instrumental CD is a tool to usher in an atmosphere of the Soaking Presence of God.[17]

While I have no objection to beautiful music, when used to alter consciousness and invoke spiritual influence it is obviously occult.

---

15. Chad Taylor, "Repentance, Reconciliation, and Renewal: The Keys of Revival," *http://www.consumingfire.com/rrandr.htm.*

16. Peter Carlson, *Washington Post,* April 27, 1997, quoted in Anderson, 2.

17. John Belt, offered at *www.mttnweb.com/email_communques.*

Submission to the Force

Readers will have observed that mystics emphasize "surrendering your will" and "opening up" to divine spirit. Charismatics believe this is biblical submission, and that we must "let go and let God." They discourage prayer because they have discovered it can interfere with "receiving." Following are examples of charismatic exhortations to open up:

> Perhaps it's time we allowed God more space to lead His own Church. We have seen, as we give the Holy Spirit room, that He is calling His people to be much more willing to risk vulnerability during worship.[18]

> We need the love of the Father flowing freely through us... So throw away that umbrella of fear and soak in the Holy Spirit.[19]

> We need to lose control and the Holy Spirit needs to gain control. I want to see more of God doing what He wants to do. Now I'm grateful and humbled when God works sovereignly and does things all by Himself.[20]

Now see similar pagan teachings:

> this Source does not care who you are (or who you think you are) or what you did in the past, or want to do with your future. All it cares about is when you are available to being open to its love in the here and now.[21]

And:

---

18. From *http://www.tacf.org/stf/archive/2-5/article4.html*. Site changed, no further info available.

19. C. Carter, *Union Leader*.

20. From *http://www.tacf.org/stf/archive/2-5/article4.html*. Site changed, no further info available.

21. Jafree, "Who is?"

when deity is present and fully manifested, ritual structure cannot and should not be tightly controlled. Deity will direct the energy of the ritual…For those of us who are used to being in control, it is a humbling and somewhat daunting experience…They involve risk—the risk to let go of the bonds of "decorum" and release one's self into the heart of the deity's energy.[22]

This last quotation is a disturbing echo of many charismatic teachings about letting the spirit "direct" worship.

What should we make of these teachings about surrender to a superior power? How do they stand up against orthodox biblical thought?

BIBLICAL SUBMISSION

At first I was uncertain about charismatic teachings on surrender to the Holy Spirit, but since all mystics teach the same thing, I knew there was a problem. Turning to the Bible for help, the answer soon became clear.

Using the old-fashioned method—the King James Version with Strong's Exhaustive Concordance—I discovered that Scripture never—not once, not ever—speaks about opening up to or surrendering to the Holy Spirit! Although the Bible speaks of opening blind eyes to see, deaf ears to hear, barren wombs, etc., there is not one single exhortation to "open" yourself to God or to the Holy Spirit.

Neither is the word "submission" ever used in the sense of submission to spiritual presence or power. In fact, the range of use is

> We must conclude that the complete absence of biblical exhortations to submit to the Holy Spirit, considered together with injunctions against the occult and the frequency of similar teaching among occult pagan groups, prove beyond a shadow of a doubt that *submission to the Holy Spirit is an unbiblical concept.*

---

22. Scott, Ecstatic Ritual.

limited, and I can do a complete review here. The concept of sub-mission occurs in the limited senses of:

(1) *Abasing or afflicting the self:* The Lord urged Hagar to *submit* to ill treatment at the hands of Sarai (Genesis 16:9);

(2) *Humbling the self to honor another:* The psalmist asked God to command kings to *submit* to Him by bringing gifts in tribute (Psalm 68:30);

(3) *Unwilling obedience; forced submission to the authority of another* as in:
   - *submission* to persons in authority by obeying them (2 Samuel 22:45, also Psalm 18:44)
   - through the greatness of God's power enemies of the Jews would *submit.* (Psalm 66:3)
   - God said He would cause Israel's enemies to *submit* if only Israel would walk in His ways (Psalm 81:15); and

(4) *Willing obedience or submission to the authority of another* as in the following Scriptures:
   - all the princes and mighty men willingly *submitted* to Solomon as king (1 Chronicles 29:24)
   - we are exhorted to *submit* as follows:
     - believers to godly leaders in Christian ministry (1 Corinthians 16:16, I Peter 5:5, Hebrews 13:17)
     - wives to husbands (Ephesians 5:22, Colossians 3:18)
     - believers to God (James 4:7)
     - believers to human institutions and authorities (1 Peter 2:13)
     - believers to fellow believers (Ephesians 5:21)
   - Lastly, Paul noted in Romans 10:3 that there are many who have zeal for God, but not according to knowl-edge; these people fail to *submit* to the righteousness of God.

In fact, the entire idea of submitting passively to a manifest spirit is occult. It is Satan's counterfeit of the godly way. Biblical submission is never passive or mindless; it is *active* and *mindful*. It means using our minds to learn God's will; and using our wills to obey. Biblical submission is a *reasoning, deliberate response*. I need to emphasize again that Jesus Himself said that whoever *does*—that is, actively performs—the will of God is part of His family (Mark 3:35). The writer to the Hebrews said, "For you have need of endurance, so that after you have done the will of God, you may receive the promise" (Hebrews 10:36). Scripture is clear that obedience is precious to God:

> So Samuel said: "Has the Lord as great delight in burnt offerings and sacrifices, as in obeying the voice of the Lord? Behold, to obey is better than sacrifice, and to heed than the fat of rams" (1 Samuel 15:22).

Godly submission is the practice of obedience. It's that simple.

What does it mean to be filled with the Holy Spirit?

Before leaving this chapter, I should address some nagging questions. If the Holy Spirit is not a force or energy, or a river or wave, or the power of God, or an ethereal, flowing spirit, then what does it mean to be "filled with" the Holy Spirit? Why is the Spirit referred to as "living water"? Why do Scriptures promise that God will "pour out" His Spirit? And what did Paul mean when he said to the Ephesians, "be not drunk with wine, in which is dissipation; but be filled with the Spirit" (Ephesians 5:18)?

The short answer is that these verses must be read not only in light of God's injunction against the occult, but also considering that biblical teaching on the Holy Spirit makes generous use of metaphor to illustrate spiritual realities not easily expressed in human language. Puritan writer John Owen explains:

> The appearance of the Holy Spirit under a visible sign suggests that he is a Person (Matt. 3:16; Luke 3:22; John 1:32). He has personal attributes such as understanding and wisdom (1 Cor. 2:10-12; Isa. 40:28; Psa. 147:5; 2 Pet. 1:21;

[handwritten margin note: Overindulgence in sensual pleasures. "a descent into drunkeness & sexual dissipation"]

[etc.]). He acts according to his own will (1 Cor. 12:11).
He has power (Job 33:4; Isa. 11:2; [etc.]). He teaches
(Luke 12:12; [etc.]). He calls to special work (Acts
13:2,4)—an act of authority, choice and wisdom. He called
Barnabas and Saul. He commanded them to be set apart.
He sent them out. All this shows his authority and personality. He appointed men to positions of authority in the
church (Acts 20:28). He was tempted (Acts 5:9). How can
a quality, an accident, a power from God be tempted?
Ananias lied to him (Acts 5:3)...The Holy Spirit can be
resisted (Acts 7:51). He can be grieved (Eph. 4:30). He can
be rebelled against, annoyed and blasphemed (Isaiah
63:10; [etc.]). Clearly, the Holy Spirit is not merely a quality to be found in the divine nature. He is not simply an
influence or power. He is not the working of God's power
in our sanctification. He is a holy, intelligent Person.[23]

Consider: a man or woman is one individual, yet being one is
also three—a body of flesh, a human soul and a spirit. Does it not
follow, then, that the God in whose image we were made is also
triune, being Jesus who came in the flesh, God the Father and the
Holy Spirit? Understood this way it becomes clear that the Spirit
of God could never be an emanating force or a power to be
"tapped into" or to flow through us, any more than our spirit
could be or do such things.

As to "pouring out," see again the writing of John Owen:

God is said to pour out the Holy Spirit frequently (Prov.
1:23; Isa. 32:15; [etc.]). Wherever this expression is used it
refers to the gospel era. It implies comparison, pointing us
back to some other time or previous act of God, when he
gave his Spirit, but not in the same way as he now intends
to give him...It implies the outpouring of the gifts and

---

23. John Owen, *The Holy Spirit: Abridged and Made Easy to Read by R.J.K. Law*
(Edinburgh: Banner of Truth Trust, 1998), 7-8.

graces of the Spirit, not his Person (for where he is given, he is given permanently). It refers to special works of the Spirit such as the purifying and comforting of those on whom he is poured (Mal. 3:2,3; Isa. 4:4; Luke 3:16; [etc.])[24]

So there we have it: the god of forces is a satanic counterfeit of the true Holy Spirit.

24. Owen, 11-12.

Chapter Thirteen

DESOLATIONS OF THE FORCE

On the altar of the Devil up is down, pleasure is pain, darkness is light, slavery is freedom, and madness is sanity.
—Anton Szandor LaVey, Satanic priest

Their sorrows shall be multiplied who hasten after another god.
—Psalm 16:4

If Satan is who the Bible says he is, then men and women involved in the occult are in serious danger—present *and* future.

THE DESOLATIONS OF A KUNDALINI AWAKENING: GALL AND WORMWOOD

Honest yoga instructors will warn their students about the risks of awakening kundalini. Yoga can make you sick. Very sick. Does this sound crazy? Read on.

One yoga master wrote that the decision to practice yoga:

> is a serious decision. Yoga is not a trifling jest if we consider that any misunderstanding in the practice of Yoga can mean

death or insanity. That a misunderstood Yoga can be dangerous has been proven by many a student.[1]

The effects of a kundalini awakening during yoga practice can
be troubling, even devastating. (As might be expected since we are
dealing with the same force, this is also true of Qigong and tai
chi.) See for example the Web site at www.kundalini-support.com,
set up by a devotee who suffered horribly after experiencing the
bite of the serpent. On his Web site other, desperate people share
their stories. The Energy Ball Man (chapter 3) wrote:

> My mind became uncontrollable and irrational which
> was caused from the disruption to normal brain func-
> tion from the event itself and also the insomnia. I
> became ridden with anxiety...When the anxiety reached
> a certain threshold I would feel nervous/fear/heat energy
> sweep through my nervous system...I had full blown
> panic attacks which were absolutely horrific...Symptoms
> that haven't improved...relentless anxiety based
> dreams...racing thoughts, panic attacks...difficulty
> thinking or concentrating, obsessive thoughts...It is no
> accident that Gopi Krishna in his popular book *Living
> with Kundalini* said that "in whom the awakening occurs
> all at once as the result of yoga or other spiritual prac-
> tices, the sudden impact of powerful vital currents on
> the brain and other organs is often attended with grave
> risk."[12]

Gopi Krishna, to whom the Energy Ball Man referred above,
was a kundalini researcher who experienced the sudden uprising
of serpent power during meditation. He wrote:

---

1. Hans-Ulrich Rieker, trans. Elsy Becherer, *The Yoga of Light, Hatha Yoga
   Pradipika—India's Classical Handbook* (New York: Herder and Herder, 1971),
   9, quoted in Johanna Michaelson, *Like Lambs to the Slaughter: Your Child and
   the Occult* (Eugene, OR: Harvest House), 96.
2. "adsiwan," 5,6,10.

I felt as if I were in imminent danger of something
beyond my understanding and power, something intangi-
ble and mysterious, which I could neither grasp nor analyze…A condition of horror…began to settle on
me…Little did I realize that from that day onward I was
never to be my old normal self again…and that thence-
forth for a long time I had to live suspended by a thread,
swinging between life on the one hand and death on the
other, between sanity and insanity, between light and
darkness, between heaven and earth.[3]

Does all this sound unbelievably extreme? That's what I
thought at first. But to my horror I discovered that there are thousands of kundalini sufferers around the world, also those who
have dabbled in meditation and other eastern practices, who
report serious problems with numbness, phobias, sexual dysfunc-
tion and the afflictions of the Energy Ball Man. These problems
can and do lead to complete inability to function, compulsive
behavior and suicidal desires. In fact, insanity from yoga is so
common, it has a name: "Kundalini Psychosis." A Swedish support
site for victims explains:

A Kundalini release can be triggered by erroneous meditation, yoga, breathing exercises, reiki, qigong, healing,
tantra, transcendental meditation and other eastern or
new age spiritual exercises. When the Kundalini energy
is rising through the chakras, it can cause big problems
for the bodily and mental health. We have received hundreds of emails from people around the world who have
been damaged by these artificial spiritual exercises…Many
people have gone insane from the tremendous Kundalini
energy and been diagnosed with psychosis, schizophre-
nia and other similar mental diseases. Modern medical

3. Gopi Krishna, *The Evolutionary Energy in Man* (Boston: Shambhala, 1971),
16-17, quoted in Johanna Michaelsen, *Like Lambs to the Slaughter*, 95-96.

science has limited knowledge and experience in this area, and often denies the existence of the Kundalini energy.[4]

The Swedish site lists further symptoms of kundalini illness, which I relate here for the benefit of sufferers, so they may compare their own experience:

- feeling hot or cold streams, or bubbles, moving up the spine
- pain in various locations throughout the body
- genital titillation and difficulty controlling powerful lusts
- "overpressure" in the head
- faster or irregular heartbeat
- hypersensitivity to light, sound or smell
- religious experiences, visions, "cosmic glimpses," paranormal abilities
- anxiety, mania, depression, insomnia
- inability to speak
- memory impairment
- poltergeist experiences and complete demonic possession [These are very frightening]

The word *poltergeist* is German, from *polter,* meaning uproar, and *geist,* meaning spirit or ghost. A poltergeist experience is an encounter with a supernatural spirit who causes objects to move without natural cause, makes noises or inflicts bodily injury.

Demonic possession (or oppression, I will not enter into that debate) occurs when a demonic spirit, or spirits, control the mind causing insanity and loss of control, temporary or permanent. Evidences include voices in the head, compulsive behavior and uncontrollable blasphemy.

---

4. "Kundalini: Risker & Information," *http://www.kundalini.se.*To see the English translation, click on "Kundalini Network & Information" near bottom of page.

Now who could ever doubt that spirits who cause such suffering are evil and destructive? They rob health and sanity and destroy lives. But despite these terrible dangers, or in ignorance of them, yoga students pursue the serpent force with blind zeal, believing in error that it will be good for them.

CHARISMATIC EXPERIENCE:
AGONY AND BLASPHEMY

As I continued my research I decided to investigate experiences of charismatics and the onset of symptoms like those listed above. I am personally aware of many charismatics who suffer from depression or anxiety, hypersensitivity to light and sound, nighttime demonic attacks and other problems also suffered by yoga practitioners. Following are charismatic testimonies taken from the Web, provided by courageous souls who want to warn others.

Matt D. said:

> I experienced all the manifestations, from falling, to swimming, to growling, laughing, crying, convulsing, shaking - the works. I really thought I was going through life-changing spiritual experiences. But the fruits were superficial. I had a "love" for Jesus, I sang of His kisses, of seeing Him run over mountains and peer through doors. Yet I always seemed to wonder where my "lover" was. I experienced times of absolute depression and anxiety…It was unbearable…I remember the final turning point really came when I asked God to protect me. I don't know why I did it, I just did. The meeting ended up in the usual TB standard…People were falling, convulsing and groaning. There I was…standing. I was convinced![5]

Jill B. reported what happened to her after TB prayer:

---

5. Matt D., "One Fish That Jumped Out of the River," quoted in "The Way of Cain: New Teachings in the Christian Church—Where Are They Leading Us?" *http://www.apologeticsindex.org/r06a22.html*, 3.

she [prayer team member] had her hand over my head, and
I thought, "I feel a little bit dizzy." The feeling wasn't very
strong. But everyone else was falling around, and I desper-
ately wanted to be touched by God. So in the end I just
decided to "go with the flow" of this dizziness, and I let
myself fall back. I felt this horrible, uncomfortable, heavy,
oppressive feeling go all over my head and down my body.
It felt two inches thick, and it also felt "buzzy," although I
couldn't hear anything…This lady said to me, "Just rest in
the Spirit, rest in the Spirit"…A few days later, all those
problems that I'd wanted the lady counselor to pray about
in the Blessing meeting were worse; every difficulty I'd ever
had [fears and phobias] was magnified a hundred-fold.[6]

Later Jill went back to the same "prayer counselor" for more
prayer, and:

by the evening I was hearing voices…telling me to kill
myself, and blasphemous swear words about Jesus. After
two hours of this, I wasn't actually tearing my hair out, but
I felt like it. I knew if those voices continued, I would kill
myself. It was absolutely awful…the voices continued all
the time, together with blasphemous swear words against
the Lord.[7]

Jill's testimony about blasphemy struck an alarming note for
me. I had heard about other people experiencing such torment.
So I wondered, were these incidents isolated and coincidental, or
is the risk of falling under the control of blasphemous spirits
something charismatics need to know about? The answer to this
is, yes, definitely.

In his book *When the Spirit Comes With Power*, John White
tacitly acknowledged that blaspheming is a problem. It apparently

6. Jill Barnes, posted at *http://www.niksula.cs.hut.fi/ahuima/toronto/testimony.html*.
7. Barnes.

occurred so frequently in his experience that he considered setting up a controlled study using groups of victims. He asked:

> What is the most effective method of changing blasphe-
> mous outbursts of rage? We would have to assign blasphe-
> mers randomly to different treatment methods—exorcism,
> counseling, psychotherapy (and ideally to a control group
> also), a procedure which raises both technical and moral
> difficulties. If we did not assign subjects randomly to dif-
> ferent groups, the subjects would choose the method they
> believed in most. In that case we could not possibly rule
> out placebo effects. There is no way in which a single-
> blind, let alone a double-blind, study could be carried out.
> All the blasphemers would know what method was being
> used.[8]

Unwanted and uncontrollable blasphemy is not a recent phenomenon. If we go back in biblical history, we find another group
of believers who had gotten out of hand. Their meetings were dis-
orderly, they were involved in mysticism, and, yes, some of them
were even blaspheming Jesus. These were the Corinthians, to
whom Paul wrote:

> You know that you were Gentiles, carried away to these
> dumb idols, however you were led. Therefore I make
> known to you that no one speaking by the Spirit of God
> calls Jesus accursed... (I Corinthians 12:2-3).

Paul was warning the Corinthians that only evil spirits cause a
person to curse Jesus. Indeed, can there be any doubt about it? To
those Christians who suffer I offer the hope of freedom through
repentance, prayer and a return to biblical practice. Seek out obedient saints, confess your trials and know that my prayers are with
you also!

---

8. White, 115-116.

Meanwhile, the carnage continues. Gayle R., involved in TB, began to hear what she believed were prophecies from Jesus. But then:

> I started to hear voices, thoughts in my mind, other than my "Jesus." There was a mocking voice, a sexually perverted voice. Another one threatened me and imitated voices of people I knew. I didn't know what was happening. I thought I was being attacked by Satan and his army because the "Lord" had so gifted me for a special mission. I couldn't control their thoughts going through my mind and they were beginning to take over. I was so frightened. Week after week the battle for my mind continued...I testify from personal experience that demons can enter a Christian's thoughts with loving Christian words and offer spiritual-sounding exhortations. Demons know Scripture and how to use it for their purposes. Many unguarded believers are manipulated and demonized this way. They are gently guided to lead others astray with awesome spiritual feelings and manifestations...[9]

L. Thomson gives this testimony:

> I was never advised to "test the spirits" according to Scripture...when I was myself roaring - laughing - shaking or crying - no one ever challenged any of it. I was not in any kind of torment while experiencing these manifestations - it was great - I never saw anyone else appear to experience torment...Then I attended a prophetic conference at Mott Auditorium, the Vineyard of Pasadena...one of the speakers (from Kansas City) began to "shoot arrows in the Spirit" at us...he told us to receive what God's angels had for us - he said "it's ok to paint a target for where you want

9. Gayle Rogers, quoted in "The Way of Cain: New Teachings in the Christian Church—Where Are They Leading Us?" http://www.apologeticsindex.org/r06a22.html, 2.

the arrow to hit you." Myself having suffered from serious childhood hurts - began to place my hand on my heart and cry out to God. Suddenly I could hardly stand - but this was not the drunk kind of swoon I had experienced before - this was painful - I ached all over as if I was coming apart inside - I wanted to sit down and catch my breath but at that very moment the speaker called out "Take it" so I forced myself to stand upright. A feeling of anguish came over me that was awful and indescribable...I layed face down on the cold floor there. Soon - I was frozen to the floor - I could not have gotten up if I had wanted to - I could not speak...The next 10 days were so incredibly bizarre I have difficulty describing what happened. I will say that there were some very bizarre 'impulses' being hurled at my spirit, as to the like I had never experienced. I began to wonder if someone had put speed into my drinking water...it was fearful and oppressive...my [prophetic] gifting seemed to turn on me as I experienced terrifying feelings and apparitions...What frightens me about the Toronto movement is that these people, as I was, are sincerely deceived...it's wow, look at that—and wow feel this...feel, feel, feel.[10]

The serpent may bestow sweet *phos* light, but he will also use the opportunities afforded him through occult practice to afflict his victims cruelly. Speaking through the prophet Jeremiah, God mourned:

"My people have changed their glory for what does not profit.
Be astonished, O heavens, at this, and be horribly afraid;

Dear Reader, run—flee—from the spirits who assault you and torment you through occult practice.

10. L. Thompson, quoted in "The Way of Cain: New Teachings in the Christian Church—Where Are They Leading Us?" 2-3.

Be very desolate," says the Lord.
"For My people have committed two evils:
They have forsaken Me, the fountain of living waters,
And hewn themselves cisterns—broken cisterns that can
  hold no water" (2:11-13).

DEMONIZATION OF KUNDALINI PRACTITIONERS

Kundalini practitioners are also vulnerable. The so-called "risk of insanity" to which yoga teachers refer is probably the risk of demonization. Following are testimonies that were posted at the kundalini support Web site when I was doing my research.[11] (I have reproduced them as posted.)

From Sol (who considers himself a Christian. Interestingly, he got worse after being slain in the Spirit):

> I had a spontaneous Kundalini awakening a few years ago. Things have settled down considerably since the year of the explosion but I had some horrendous experiences some years after the awakening which are connected to a visit to a spiritual healer, and which continue to bother me from time to time.
>
> After a time I began to suffer terrible psychic attacks which ranged from assaults on the nervous system to mental disturbance. On one occasion I went to a Christian healer, having given myself back to Christ (I was brought up an evangelical Christian), and the ensuing attacks from the original psychic healer, after this slaying in the Spirit experience, were horrendous.
>
> Some of the symptoms are as follows. I feel an evil presence which I am able to identify, my mind plays a train of thought which is other to my own, accompanied by a decidedly unpleasant feeling in my spirit, I have a kind of alien depression forced on me, my body is frequently jolted or made to feel an unnatural tension, my dreams are

---

11. Letters and testimonies appear to be deleted periodically from the Web site and may not be available after the passage of several months. However, new ones are posted in their place as victims continue to fall prey to occult spirits.

invaded and so on and so forth. There have been two or
three periods which lasted a month or so where I was
completely debilitated.

From Christine:

> looking back (thus far) i would say most of my negative
> experiences seem to have had a correlation with when my
> root opened up. i had entities harrass me by slapping me ,
> and the worst was when i was almost asleep once.. in
> between sleep and non sleep.. and i saw a being in my
> inner sight and before i could react .. it scratched my left
> leg viciously.. and drew blood.

From Safira:

> i was lying in bed, had been reading a psychology book,
> and all of a sudden i felt some energy i had never felt
> before. i felt like i was making a connection w/some divine
> being! maybe i was in a higher state of consciousness, but
> it was some kind of natural "high" and i was in a blissfull
> state and felt a freedom from anxiety like never before
> (and i have always suffered w/extreme anxiety). so, under-
> standably, i was happy and told my relative and her hus-
> band and this high went on for about an hour…ok, so
> around 3 weeks later… i woke up one night with horrible
> depression! i got up and could not sleep and started pac-
> ing around the apartment. i did not wakeup my sister
> because her husband had to go to work early. ..so, i am
> disabled now. i cannot read like i used to after that. i can-
> not focus or concentrate. my education came to a halt… i
> feel my life as i knew it is over…i cannot do a lot of things
> most people can do w/this depression. i did not deserve
> that, i never killed anybody. it made me very resentful. . . i
> tried to watch tv, play w/the cat, nothing helped. the
> depression was building and building and i became SUI-
> CIDALLY DEPRESSED!!! at then after maybe an hour or
> so i could not take it any more and started screaming. i

had looked at a knife in the kitchen sink wanting to kill
myself to end the depression but i could not do it.
i was screaming in mental agony and mysister woke up
and came out and said whats wrong!? she hugged me and i
said help me! and she took me to the emergency room.

Occult spirits can, and obviously will, inflict great suffering upon those who make the terrible mistake of turning to Eastern religious practices.

SPIRITUAL STARVATION

We can be sure that engaging in occult practice grieves the Holy Spirit. If we choose sin and disobedience, God will—indeed must, if He is merciful and just—cause us or allow us to experience the consequences. The pain is a clarion call, a warning to those who err. The psalmist said, "If I regard iniquity in my heart, The Lord will not hear" (Psalm 66:18). King David said that because of sin his bones grew old, and he groaned all the day long (see Psalm 32:3). God's love does not abide in the hearts of those who depart from His ways.

One of the consequences of occult practice is a counterfeit thirst for "God"—a painful ache for *phos* light encounters that can be satisfied only by more occult experience; yet practitioners find that as time goes on the rewards of their practice diminish and they become desperate, seeking anxiously for the spiritual ecstasies they first knew with a god who, for his own evil purposes, becomes increasingly elusive.

Desperate for God

Most charismatics, believing in error that occult *phos* light experiences are encounters with God, find they need more and more to appease a growing thirst. Several leaders told me, when I was a new believer, that we should "*always* be desperate for God." In fact, they insisted that times of depression are an inevitable part of every believer's walk! But in so saying, they reveal the famished state of their own souls.

Examples abound. Pastor John Arnott of the Toronto church, speaking to pastors at a conference, invited them to come forward if they "felt they would die if they did not soon receive a touch from God."[12] John and Paula Sandford of Elijah House say they need to soak regularly so they can keep going:

> Depression and spiritual angst are satanic counterfeits of true, godly hunger, which anticipates with delight the joys of obedience and prayer and the Word.

> That's the secret for us now, experiencing prayer through the power of His presence. Now it is an extremely important part of our lives, refreshing us as we go. Although we sometimes still grow weary, by receiving "soaking" prayers through our loving friends at Toronto we now experience "re-refreshing" so we can go at it again.[13]

But the reality is, the continual need for occult *phos* light experience is one of the desolations of the force. It is a counterfeit of true spiritual thirst, and is uncommonly painful to the soul.

Scripture does not promise an abiding thirst for God. It promises abiding joy and peace. Jesus said to the Samaritan woman at the well, "Whoever drinks of this [well] water will thirst again, but whoever drinks of the water that I shall give him will never thirst. But the water that I shall give him will become in him a fountain of water springing up into everlasting life" (John 4:14).

When a believer has the Holy Spirit indwelling and walks in God's will, his soul is revived, and continues to be revived unto eternal life. I'm not saying that life is always a breeze—of course it isn't. Many troubles can, and will, arise. But as Jesus said, in a spiritual sense, the believer's thirst has been forever quenched.

---

12. Quoted in, "Confusion about 'Spirit Slaying,'" Way of Life Literature, *http://www.wayoflife.org/fbns/endtimesconfusion.htm.*

13. John Sandford, *Spread the Fire Magazine 2000,* Vol. 6, Issue 5, *http://www.tacf.org.stf/archive/6-5.*

Jesus fills, but Satan's cup is empty

As one grows in true faith and practice, he or she will know a continuing, sometimes overflowing delight in ordinary things. This is one of the sweet ingredients our Lord casts into our cup. Reading the Bible, home life, ordinary things—and following the rules—these give peace and pleasure.

But such pleasures are sacrificed to the need for supernatural experience when occult influence predominates. Charismatic Matt Sorger admits that he has been "ruined for the ordinary." He says, "Once you've experienced the true presence and power of God you're ruined for anything less. Mere religious form and practice will never satisfy. There is an insatiable longing in man to experience a living, supernatural God."[14] Matt and other charismatics live for occult encounters. But so do yoga practitioners; earlier (chapter 2) we read this statement:

> The desire to know God and to be one with God is felt like
> an ache, sending you into hours of meditation, intense
> devotion and deeper commitment. Nothing less will do,
> the Kundalini requires that you give everything.

As C.S. Lewis once pointed out, Satan compels us to strive harder and harder for diminishing rewards. Thus time is lost in the vain pursuit of spiritual experience, and hours are misspent soaking or meditating to feed the starving soul. In the end the practitioner is, as Matt said, ruined for the ordinary. If only Matt realized how great a loss he has suffered.

KUNDALINI IN THE MEDICAL PROFESSION

I cannot leave this chapter without drawing the reader's attention to a disturbing trend in modern psychiatry.

I have learned that there are psychiatrists now who specialize in treating kundalini sufferers. The problem is, they believe kundalini is a good spiritual force. Amazingly, blindly, they believe intense

---

14. Matt Sorger, "The Coming Healing Revival,"
http://www.elijahlist.com/healing_columns/052303_Sorger.htm.

suffering to be a sign of spiritual growth. An organization called the Spiritual Emergence Network (SEN) comprised of mental health "professionals" formed a referral network to treat victims of the serpent force. SEN posted the following on its Web site:

> The SEN@CIIS mental health professionals…are respectful of spiritual experience, familiar with a number of spiritual traditions and indicate that they are qualified to work with at least one of the following areas of difficulty
>   Loss or change of faith
>   Existential and/or spiritual crisis
>   Experience of unitive [sic] consciousness or altered states
>   Psychic openings
>   Possession
>   Near-Death Experience
>   Kundalini
>   Shamanic journey
>   Difficulties with a meditation practice
> Drawing on transpersonal psychology and the knowledge from the spiritual traditions which have investigated the stages and characteristics of spiritual growth, the mental health profession in the United States is beginning to understand that some of the characteristic [sic] of spiritual development can be confused with symptoms of mental illness. When accurately understood these characteristics can be recognized as evidence of the normal, potentially life-enhancing aspect of human development.[15]

Potentially life-enhancing? What delusion. SEN has a crisis line for what they refer to as "the spiritual emergence population." Of course, since SEN believes kundalini suffering is a sign of spiritual growth, they encourage victims to continue practices that are harming them.

---

15. Web site, Spiritual Emergence Network at the California Institute of Integral Studies (SEN@CIIS), *http://www.ciis.edu/comserv/sen.html.*

Message for non-Christians

To non-Christian sufferers, this section is for you. I say with a heart full of compassion: Do not go for help to "professionals" who advise you to continue practices that hurt you, endanger you and cause suffering—not even if they tell you it is only temporary and you just need to "manage it properly." Not even if they say they have peace in their own lives since they went through it. These counselors and professionals are terribly misguided. They are leading you to spiritual disaster because they do not understand where they have been, nor where they are going.

Your suffering and pain mean you are being damaged and polluted, not that you are being purged and detoxified. Don't be like the foolish moth, which loves the light that burns! Your symptoms indicate that you are getting sick. Do not deny the evidence! Hear, hear, what your soul, your mind and your body are trying to tell you!

Only harmful spirits will sicken and depress you. Only malicious ones will afflict you with anxiety and mania. It is important to realize that there are evil spirits who want to ensnare you with lies and false gifts. They want to hurt you. When, through occult practice, you pierce the veil that separates them from us and open yourself to anything that comes along, you are endangering your health, your family, your sanity and your very soul.

Salvation and safety lie only in the paths set by the true God. See what the psalmist wrote:

> Their sorrows shall be multiplied who hasten after another
>   god...
> [But] You, O Lord, are the portion of my inheritance and
>   my cup;
> You maintain my lot.
> The lines have fallen to me in pleasant places;
> Yes, I have a good inheritance
>   (Psalm 16:4-6).

For any precious soul who is willing, I say, investigate Christianity! I pray that you will find the answers you need and I promise that if you do, you will feel like you have finally landed on solid ground. Simple, sensible, sweet ground.

MESSAGE FOR RAGGED CHARISMATICS

I often wondered about the prevalence of spiritual and emotional problems among my charismatic friends and acquaintances. Anxiety, depression and marital woes are commonplace. They go from crisis to crisis. There is constant demand for counseling courses and healing therapies, which never seem to help.

I once attended a Sunday gathering where the pastor's wife stood at the front and lamented for 30 minutes both the material and emotional poverty of their church. "Where is God?" she cried in desperation. "Why is it so hard and so painful?"

Charismatics typically combine sad lamentations about their lot in life with exhortations to have faith, fight demons and pray for things to get better. Chuck Pierce published the following "prophecies" on the Web, a testament to their "grief," "fragmentation," and suffering:

> The trumpet blows:
> …All the fragmentation in our soul and body—if we grab hold of this, this year, there will be a realignment and the fragmentation of soul can be mended…We are actually going to have to let Jehovah Rohi (the Lord my Shepherd) become real this year and follow Him into some new places. That is going to be the requirement to break off the old fragmented nature and woundings that have occurred in me and separated me…
>
> Feast of Tabernacles, Year 5764:
> …You are going to understand why you have gone through this loss you have gone through, why you have been sick, why that last business dried up. God's covenant plan is going to be activated in a new way this year—like never before…
> Tonight there is a grief that God wants us to leave. He knows your grief and how long you have carried it.

Finances, relationships out of sync, business, lay it
down…Grief—we've got to lay it down…thirst no more—
let the river begin to flow.[16]

Among other things, charismatics are strained by demands
they make of themselves in the area of spiritual warfare. They
strive for power in intercessory prayer, where they "come against
the enemy." Frequently they claim that God "woke them up" in
the middle of the night to pray for an unknown person halfway
around the globe, and then they walk haggard during the day.
They maintain long prayer vigils to beat away forces of darkness.
Mr. Pierce wrote, "You are going to have to go where God tells you
to go…There will be divine assignments in the grocery store etc.
at 8am because God wants you to give the word of the Lord."[17] He
promised that if people will strive, seek in the occult, travail cease-
lessly in prayer and get up early when prompted…then they will
"prevail."[18] He predicted, "This year we will be more dependent
on God than drugs," and, "We will enter into a new dimension of
healing—they are keeping us out of revelation."[19]

Promises, empty promises.

Vain travailing prayer drains charismatics, who feel responsible for the spiritual and economic well-being of entire cities and
countries. Cindy Jacobs, self-proclaimed "General of Intercession,"
gave the following prophecy for 2000:

So, the Lord would say, My Children, I know that you feel
ragged. I know that you feel beat up and I know that you
have gone through difficult days. For the enemy is coming
against your soul, but I would say, children, I don't want
you to think that what you see at this moment is reality
because there is a greater reality and the I AM that I AM

---

16. Chuck Pierce, "A Gospel for the New Year (Jewish calendar)," *http://www.gen-
erals.org/articles*, 1-2.

17. Pierce, 1.

18. See Pierce, 1.

19. Pierce, 6. Ironically, Mr. Pierce is linked with the so-called "Healing Rooms".

says I AM the greater reality than what you can see and what you know.[20]

While I agree with Ms. Jacobs that the enemy is coming against her soul, it is sad that she, like yoga teachers, strives to get beyond her troubles by persevering in an occult search for a mystic "reality" that is always just out of reach. Ms. Jacobs explains away the unhappiness experienced by so many charismatics as follows:

> And the Lord showed me it was as if the people of this church and even the Christians of this nation have pushed and pushed and it is even like postpartum depression. After you have had a baby, then there comes this time where you women can feel really depressed. And the Lord would say to you, surely the baby has been born! Surely you have done well. Well done, good and faithful servants. And do you not think that I am a debtor to you![21]

To those involved in charismatic practices I say, pay heed to exhaustion, spiritual thirst and times of depressive suffering. Do not listen to blind leaders who tell you these are a normal part of Christian experience! You should be growing in joy and in the fullness of the abiding presence of God. Every year should be better than the last. This is one of the ways almighty God is glorified in His children.

Turn from occult practices and, after a while, you will understand. Your spirit will bear witness that you have escaped a black hole and found the narrow path leading to the knowledge of God.

---

20. Cindy Jacobs, "A Word of Exhortation," *www.generals.org/articles*, 1.
21. Jacobs, "Word of Exhortation," 1. I need to comment on Ms. Jacob's unbiblical belief that the Lord is her debtor. In his letter to the Romans, Paul said, "Oh, the depth of the riches both of the wisdom and knowledge of God!...who has first given to Him and it shall be repaid to him?" (Romans 11:33-35). God is indebted to no one.

WHAT ABOUT GOOD FRUITS?

We have explored the desolations of the force. But what about charismatics with good fruit in their lives? And what about yoga students? They claim good fruits, too. I don't know how many of these are true. But if so, I could point out that Satan is too smart to give everyone a bad experience. If he did, no one would be fooled, and he would defeat himself.

However, claims of good fruit can be misleading. Witness admissions from Mrs. Arnott of the Toronto Airport Church (who despite the bad fruits confessed here remains convinced of her godly ways):

> maybe you are asking, "Why does the devil seem to be so powerful? Why is he always attacking me when others don't seem to be attacked nearly so much?"
> Throughout our ministry, even before renewal began in 1994, we have seen many casualties in ministry as well as in the pew. Even since the new outpouring of the Spirit started, we have seen people continue to stumble and fall. In one case we saw a man and his wife who were power-fully touched by the outpouring, but...Two years later, [the husband] left his wife and ministry for another woman half his age...
> Another pastor would not deal with sexual sin in his life...
> Another pastor of a large church fell into major depression to the degree that he could not function...
> All the people I'm describing had been powerfully touched by this River of God's presence, were mightily anointed by the Holy Spirit and had gone out across the world spread-ing the fire. All of them had something else in common: none had allowed the Lord to dig in the garden of his heart.
> But why did the anointing seem to remain with them?[22]

---

22. Carol Arnott, "Inner You," 1.

Mrs. Arnott asks why "God" would continue to bless the ministry of unrepentant sinners in leadership positions in the charismatic church. Of course He wouldn't, and He doesn't, and He never will.

The true God *does not* turn a blind eye to adultery and sin. The anointing that remains with these leaders is definitely not from Him. Jeremiah cried:

> Also I have seen a horrible thing in the prophets of
> Jerusalem:
> They commit adultery and walk in lies;
> They also strengthen the hands of evildoers,
> So that no one turns back from his wickedness
> (Jeremiah 23:14).

Let the words of the apostle John close this chapter:

> Little children, let no man deceive you: he that doeth
> righteousness is righteous, even as he is righteous. He that
> committeth sin is of the devil; for the devil sinneth from
> the beginning (1 John 3:7-8 KJV).

Chapter Fourteen

GOLD DUST AND ASHES

This is an evil generation. It seeks a sign, and no sign will be given to it except the sign of Jonah the prophet. For as Jonah became a sign to the Ninevites, so also the Son of Man will be to this generation.

—Jesus the Christ, (Luke 11:29-30)

*G*old dust, gold fillings and miraculous healings; these are some of the signs and wonders accompanying charismatic ministries.

Miracles stir hope. But we know from Scripture that while God performs miracles, Satan does, too.

HOPE, HEALING AND HOLY ASH

Guru Sai Baba is a miracle-working guru from India who claims over twenty million followers. A young American named Tal Brooke was, for a time, one of Sai Baba's most trusted Western disciples.[1] Mr. Brooke was captivated by Sai Baba's extraordinary

---

1. After his conversion to Christianity, Mr. Brooke became president of the Spiritual Counterfeits Project in California, an organization dedicated to exposing deceptive spiritual practices.

power and charisma. He personally witnessed many signs and wonders, including the miraculous materialization of gold and metal items. Sai Baba turned water into gasoline when he ran out of fuel in the desert. He was uncannily psychic, and knew secrets about Tal's past that no one could naturally know. He frequently materialized "holy ash" out of thin air, which people rubbed on themselves for healing, and he also materialized gold ornaments. Mr. Brooke writes that he witnessed these wonders up close, and they could not have been faked.[2]

Miracles, healing and magic arts have for many ages been the boast of gurus, shamans and magicians. But charismatics now echo these boasts, and promote their ministries partly by the advertisement of signs and wonders. I once heard a pastor claim that God sends gold dust and gold fillings to his meetings. The Toronto Airport Church posted Web photographs of people with open mouths displaying new, supposedly God-given, gold fillings.[3]

Let's assume these claims are true, and these wonders are really happening. We still need to ask, are they from God?

FOR WHAT PURPOSE, MIRACLES?

The purpose for advertising signs and wonders is—indeed must be—the same for charismatics as for Sai Baba and other gurus. I am not trying to smear anyone, just stating a fact. Leaders promote miracles in connection with their ministries for three purposes: to attract people, to demonstrate connection with supernatural power and to validate their ministry.

This is true when they are sincere, but also when they are not.

I know people who have been miraculously healed through prayer with well-meaning pastors in charismatic healing ministries. I also know a woman who, formerly confined to a wheelchair, is now walking normally as a result of faith healing through an occult channeler in Tibet. She said he was a wonderful man.

---

2. See Mr. Brooke's autobiography: Tal Brooke, *Lord of the Air* (Eugene, OR: Harvest House, 1990), now published under the title 'Avatar of Night.'

3. For example, see *www.surewordministries.com/dentalmiracles.html.*

My guess is that most people involved in healing ministries, aside from those who reap in money by taking advantage of gullible people, are sincere, whether or not they consider themselves Christian. But sincerity is not a seal of godliness. And the fact is that now, as in times past, many miracle mongers are not godly. Like Simon the sorcerer, they derive power from another source.

That Satan has awesome power to work miracles is amply demonstrated in Scripture. In the book of Exodus the first three miracles Moses performed by the power of God were duplicated by Pharaoh's sorcerers through the power of Satan. Both threw down their staffs, which became snakes (Exodus 7:12). Both turned water to blood (7:21-22). And both made frogs come up in Egypt, hordes of them (8:6-7). It is noteworthy, moreover, that nothing in the nature of these miracles revealed whether the power behind them was godly or satanic. They were identical. The frogs were unpleasant and the bloody rivers deadly: an observer could easily have concluded that the same spirit—and an evil one at that—was behind both miracles. From this we can conclude that a miracle in itself proves nothing.

Many Scriptures confirm that signs and wonders are no yardstick for truth. In fact, they can deceive. Paul said, "The coming of the lawless one is according to the working of Satan, with all power, signs, and lying wonders, and with all unrighteous deception among those who perish" (2 Thessalonians 2:9-10). Therefore no ministry, and no minister, should be judged godly just because they can boast about signs and wonders.

OF WHAT VALUE, MIRACLES?
Evangelizing through signs and wonders

Every believer wants others to share their faith. Many think signs and wonders prove that God is real, and therefore are useful for evangelism.

When I was a new Christian I experienced several miracles, including healing, and I told my family and friends. Why? Partly to prove that my faith is real, hoping they would believe and turn to God. However, they were not convinced, and I needed to learn more about how God brings people into His kingdom.

Believing God is real—that is, believing in God—does not make someone a Christian. Nor does believing in miracles. No, because a Christian is someone who, granted the gift of faith, believes the gospel from the heart. Author Robert Coleman observed that Jesus, when He was teaching about the kingdom of God, easily could have had all the Kingdoms of men at His feet, for:

> All He had to do was to satisfy the temporal appetites and curiosities of the people by His supernatural power…these spectacular things [miracles] would surely have excited the applause of the crowd…But Jesus would not play to the galleries. Quite the contrary. Repeatedly He took special pains to allay the superficial popular support of the multitudes…He would even ask those who were the recipients of His healing to say nothing…[4]

Although the miracles Jesus performed helped true believers understand who He was and why He had come, He never used them to win people to faith. Relying on miracles to prove the existence of God is not the way to save a soul. In fact, trying to prove the existence of God is always pointless; even the devil believes in God. Such belief, although true, is not saving faith. But the following quote from charismatic Matt Sorger demonstrates how far the erroneous reliance on signs and wonders—so-called power evangelism—has penetrated some outreach ministries:

> The miraculous establishes the Kingdom of God in the Earth. Miracles serve as signs to the unbeliever. They point the way to God and soften the hardness in man's heart…They prove the existence of God and reveal the way to God.[5]

---

4. Robert E. Coleman, *The Master Plan of Evangelism,* 45th ed. (Old Tappan, NJ: Spire Books, 1987), 29.
5. Sorger, "Healing Revival."

Mr. Sorger tries to raise faith in God through miraculous demonstrations because that is apparently how he came to "believe," he and his whole family:

> I was birthed into the Kingdom through a miracle power encounter…My whole family was saved. God's Kingdom was established in our hearts through the miraculous demonstration power of God.[6]

But earlier (chapter 12) we read a similar story about a cult leader:

> Subuh claims that he went through a series of deep inner changes and received what he termed the "Great Life Force," a manifestation of the power of God.

Do demonstrations of power make true Christians? No. Do miracles soften the hardness in the human heart and "reveal the way to" God, as Mr. Sorger believes? Again, no. Scriptures say that even a miracle as fantastic as raising someone from the dead cannot convince an unbeliever. Jesus said, "If they do not hear Moses and the prophets, neither will they be persuaded though one rise from the dead" (Luke 16:31). The apostle John wrote:

> But although He had done so many signs before them, they did not believe in Him, that the word of Isaiah the prophet might be fulfilled, which he spoke: "Lord, who has believed our report? And to whom has the arm of the Lord been revealed?" Therefore *they could not believe*, because Isaiah said again: "He has blinded their eyes and hardened their heart, lest they should see with their eyes and understand with their heart, lest they should turn, so that I should heal them" (John 12:37-40). (emphasis added)

---

6. Sorger, "Healing Revival."

John is saying here that even with all the miracles Jesus did, the people could not believe, due to spiritual blindness. Unless the Holy Spirit opens his eyes a man simply cannot see, and understand and believe. Miracles do not open our eyes!

God converts souls to Him not by proving His power, but through enabling us to see and believe the truth of the gospel. He brings us forth by the word of truth (James 1:18). The light of this truth reveals the way to Him. Note, God can and does use errant ministries to rescue lost souls if essential truths are spoken. When Paul was in prison he rejoiced that the gospel was being taught, even by insincere people. He wrote to the Philippians, "…whether in pretense or in truth, Christ is preached; and in this I rejoice, yes, and will rejoice" (1:18). I myself came to faith through the Alpha course, although many of their teachings are occult and I was led astray for a time.

But while miraculous signs are given to those who believe (see Mark 16:17; John 14:11), true faith is granted only to those who are believing and repentant before the gospel message:

> So then faith comes by hearing, and hearing by the word of God (Romans 10:17).

> our Savior Jesus Christ…abolished death and brought life and immortality to light through the gospel… (2 Timothy 1:10).

> I am not ashamed of the gospel of Christ, for it is the power of God to salvation for everyone who believes, for the Jew first and also for the Greek (Romans 1:16).

It is gospel teaching that saves souls. Dr. J.I. Packer says we must impress upon people that the gospel is *a word from God,* and teach and reason with them:

> Luke's regular way of describing Paul's evangelistic ministry is to say that he *disputed,* or *reasoned (dialegomai:* RSV renders "argued"), or *taught,* or, *persuaded* (i.e. sought to carry

his hearer's judgments). And Paul himself refers to his ministry among the Gentiles as primarily a task of instruction: "unto me…was this grace given, to preach unto the Gentiles the unsearchable riches of Christ; and *to make all men see* what is the dispensation of the mystery…" Clearly, in Paul's view, his first and fundamental job as a preacher of the gospel was to communicate knowledge—to get gospel truth fixed in men's minds. To him, teaching the truth was the basic evangelistic activity; to him, therefore, the only right method of evangelism was the teaching method. (emphasis original)[7]

Biblical evangelism, therefore, involves teaching, explaining and persuading people of the truth.

The great evangelist and preacher Charles Spurgeon once wrote, "Do you not know…what God's estimate of the gospel is? Do you not know that it has been the chief subject of His thoughts and acts from all eternity? He looks on it as the grandest of all His works." Such is the supremacy of the gospel that the apostle Paul invoked the curse of God upon anyone who perverts it or preaches anything different (Galatians 1:7-9). God will not be pleased with those who diminish the place of His gospel to proclaim the empty glitter of miracles, signs and wonders.

7. J. I. Packer, *Evangelism & the Sovereignty of God* (Downers Grove, IL: InterVarsity, 1961), 48-49.

Chapter Fifteen

THE PURSUIT OF
PROPHETIC AUTHORITY

*Do not listen to the words of the prophets who prophesy to
you. They make you worthless; they speak a vision of their
own heart, not from the mouth of the Lord.*
—Jeremiah 23:16

*H*ow the world loves a prophet!
A young man from Kentucky, a serious Bible student
with no medical training, discovered he had a supernatural gift to
discern illness in people without any examination. Then he developed a gift of healing which he could exercise even for people who
lived far away.

In wonderment this young man searched the Scriptures for
understanding. He studied chapter 9 of John's Gospel for
insight into the relation between sin and sickness, and formed
the conclusion that with sufficient faith in God, all believers can
perform healing miracles. Later this young man began to
prophesy, predicting future events with amazing accuracy. But
despite pressure from others he refused to charge a fee for helping others. He said that because his gifts were from a pure and

holy God, he also must keep himself pure, and taking money would be wrong.[1]

Who was this altruistic young man? He was Edgar Cayce, one of the secular world's most renowned spiritists and "medical intuitives" (a term used by psychics to describe those who have supernatural ability to discern illness). He purportedly worked many miracles and healings, relying heavily on Bible teachings to explain and interpret his work. He died in 1945, but still has many followers.

Then there was a prophetess, also a student of the Bible, who prophesied about the Antichrist. She wrote:

> There are those who will try to sound a warning, for he
> will be glib and egotistical; but others will say that he
> deserves leadership, and his fame will spread to other areas
> of the world, so that for a time he will seem to be the
> promised savior. His strength will lie in his charismatic
> leadership qualities, for except to those who know him
> well, he will exhibit a side of his nature that indeed seems
> benevolent. As he seizes world power there will be some
> awesome days...[2]

This same prophetess had a vision about the final cleansing of the Earth. She said it will be like: "a giant wave, higher than a ten-story building, racing toward shore."[3] And who was she? She was Ruth Montgomery, an occultist who received information from unseen spirit guides. She called these guides her "friends who have been dictating through my typewriter since 1960."[4]

---

1. Jess Stearn, *A Prophet in His Own Country: The Story of the Young Edgar Cayce* (New York, William Morrow & Company, 1974); 157, 259.
2. Ruth Montgomery, *Strangers Among Us* (New York: Fawcett Crest, 1979), 220.
3. Montgomery, 229.
4. Montgomery, 14. Ms. Montgomery, through her guides, wrongly predicted a World War in the 1980s that would dramatically reduce the earth's population from billions to millions (see p. 228).

Over the centuries, occultists like Ruth Montgomery and Edgar Cayce have proclaimed themselves prophets, relying upon, and teaching from, the Bible. Therefore, we need discernment to distinguish true prophecy from the occult counterfeit.

PROPHECY:
THE ORTHODOX VS THE OCCULT APPROACH

That there is a biblical gift of prophecy cannot be denied. However, in this matter, as in so many others we have seen, there are right ways and there are occult ways.

Prophecy the orthodox way

Let us turn to the teaching of John MacArthur, who helped me understand the true meaning of biblical prophecy. He explains:

> The New Testament prophetic gift (Rom 12:6, 1 Cor 12:10) primarily has to do with declaration, not revelation. The New Testament prophet "speaks to men for edification and exhortation and comfort" (1 Cor. 14:3). He is a preacher, not a source of ongoing revelation. His task is one of forth-telling, not foretelling. That is, he proclaims already revealed truth; he is not generally a conduit for new revelation.[5]

True prophecy declares, clarifies, repeats and explains doctrine *already revealed* in Scripture. The gift of prophecy enables a believer to understand, teach and proclaim God's truth accurately and movingly in the power of the Holy Spirit. In the book of Acts, Luke used the expression "filled with the Holy Spirit" several times to describe people who were gifted to preach; for example, "Then Peter, filled with the Holy Spirit, said to them…" (Acts 4:8); and Stephen, who spoke with great eloquence to the synagogue leaders, was described as "a man full of faith and the Holy Spirit" (6:5).

---

5. John F. MacArthur, Jr., *Charismatic Chaos* (Grand Rapids, MI: Zondervan, 1992), 81.

Real prophets today do not offer new revelation. Nor do they predict the future, for this is divination. Real prophets declare God's Word so others are convicted and convinced, and souls are nourished by truth.

True prophetic utterance may be inspired, in the sense that biblical understanding is given supernaturally to an individual on a particular occasion. For example, I believe I prophesied when, as a newly converted believer who had barely looked at the Bible, I said to my pastor, "I have confidence that God will complete the work He has begun in me." This was a biblical statement of truth, although I did not realize it.

I believe my partner at the time, a man exceedingly hostile to Christianity and furious with me for looking into it, also prophesied. It was the night of my conversion. I was radiant in the Spirit, having received forgiveness and the gift of eternal life only hours before. I asked my partner if he knew who God was and he confounded me—and likely himself, also—by answering, "God is love." I then asked if he knew what sin was. He prophesied again—that is, he declared God's truth again—and answered, "Sin is a barrier between us and God." To my knowledge he had never read Scripture and no one had explained these doctrines to him. But even if he had heard them before, he never really believed them. In fact, he soon terminated our relationship because I had come to faith.[6]

Prophecy the occult way

In any of its forms and varieties, occult prophecy is really divination and includes "new revelation." It includes giving words about things "seen" or experienced through occult practice, or under occult influence. It includes the belief that truth is revealed in our actions or behavior (see Chapter 19). Channeling "teachings" from spirit guides or angels, necromancy (speaking with dead people), reading minds, discerning illnesses, revealing the past or the future

---

6. There is biblical precedent for inspired prophecy from the lips of an unbeliever. Caiaphas prophesied that Jesus would die for the nations (John 11:49-52). Balaam also prophesied (see Numbers 24:1-9).

from "knowledge" gained through visions or dreams, advising people through reading tea leaves, devising symbolic behavior ("prophetic acts") to meet with God or deliberately "opening" yourself to receive mental impressions: these are occult ways.

Scripture teaches that false prophets may speak under the influence of Satan (see Jeremiah 2:8) or from their own hearts and imaginations (Jeremiah 23:26). There are many false prophets, literally thousands among charismatics worldwide. Pastor MacArthur says:

> The contemporary charismatic perspective that makes every prophet an instrument of divine revelation cheapens both Scripture and prophecy. By permitting these so-called prophets to mix error with messages supposedly "fresh from God's lips," charismatics have opened the floodgates to false teaching, confusion, error, fanaticism, and chaos.[7]

One telling verse in Scripture divides the true prophet from the false. Jeremiah said:

> "The prophet who has a dream, let him tell a dream; and he who has My word, let him speak My word faithfully. What is the chaff to the wheat?" says the Lord. "Is not My word like a fire?" says the Lord, "And like a hammer that breaks the rock in pieces?" (23:28-29).

Here Jeremiah is saying that false prophets who tell their dreams are like "chaff." Chaff is the dead skin of a kernel of wheat, the part which does not nourish. On the other hand, those who have His Word and speak it faithfully are like "wheat"—their words nourish life because the Word is powerful, like fire to convict, and like a hammer to destroy strongholds of false beliefs.

GOD HATES FALSE PROPHETS

Scriptures fairly burst with the wrath of God against false prophecy. Verse after verse warn against this sin:

---

7. MacArthur, *Chaos*, 82.

I have heard what the prophets have said who prophesy
lies in My name, saying, "I have dreamed, I have
dreamed!" How long will this be in the heart of the
prophets who prophesy lies? Indeed they are prophets of
the deceit of their own heart, who try to make My people
forget My name by their dreams which everyone tells his
neighbor, as their fathers forgot My name for Baal
(Jeremiah 23:25-27).

Here Jeremiah describes false prophets as people who speak
lies in God's name, from the impulses of their own hearts, and
lead His people astray. A warning to these:

"both prophet and priest are profane; yes, in My house I
have found their wickedness," says the Lord. "Therefore
their way shall be to them like slippery ways; in the darkness they shall be driven on and fall in them; for I will
bring disaster on them..." (Jeremiah 23:11-12).

I need to pause here, and acknowledge that I personally fell
into sins of false prophecy, both under the influence of occult
spirit (as I explained in chapter 1), and by speaking out of my
own imagination. For some reason the latter is more disturbing to
me. I was forced to my knees to ask forgiveness when I realized I
had proclaimed my own ideas before other people as if they were
divine prophecies. I still cringe to think about it. I wrongly and
pridefully claimed prophetic authority, motivated by the desire to
please or impress. Even worse, I modeled occult practice before
young believers who considered me a leader.

VAIN PURSUITS: DREAM INTERPRETATION

The Bible contains stories of genuine prophets who received
significant dreams from God, or were given insight to interpret
dreams. I believe God still speaks to people through dreams at
special times, and that He enables others to interpret. However,
there is an occult counterfeit of these God-given gifts, namely the
practice of sifting through dreams deliberately and purposefully

CHRISTIANITY and PROPHECY

ILLUMINATION
The Holy Spirit illuminates God's
revealed truth (the Word).
Prophets are gifted to understand and
declare God's Word.

OCCULTISM and PROPHECY

REVELATION
Occult spirit reveals new "truth" and hidden secrets,
sights & sounds.
Prophets are gifted to divine and declare God's
present will, future events, etc.

to identify and analyze symbols for guidance and understanding of problems: This is divination.

A fascination with dreams goes hand-in-hand with occultism. Witches and shamans have for centuries probed dreams for guidance and hidden meaning. New Agers usually own at least one dream dictionary. Now, leading charismatic "prophets" rely increasingly on their dreams for personal and corporate guidance, and even national and international guidance. A leader posted on the Web details of a "prophetic dream" he had concerning a pending missile attack on the U.S. He said that when he awoke he heard a "stern, loud" voice say, "This will happen; you must warn them." He was so genuinely concerned, he considered warning the U.N., but was advised by an associate that the time was not right.[7]

7. Alistair Petrie, "Lion on the Wall: Prophetic Dream—Wednesday, May 29th/02—4:00 a.m.," *Watchman, South Africa,*
http://www.christiannet.co.za/watchmansa/wall.htm .

Many charismatics take dream analysis as seriously as pagans do. Elijah House includes dream analysis in its counselor training program. Indeed, many charismatics now offer dream analysis to individuals for personal and counseling purposes; one group has made a real ministry out of it, offering an on-line bookstore and courses on "Dream Interpretation Mentoring." They even posted "Dream Interpretation Guidelines" on the Web.[8] But, so have many secular groups.

If we compare their teachings we discover that both charismatic and non-Christian groups who promote dream analysis hold similar beliefs as to the significance of dream symbols. Both hold that certain symbols have universal meaning and others are uniquely personal. Both advise keeping "dream journals." Both offer "expert interpretation" and personal counseling—for a fee. Both also offer courses—for a fee.

Vain pursuits: training prophets

Another pursuit common among mystics—pagan and charismatic alike—is the attempt to "develop" divination gifts in new initiates, including powers to foretell the future, discern illness, know what others are thinking and receive divine revelation.

Charismatic leaders believe it is their responsibility to "raise up prophets" for the church, and that prophetic "gifts" can be enhanced through practice, training and testing. For example, self-proclaimed prophetess Cindy Jacobs, who says she has possessed supernatural insight since childhood, writes books teaching Christians how to prophesy the occult way. She believes any child of God can cultivate this "gift." My own church taught a course based on Cindy Jacob's teaching, and I have seen her books in Christian bookstores everywhere.

But secular stores are jammed full of their own books teaching the same thing, only using different terminology. In most you will find books on "developing ESP," "reading auras" or "becoming a prophet." In the course of my research I looked through the shelves in a used bookstore and found so many New Age, magic

---

8. See *http://www.lapstoneministries.org.*

and Wiccan books on prophecy that I hardly knew where to begin. Everyone wants to be a prophet.

For example, let's turn to a self-styled "magic primer," which contains a chapter entitled "The Art of Prophetic." The author instructs people in the art of "precognition," meaning that branch of divination which involves prophesying the future:

> Precognition therefore is nothing less than the conscious mind's awareness of the timeless vision presented to the subconscious…In general these glimpses of the future are quite involuntary, so that the primary aim of divination is to encourage the voluntary departure of the subconscious into absolute time. The conscious mind has then to be kept in a state of receptive passivity so that it will accept whatever images are conveyed to it…[9]

Here we see the occult practice of waiting on mental impressions—visions or words—like charismatics do. The only difference is that charismatics claim the God of the Bible is the source of their "knowing," while Mr. Conway credits the "subconscious."

I'll mention just one more secular book, by a self-proclaimed "seer" who wrote *The Reluctant Prophet.* The inside flap says:

> Are we all reluctant prophets? Do we all possess the latent talent—"A sixth sense"—to predict the future, to communicate with the spiritual world? Daniel Logan, the young and widely-known American mystic, firmly believes that we do! He believes every intelligent human being possesses this psychic ability – an ability, *when cultivated,* that can manifest itself in extraordinary ways for the benefit of mankind as well as the individual.[10] (emphasis original)

---

9. David Conway, *Magic, an Occult Primer,* 2nd ed. (New York: Bantam Books, 1972), 188-189.

10. Daniel Logan, *The Reluctant Prophet* (Garden City, NY: Doubleday, 1968), on the dustcover.

A comparison of *The Reluctant Prophet* and Ms. Jacobs' books (such as *The Voice of God*) reveals that both authors believe they were gifted with paranormal perception from childhood. Both teach how to cultivate the gift of prophecy. Both appear to be well-intentioned, wanting to help others. But, one calls herself a Christian, apparently not realizing that her practice and beliefs are glaringly occult.

NECROMANTIC VISIONS
Receiving prophecy

The Muslim prophet Muhammad believed God gave him the content of the Islamic Scriptures, the *Koran*, by revelation during trance states over a period of time. An historian writes as follows:

> Muhammad had no control over the flow of the revelation; it descended on him independent of his will. When it arrived he was changed...Both his appearance and the sound of his voice would change. He reported that the words assaulted him as if they were solid and heavy: "For We shall charge thee with a word of weight" (chapter 73, verse 5, the *Koran*). Once they descended while he was riding a camel. The animal sought vainly to support the added weight by adjusting its legs. By the time the revelation ceased, its belly was pressed against the earth and its legs splayed out.[11]

Muhammad also claimed he met the angel Gabriel during trance states.

Charismatics believe similar claims by Rick Joyner, one of their favorite prophets. Mr. Joyner believes God gave him the content of his book *The Final Quest* by revelation during trance states over a period of time. He also claims to have spoken with Jesus, angels and even a talking eagle during these "visions." In his own words:

---

11. Smith, 232-233.

> Some of [the book] came under a very intense sense of the
> presence of the Lord, but the overwhelming majority was
> received in some level of a trance…Once the experience
> became so intense that I actually got up and left the
> mountain cabin where I go to seek the Lord, and drove
> home. Over a week later I returned and almost immedi-
> ately I was right back where I left off.[12]

Popular Mormon prophet Joseph Smith also said God gave
him the content of his books, the *Book of Mormon* and *The Pearl
of Great Price,* by revelation over a period of time. He said he
spoke with an angel named Moroni, and even Jesus Himself. Here
is part of Mr. Smith's story:

> The year 1820 proved to be the real beginning of the
> prophet's call, for in that year he was allegedly the recipi-
> ent of a marvelous vision in which God the Father and
> God the Son materialized and spoke to young Smith as he
> piously prayed in a neighboring wood…he reveals that the
> two "personages" took a rather dim view of the Christian
> church…and announced that a restoration of true
> Christianity was needed…With the appearance of the
> angel Moroni at the quaking Smith's bedside [Smith]
> began his relationship to the fabulous "golden plates"…
> the progression of [the] "translation" and spiritual zeal
> allegedly attained such heights that, on May 15, 1829,
> heaven could no longer restrain its joy; and so John the
> Baptist in person was speedily dispatched by Peter, James,
> and John to the humble state of Pennsylvania…[13]

Mr. Smith believed he merited the privilege of being God's
prophet to restore Christianity due to his great religious zeal. Mr.

---

12. Joyner, *Quest,* 11.
13. Walter R. Martin, *The Kingdom of the Cults,* 15th ed. (Minneapolis, MN:
    Bethany Fellowship, 1974), 150-152.

Joyner also believes God chose him to express His dim view of the church, claiming Jesus spoke these very words to him:

> My church is now clothed with shame because she does not have judges. She does not have judges because she does not know Me as the Judge. I will now raise up judges for My people who know My judgment. They will not just decide between people or issues, but to make things right, which is to bring them into agreement with Me.[14]

These so-called prophets certainly consider themselves exalted in God's eyes.

Spiritism and necromancy

It is noteworthy that Mr. Joyner and Mr. Smith both claim to commune with the spirits of dead people. Numerous times in *The Final Quest* Mr. Joyner said that, while in a trance, he saw or communicated with Adam, Martin Luther, Luther's wife and the apostle Paul. Joseph Smith, in the quotation on the preceding page, claimed he spoke with John the Baptist.

But what do Scriptures say about communicating with dead people? In fact, it is spiritism and necromancy, and is abominable to God:

> When you come into the land which the Lord your God is giving you, you shall not learn to follow the abominations of those nations. There shall not be found among you anyone who...practices witchcraft, or a soothsayer, or one who interprets omens, or a sorcerer, or one who conjures spells, or a medium, or a spiritist, or one who calls up the dead. For all who do these things are an abomination to the Lord... (Deuteronomy 18:9-12).

While nonbelievers may be forgiven for failing to recognize the sin and danger of communicating with the supposed spirits of dead

---

14. Joyner, *Quest,* 128.

people, professing Christians should know better. Charismatics usually condemn spiritism, but at the same time blindly condone it in their favorite prophets. Mr. Joyner has been crowned "prophet and judge" by an undiscerning church; my former pastor told me *The Final Quest* is advanced reading—for mature Christians only.

MESSIANIC PROPHETS?

Cindy Jacobs and some of her associates posted a lengthy "group prophecy" on the Web in 1999, which they called "Word to the Nation."[15] They waived copyright, and I have attached the script to my book as an Appendix (at p. 303), for reference and as an example of charismatic teaching that suffers profoundly from occult influence.

Ms. Jacobs' group included John and Paula Sandford, Rick Joyner and Bill Hamon, teachers we have already considered. Dutch Sheets, a popular prayer teacher, was also part of the group. These people wrongly predicted that in the year 2000 there would be "disruption of communication like the Tower of Babel, and for a season, communication will be shut off."

But Ms. Jacob and her associates did more than falsely predict a communication catastrophe. They demonstrated such an exalted view of themselves we can be certain they have accepted the serpent's temptation. Under the influence of occult spirit they have been led to believe that they are equal to God. Below, we will examine how they worked up to this amazing self-estimate. (Please pause here to review the Appendix, if you like.)

God's counselors?

In their "prophecy" (p. 303, Appendix), the Jacobs group claims to be counselors with God. Cindy says:

> Finally in the day, John Sandford began to share something that he has shared with me in private, and I won't go into the whole thing, but essentially that God takes counsel with

---

15. "Cindy Jacobs Word to the Nation,"*Rocky Mountain Awakening, National School of the Prophets,* http://www.awake.org/testimony/nsop.htm.

his people and his prophets, that he doesn't move in a
vacuum…He is looking for a people to take counsel with
(p. 308, Appendix)

and,

as we began to pray and we began to worship, a sensing
came in our midst, the Lord was calling us up together in
His throne room. It was such a holy moment, I do not
have words to describe it to you. I don't know how everybody else felt. But God began to share how the Lord was
putting like chairs in heavenly places, and we were coming
up together. That He would speak to us about the judgments and the things to come, to take counsel together. It
was such a holy moment (p. 309, Appendix).

Ms. Jacobs and Mr. Sandford reveal here that they consider
themselves so wise, and their understanding so godly, divine and
exalted, that Jehovah God—the holy and mighty One whom no
one can see, He who created the universe and whose thoughts and
ways are far above ours—has chosen them with whom to "take
counsel." God, they say, called them together and set chairs for
them in His throne room.

Is this possible? Decidedly not; it is eminently delusional. God
does not take counsel with His creatures. In his letter to the
Romans, Paul indicated that we are so far beneath the Lord, the
very idea is absurd:

O the depth of the riches both of the wisdom and knowledge of God! How unsearchable are His judgments and
His ways past finding out! "For who has known the mind
of the Lord? Or who has become his counselor?"
(Romans 11:33-34).

These verses tell us plainly that no man or woman could ever
hope to take counsel with God. Indeed, in case we didn't already
realize it, only a fool would entertain the notion:

O Lord, how great are Your works! Your thoughts are very deep. A senseless man does not know, nor does a fool understand this (Psalm 92:5-6).

The Bible teaches—and true Christian experience confirms—that the closer a man comes to God, the more he realizes his own sinfulness and unworthiness. When he saw the Lord high upon a throne, Isaiah cried, "Woe is me, for I am undone! Because I am a man of unclean lips" (6:5). Job said, "Behold, I am vile; what shall I answer You? I will lay my hand over my mouth" (40:4). But Ms. Jacobs says, "It was such a holy moment!"

New saviors?

However, there is a claim even more startling in the "Word to the Nation," published by the Jacobs group, namely a claim to Messiahship (see Appendix). These self-proclaimed prophets and counselors to God again blow the trumpet for themselves, this time to announce that God is raising them up to take Jesus' place! How so? They say they are *saviors*, collectively a new, divine "light" from God. Incredible. Here is exactly what Mr. Hamon said:

> God is raising up saviors on Mount Zion, and we're to be that light and that person, Amen (p. 316, Appendix).

Ironically, this pronouncement of personal messiahship was expressed by Bill Hamon shortly after he said that God had spoken to him "deeply" about the "need for humility."

How can anyone—let alone a person who professes to follow Jesus—take these people seriously? Yet many do. When I complained to a charismatic teacher about this, I was warned not to "criticize God's anointed."

Many will come in His name, claiming to be the Christ

What, we might ask, would Jesus say about a group of people who claim to be saviors, collectively a "new Christ"? In Scripture is a warning, one that warrants close attention:

Take heed that no one deceives you. For many will come in
My name, saying "I am the Christ," and will deceive many
(Matthew 24:4-5).

Jesus warned that people will come *in His name*—that is, confessing Him as Savior—but they will *also* claim that they *are* the
Christ. How, we might ask, could they get away with both professing Jesus as Lord and also claiming to be the Messiah themselves?
Well, Mr. Hamon and his crew made such a claim in 1999...and
are still getting away with it.

These prophets profess Christian faith. They give lip service to
the need for humility. But at the same time they make the incredible—some might say insane—claim that they are messianic saviors.
But who has realized it? For as Jesus said, they will deceive many.

GOD TESTS HIS PEOPLE
THROUGH FALSE PROPHETS

Moses warned the Israelites:

If there arises among you a prophet or a dreamer of
dreams, and he gives you a sign or a wonder, and the sign
or the wonder comes to pass, of which he spoke to you,
saying, "Let us go after other gods which you have not
known, and let us serve them," you shall not listen to the
words of that prophet or that dreamer of dreams, for the
Lord your God is testing you to know whether you love
the Lord your God with all your heart and with all your
soul (Deuteronomy 13:1-3).

From this we must understand that God allows signs, wonders
and false prophets, even permitting them to speak accurate
words. By these He tests us, to prove whether we love Him or
them; whether we will be wheat, as those who love His Word, or
chaff, as those who follow teachings that tickle their ears.

(2 TIMOTHY 4 vs 3-4)

Chapter Sixteen

THE PURSUIT OF
SPIRITUAL AUTHORITY

Not everyone who says to Me, "Lord, Lord," shall enter the kingdom of heaven, but he who does the will of My Father in heaven. Many will say to Me in that day, "Lord, Lord, have we not prophesied in Your name, cast out demons in Your name, and done many wonders in Your name?" And then I will declare to them, "I never knew you; depart from Me, you who practice lawlessness!"
—Jesus the Christ (Matthew 7:21-23)

*M*om, Dad and I had just finished eating dinner at their place, and were discussing recent strange events. They said they were hearing unexplained crashing sounds from the attached garage. Dad showed where the noise was coming from, and demonstrated by dropping a metal toolbox onto the floor, from about three feet. It was loud all right, and startling. I was convinced there was an evil spirit in the garage that needed to be cast out, and that I could do the job. After all, I had been taking lessons in spiritual warfare from a charismatic leader with a deliverance ministry.

My mother and father are not Christians, but they have been accepting and respectful of my faith. They talk with me about it, sit patiently through my Christian videos and let me pray with them sometimes. That evening they allowed me to anoint them with oil as I tried to cast the evil spirit out of the garage.

Looking back, I deeply regret my actions.

SPIRITUAL WARFARE: THE ORTHODOX VS THE OCCULT APPROACH

Spiritual warfare is real, but there is an occult counterfeit.

I discovered that warring against evil spirits is a significant part of occultism in other religions. Moreover, it is an extremely dangerous practice, involving misguided attempts to challenge and defeat an invisible enemy, one far more powerful than we, in direct combat on his own turf.

Orthodox Christian warfare

In biblical Christianity, personal spiritual warfare is humble and simple. It involves primarily resisting the temptations of Satan and the flesh, and walking in obedience to the commands of God.

We are doing spiritual warfare when we say "no" to ungodly temptations and opportunities: yes, this is godly spiritual practice! This protects us from Satan. Declaring God's truth during difficult times, either quietly in one's mind or out loud if circumstances permit, is to use the sword of the spirit—that is, God's word—and is an effective way to resist. This is what Jesus did when faced with temptation in the desert (see Matthew 4:1-9). Satan hates truth and will flee from it. For this reason the belt of truth was the first item Paul mentioned in the armor of Christian spiritual warfare (Ephesians 6:14).

Therefore, our greatest protection from satanic attack is the cultivation of holiness in character and conduct—that is, walking in God's will. The apostle John wrote:

> We know that whoever is born of God does not sin; but he who has been born of God keeps himself, and the wicked one does not touch him (I John 5:18).

Dr. J. I. Packer commented:

> Holiness effectively thwarts Satan in his designs on our
> lives. By contrast, unconcern about holiness and failure to
> practice the purity and righteousness to which we are
> called play into his hands every time...Righteousness,
> meaning holy integrity and uprightness, is the breastplate
> in the armor of God that Christians are called to wear in
> order to counter the devil's attacks.[1]

Of course, believers—especially new believers or those
plagued by besetting sin—should never hesitate to fast, pray and
plead to God for help and deliverance.

As to intercessory warfare, the orthodox approach is first to
pray, plead and reason with God on behalf of those who need
His mercy and power. Second—and equally important—we
intercede for people by teaching and declaring God's truth (this
we saw partly in chapter 14, and will touch on below from a different perspective).

Occult spiritual warfare

The occult approach to spiritual warfare is to exercise authority over the spirits, or even over Satan, in the "name of" God,
Jesus or other "greater" power. Spiritual authority is believed to
be delegated or derived from "Jesus," the God of the Bible or
some other deity. Medieval magicians exercised spiritual
authority in the name of "God" to invoke (invite), evoke (dismiss) or otherwise control spirits. Charismatics believe they
have the same authority that Jesus has over spirits, through
being in the faith and using His name.

"Building" faith

Personal warfare for charismatics involves striving for confidence about one's "position in Christ" and "realizing who you are

---

1. J. I. Packer, *Rediscovering Holiness* (Ann Arbor, MI: Servant Publications,
   1992), 36-37.

in Christ" in order to build up faith and resist demons (not temptation). An individual will try to "believe for victory," a positive thinking approach that is really no different from the affirmations secular people use, such as, "I am beautiful," or "I have nothing to fear." An example:

> Confession of Faith and My Position in Christ (to be prayed out loud): Now I am seated with You in heavenly places. In You I have authority over Satan and all his demons. I stand strong in You, Lord Jesus, and resist Satan and all his evil schemes. I am covered and protected by Your precious Blood…I bind and rebuke all evil spirits and powers of darkness…[etc.]

I don't know anyone for whom such affirmations have ever worked—they never worked for me—but this sort of thing is common practice. It is an example of satanic reversal: Lucifer gets us focused on building ourselves up and "strengthening our faith" through vain affirmations. However, the Lord says it is not the strong who succeed, but the weak. The victor is the abject one who relies not on himself or his faith or his own efforts, but on God alone; in such weakness God is glorified, and He can then be strong.

Demons, demons everywhere

In my former church, leaders claimed they could see demons hovering over the congregation during worship. They stood at the back waving flags to do spiritual warfare, supposedly expelling demons from the building and protecting worshipers. A leader told me, "There's power in the flags!" (Like a magic wand?) I don't know what, if anything, these people were "seeing." However, we have learned that demons will manifest to those who dabble in the occult (see chapter 13). Experienced magicians know this for a fact. D. Conway, in his magic primer, explains as follows about demons (called "forms"):

> everyone who reads occult literature or has any experience
> of magic will soon be brought up against forms which

seem every bit as personal as the adept [magician] himself.[2]

Because demons eventually show up, occult practitioners become concerned about how to fight them off. Some inevitably develop a "specialty" in deliverance or demonology, as has happened among charismatics. However, this is occult spiritual warfare, and is one more mile along the broad highway leading people into spiritual darkness. Thinking they now "see," their minds become blackened.

POWER IN A NAME?

To liberate people or places from demonic control, charismatics try to exert authority over demons by using Jesus' name, thinking this compels spirits to obey. But the unsettling reality is that using the name of a "more powerful deity" as a weapon of authority against "lesser spirits" is typical occult methodology. Magicians have been doing it for centuries. For example *Goetia* (Latin for "howling") magicians bind the spirits and command them in the name and authority of their deity in a manner very like that employed by charismatics. According to one author:

> the spirits and demons of Geotia are bound and commanded by the magician to act as his servants…Common methods of control include threats, particularly in the form of the vibration of divine names, which tells the demon or spirit that the magician speaks *with the authority and power of the god* whose name he is intoning.[3] (emphasis added)

To take—or presume to take—authority over spirits in the name of your god is magic, common practice among the nations. Says one magic teacher:

---

2. Conway, *Occult Primer*, 195.
3. David Claiborne, *Goetia*, *http://heru-ra-ha.tripol.com/topics/goetia.html*, 1.

any student; whether Jewish, Christian, or Pagan [can]
command and exercise authority over the demons...by
using the Names of Power associated with their faith.[4]

I'm not saying that Jesus will not come in power when we seek
His help. I have no doubt He can and will and does. As the One
through whom the Earth came into being, and who need only
speak the word to make a thing happen, Jesus has complete
authority over demons and may choose to exercise that authority
at any time. However, we need to realize that His name has no
magic effect. It is not a club to use against evil spirits. We cannot
speak His power into being. Jesus exercises His power if and when
He chooses, and anything else is an occult counterfeit.

CATALOGUING DEMONS

The practice of "spiritual mapping" to identify and locate
demonic strongholds over geographical areas has been widely
popularized by The Sentinel Group in their "Transformations"
videos.[5] Part of the spiritual mapping process involves identifying
and naming demons, so-called "strongmen" who have allegedly
set up spiritual camp in certain geographic areas. The idea is that
you need to understand what demons you are dealing with so you
know how to fight them and expel them.

Charismatics in general are writing about and naming specific spirits they believe to be manifest enemies of the church, or
spirits in control of a person or place. Books are written about

4. Garald Campo,*New Aeon Magick*, *http://www.ecauldron.com/newaeon02.php*,
ch. 2, p. 3.

5. Some groups, concerned about the authenticity of claims made in the
Transformations videos, investigated and report that the claims are untrue.
One author concludes: "As far as we can see, this video and movement is
coming into the churches under the stealth of prayer. Much of what had been
reported in the video is falsehood, exaggeration with only shreds of truth.
They may mean well but we should be offended and resound against such
monkey business on their part. They are giving glory to God for events that
did not transpire the way they say. Instead, they give the people who watch
this video, fabrications." *http://www.agetwoage.org/T4.htm*. Other reviews are
available on the Web.

CHRISTIANITY
Spiritual freedom and protection by:
Knowing God's truth
Practicing obedience
Resisting temptation
Seeking God in prayer for deliverance and change

OCCULTISM
Spiritual freedom and protection by:
Repeating affirmations
Realizing who you are in Christ
Rebuking demons in name of Christ
Deliverance by a leader expelling demons
(in His name and power)

Thousands of Christians misunderstand Christian spiritual warfare. They
combine occult and biblical practices
in very dangerous ways.

"unmasking the enemies of the church" and how to identify particular spirits that harass believers, for example the "Jezebel"
spirit. One pastor says "Jezebel" can be recognized by certain
personality traits:

Jezebel is fiercely independent and intensely ambitious
for pre-eminence and control. It is noteworthy that the
name "Jezebel," literally translated, means "without
cohabitation." This simply means she refuses "to live
together" or "cohabit" with anyone. Jezebel will not dwell
with anyone unless she can control and dominate the
relationship...While she uses every means of sexual per-
versity known in hell, immorality is not the issue; *control*

is what she seeks, using the power of sexual passions for the purpose of possessing men.[6] (emphasis original)

But I discovered that naming and describing demons is yet another ancient, occult pursuit, common among magicians who believe they need to identify spirits so they know how to deal with them. This is precisely the thinking behind "spiritual mapping." Again, let us consult Mr. Conway's magic primer:

> If this were an encyclopedia of demonology—and there are such things—we would now be faced with the horrible task of cataloging all known demons—and there are thousands of them of every shape, size and hue. The problem is compounded too by the fact that one demon may have myriad different shapes and often just as many names to go by. Fortunately, this work can safely be left to the encyclopedist although, unlike the magician, he is never likely to find himself conversing with the real thing.[7]

Demon encyclopedias! Classing and categorizing and naming and describing demons! This is not something new that charismatics are doing. No, it is not an area they are pioneering, not a "new thing" God is doing in these days. Centuries ago a still-famous, occult manuscript called *The Book of Solomon* cataloged an elaborate hierarchy of demonic spirits, detailing their names, abilities and areas of specialty for the use of magicians and spiritists. A modern reference manual—entitled *Dream Dictionary: The Leaders of Hell's Army*—can be downloaded from the Web for a mere $US6.95 as at September 2004.[8] The Web site promotion, written by a secular occultist so far as I can tell, reads:

---

6. Frangipane, Francis, *The Jezebel Spirit* (Cedar Rapids, IA: Arrow, 1991), 8-9.

7. Conway, *Occult Primer*, 195.

8. Garry, *http://www.angels-and-demons.com*. Garry noted on his Web site that he was also writing a book on the major angels of heaven.

there are only 72 high ranking demons that rule and command all the others. These are the leaders in Hell and will be the commanders of Satan's army at the final battle. This book is an attempt to identify these primary demons and briefly describe their influences upon mankind. I have provided the name, rank, seal, and a description of the demon and the powers each can demonstrate or control.

The fact is, there is a vast amount of literature purporting to cataloge demons, from magicians and other occult practitioners. Why don't spiritual mappers and charismatic "discernment teachers" use them? No point reinventing the wheel. However, it would be better if they stopped calling themselves "Christian."

INTERCESSION BY TEACHING AND PREACHING

In orthodox Christian thought, a stronghold is a system of erroneous beliefs. Charismatics would agree with this statement because they understand, at least in theory, the importance of believing what is true and rejecting what is false. But they do not understand spiritual warfare, and so they think we should tear down strongholds by casting out demons. Wrong.

As the father of lies, Satan exerts power by influencing what humans believe. Therefore, the strongholds we need to demolish are erroneous beliefs which blind people to the truth of God's Word. Study, teaching and even argument are godly weapons of spiritual warfare.

Viewed from this perspective it becomes clear that the apostles were engaged in spiritual warfare when they preached, taught and wrote. "Go into all the world and preach the gospel to every creature" Jesus said (Mark 16:15). Paul wrote:

> For the weapons of our warfare are not carnal but mighty in God for pulling down strongholds, casting down arguments and every high thing that exalts itself against the knowledge of God, bringing every thought into captivity to the obedience of Christ... (2 Corinthians 10:4-5).

Paul did not say to "cast out" high things or "bind every spirit to obedience to Christ." No, because the battle is not won that way. We cast down *arguments* to win the mind with truth, and bring *thoughts* into captivity. (This book is my effort to win the minds of my readers, and to set people free from charismatic strongholds.)

ON GUARDIAN ANGELS AND ENGAGING WITH CELESTIAL BEINGS

I read that charismatic Bill Hamon, speaking at the National School of Prophets in 1999, claimed God had appointed him as "General Hamon" with authority over the archangel Michael. Mr. Hamon then said that "war angels" were coming to "co-labor" with him and with others willing to go into battle.[9]

Occult ideas like joining with angels to battle demons are gaining hold in charismatic circles. But this sort of teaching is as old as magick. Abramelin the Mage, occultist and hermit of antiquity (see chapter 9), wrote on how to relate with angels and co-labor with them against evil spirits in his *grimoire* (magic guide), entitled *The Book of the Sacred Magic of Abramelin the Mage,* translated from the original Hebrew around the seventeenth or eighteenth century. This book is still considered a valuable resource by modern magicians. Below, the Mage offers advice on dealing with recalcitrant angels:

> Also you shall menace them, in case they are unwilling to obey, with calling unto your aid the power of the holy angels over them. Your guardian angel will also have instructed you to perform this convocation with modesty, and in no wise to be timid, but courageous, yet in moderation, however, without too overbearing hardiness and bravery. And in case of their being inclined to resist, and unwilling to obey you, you

---

9. Bill Hamon, quoted in Kent Philpott, "Warrior Angels," Miller Avenue Baptist Church, *http://www.w3church.org/WarriorAngels.html,* 1-2. Precise quote: "Now, everybody that's willing to be a warrior, raise your hand, because angels are coming for assignments to co-labor with us. You've had your guardian angels. This is a new angel. This is a war angel. I say this is a war angel."

must not on that account give way to anger, because thus you will only do injury to yourself; and they will ask nothing better, it being exactly what they would be endeavoring to do; but (on the contrary) with an intrepid heart, and putting your whole trust in God, with a tranquil heart you shall exhort them to yield, letting them see that you have put all your confidence in the living and only God, reminding them how powerful and potent he is.[10]

Note here that lip service is given to God's sovereignty, but all the while the magician is controlling the show.

The approach of medieval magicians to evil spirits seems to have been generally courteous and respectful:

The courteous form of words in which Cellini's priest addressed the demons in the Coliseum may have been on the lines of the following dismissal, which is typical of many found in medieval *grimoires:* "O demon, seeing that thou hast duly answered all my questions, I hereby license thee to depart without injury to man or beast. Depart, I say, and be thou willing and ready to come to me whenever conjured to do so by the sacred rites of magic. I now beseech thee to withdraw quietly, and may peace remain forever between me and thee."[11]

Talking Tough

If early magicians preferred to entreat demons with deference, such is not the case with modern "charismagicians" who confront angelic beings with aggressive presumption and authority. For

---

10. The Mage, *Sacred Magic,* ch. 13, p. 1. Abramelin condemned other occultists. We saw in chapter 8 that this is common among mystics and magicians, who accuse each other of sorcery. Abramelin wrote "certain accursed persons write…by means of seals, and conjurations, and superstitious figures, and pentacles, and other abominations, written by diabolical enchanters…this would be the coin wherewith the hideous Satan would buy you for his slave" (p. 2).

11. Conway, *Occult Primer,* footnote, 200.

232 True to His Ways

example, Cindy Jacobs, a founder of "Generals of Intercession," believes the Lord is bestowing new spiritual authority upon her and her associates. She calls it a "release of the fist anointing." Tough talk, indeed! Ms. Jacobs prophesied:

> The Lord says, "Is not my right hand symbolic of My power and My right arm? With this release of the fist anointing, that which can punch the enemy can also break down strongholds. I have given you that fivefold." The Lord says, "You must mix it with the spirit of Elijah, the turning of the hearts of the fathers to the children and the children to the fathers to have the equation that will release the former and the latter rains of revival," says God.[12]

Wow. We can give the devil a spiritual fist in his spiritual face? I think not.

Charismatics misunderstand two Scriptures, believing them to teach that ordinary believers should be doing great, supernatural works and miracles. One is Jesus' statement, "Most assuredly, I say to you, he who believes in Me, the works that I do he will do also; and greater works than these he will do, because I go to My Father" (John 14:12).

But think of it, what can rebellious, darkened, sinful human flesh possibly do that could be greater than the works of Jesus who is pure and holy, and who created the entire universe by the word of His mouth? I have come to believe that "greater things" have to do with the work of the Holy Spirit in sinful hearts. Jesus was *naturally* perfectly loving, merciful and obedient, for He was without sin. That fallen man can now, by the power of the indwelling Spirit, also be loving, merciful and obedient is a great thing indeed, for it is *unnatural*. To be

---

12. Cindy Jacobs, "Restoring the Spirit of Elijah," May 5, 2002, *http://www.generals.org/articles reports words/* . I need to comment that this "mixing" of spirits to have an equation that will "release rains of revival" is nothing more than a spell, an occult "formula" intended to magically accomplish the speaker's purposes.

unnaturally loving and obedient is the only thing Jesus could never do.

The second Scripture misunderstood by charismatics relates to Jesus giving the apostles authority over demons. Matthew wrote, "And when He had called His twelve disciples to Him, He gave them power over unclean spirits, to cast them out..." (10:1).

The short explanation for this verse is that power over spirits was given to the twelve, not to us. They (except Judas) were specially chosen apostles who walked with Jesus and were commissioned by Him for the uniquely momentous task of inaugurating the Christian church on Earth. They and the prophets form the foundation of the temple God is building under the New Covenant, Jesus being the chief cornerstone (see 1 Corinthians 3:9; Ephesians 2:19-22; Romans 15:20). Later believers are mere bricks and stones, being added one by one upon the foundation already laid until the temple shall be complete.

Further, Matthew 10:1 simply cannot mean that believers should be battling demons and rebuking evil spirits the way charismatics do. Why not? First, because these practices are occult. They are the practices of the nations. Second, because among other things angelic beings are superior to humans in knowledge, strength and might and we must not presume against them. Peter and Jude did not mince words about those who do:

> They are presumptuous, self-willed; they are not afraid to speak evil of dignitaries [angels], whereas angels, who are greater in power and might, do not bring a reviling accusation against them before the Lord (2 Peter 2:10-11).

And:

> these dreamers defile the flesh, reject authority, and speak evil of dignitaries. Yet Michael the archangel, in contending with the devil, when he disputed about the body of Moses, dared not bring against him a reviling accusation, but said, "The Lord rebuke you!" But these speak evil of whatever they do not know... (Jude 8-10).

234   TRUE TO HIS WAYS

The word "dignitaries" in these passages is better translated "angelic majesties" or "celestial powers." These Scriptures indicate that we are not to rebuke (that is, condemn, order around or "come against") angelic beings. Such matters are too deep for us; we do not and cannot understand them. But charismatic leaders regularly presume to tackle fallen angels head-on. One wrote the following instructions:

> Step eight: *Deliverance* At this point you are ready to expel
> the demons. I do so, casting them out by commanding them
> to *"leave (the person) in Jesus' Name, and begone to waterless
> places"* (where Jesus said they would go, Mt 12:43), *and never
> to return* (Mk 9:29). I do not feel comfortable sending them
> to the *abyss*. That judgment is the prerogative of God at the
> time of the end (Lk 8:31).[13] (emphasis original)

The above author believes he could send demons to "the abyss," but humility requires that he leave this task for God to do. Another leader approved the public cursing of Satan:

> More than any place I know the most prominent Christian
> leaders in Argentina, such as Omar Cabreo and Carlos
> Annacondia, Hector Gimenez, and others, overtly chal-
> lenge and curse Satan and his demonic forces both in pri-
> vate prayer and in public platforms. The nation as a whole
> is apparently engaged in a world class power encounter.[14]

Are these forms of spiritual warfare—even cursing celestial beings—not blatant violations of Jude 8-9?

No man can win a "power encounter" with Satan or his spirits; just when one thinks he is winning, the demons are probably laughing.

---

13. John Hill, *Coming to Grips with Deliverance* (self-published booklet), 51.
14. C. Peter Wagner, *Engaging the Enemy*, Jubilee Christian Centre, 22-23, quoted in Bill Randles *Making War in the Heavenlies: A Different Look at Spiritual Warfare* (Great Britain: St. Matthews Publications, 1996), 46.

REVERSE VOODOO

A form of occult warfare increasingly common in the charismatic church is what I call "reverse voodoo." Voodoo is a Haitian form of magic characterized by the frequent use of hexes, or curses, placed on people, places or animals. *Reverse* voodoo is the attempt to break or remove curses.

Whole ministries have been developed around reverse voodoo.[15] Charismatics battle against all types of curses, including those imposed by God, as with so-called "generational curses," and also witches' curses.[16]

Anyone who has spent time among charismatics will be familiar with the prayer formulas they use to break the power of a curse. See, for example, the following teaching:

> PRAYING FOR SOMEONE THAT HAS HAD A CURSE
> OR SPELL PLACED ON THEM: After having the person
> pray the above prayer on this page, you, as God's ser-
> vant, may break the curse or spell by praying the follow-
> ing words over the person: In the name and authority of
> the Lord Jesus Christ, as His servant, I now break all
> curses, spells or incantations off you... [etc].[17] (emphasis
> original)

But, what if it doesn't work? Well, reverse voodoo is practiced widely among the nations, one can always seek a remedy there. A group called "Global Psychics" published the following:

---

15. An example is *Streams Ministries.*
16. Fear of witches leads to senseless hysteria and persecution, even murder, as we saw in the witch trials of the early 1690s. Yes, the Bible teaches that witchcraft is an abomination, but no more so than any other occult practice, or other form of rebellion. But hysteria only serves the purposes of Satan. Furthermore, the obedient Christian can rest on the word of God that, "Like a flitting sparrow, like a flying swallow, so a curse without a cause shall not alight" (Proverbs 26:2).
17. "Breaking Curses, Spells and Incantations," *http://home.datawest.net/esn-recovery/free/prayer10.htm.*

> Notes on Removing a Curse: …the first remedy for clear-
> ing a curse is to raise your vibrational frequency so that
> the negative energy can no longer infect your life…[18]

Not keen on raising your vibrational frequency? Well, you can purchase yarrow root from Venice Voodoo for $2.50, good for breaking curses.[19] And witches have spells:

> This is a simple spell to do and is most effective in remov-
> ing a curse. Most important it sends the curse back to its
> original source seven times worse… Carry out the spell
> only on a full moon between the hours of twelve midnight
> and one in the morning.[20]

On the Web I also found material from magicians, Chi work-ers, "medical intuitives," and shamans who all say they know how to break off a curse. But the point has been made. Reverse voodoo is not Christian, it is occult.

DELIVERANCE

As an unwitting student of the occult I once took a course from a self-styled charismatic prophet and teacher with an inter-national deliverance ministry. He told the class he often engages in "power encounters" with evil spirits, takes control of them and casts them out. During these encounters the spirits supposedly "manifest" in weird and frightening ways; for example, by causing their victims to slither like snakes or roar like lions. The teacher said these manifestations show the demons are fighting back.

That God delivers people from addictions and demonic con-trol is a fact. He promises to set us free, and He does. But the satanic counterfeit is exorcism, namely the purported use of one's own "authority in Christ" to compel demons to leave.

---

18. from *http://www.globalpsychics.com/lp/Tips/remove_curses.htm*.
19. Venice Voodoo, "Herbs and Roots," *http://www.venicevoodoo.com/herbs.html*.
20. "Spells to Remove a Curse," *http://www.paralumun.com/spellscurse.htm*.

Exorcism and deliverance ministries are common among charismatics. I myself witnessed a few "power encounters" and I can testify that the howling, struggling, apparent release, resulting exuberance and other manifestations are convincing. However, in no case did I ever see lasting fruit. This puzzled me, but the manifestations were so real I continued to believe, in error, that my leaders were helping people.

No good fruit, but what about the bad? Consider what follows.

Poltergeist experiences

My former "spritual warfare" teacher admitted that he suffers from demonic attacks. Once he saw gremlins climbing up his arm, heading for his brain—a classic poltergeist experience, such as often happens to people involved in the occult. Sadly, however, this teacher believes Satan attacks him because he is a great prayer warrior.

Former guru Rabi Maharaj (chapter 7) tells of poltergeist phenomena he and his family suffered when they were involved in yoga; they thought their house was haunted and that a Hindu god, Shiva, was attacking them. Mr. Maharaj writes:

> One night while studying late he [a cousin who lived in the house] had been slapped by an invisible hand so hard that it had knocked him down, and the next morning the marks were still on his face for us all to see. Another night invisible hands had chocked [sic] him on his bed, and again he had felt it was Shiva…These mysterious physical attacks and the continued haunting of the house by Nana's spirit had a cumulative and unnerving effect upon all of us.[21]

Those residing with occult practitioners may also be at risk. Benny Hinn, highly empowered for TB, wrote that his mother was knocked down by an unseen force in her own home:

---

21. Maharaj, 73.

Once, my mother was cleaning the hallway while I was in my room talking with the Holy Spirit. When I came out, she was thrown right back. Something had knocked her against the wall. I said, "What's wrong with you, Mama?" She answered, "I don't know." Well, the presence of the Lord almost knocked her down. My brothers will tell you of the times they came near me and didn't know what was happening—but they felt something unusual.[22]

Charismatic teacher Neil Anderson also experiences poltergeist attacks. He runs a "counseling and deliverance" ministry and has published several books. In *The Bondage Breaker* he writes:

I was preparing to speak in chapel on the topic of deliverance and evangelism, in which I would expose some of the strategies of Satan in these areas. Early that morning I rose...When I stepped out of the shower I found several strange symbols traced on the fogged-up mirror. I didn't do it, and [the family] hadn't done it either...I went down to eat breakfast alone, and as I was sitting in the kitchen, suddenly I felt a slight pain on my hand that made me flinch. I looked down to see what appeared to be two little bite-marks on my hand. "Is that your best shot?" I said aloud to the powers of darkness attacking me. "Do you think symbols on the mirror and a little bite are going to keep me from giving my message in chapel today? Get out of here." The nuisance left, and my message in chapel went off without a hitch.[23]

Like my old teacher, Mr. Anderson also believes these demonic attacks indicate he is successful in ministry, so Satan is after him in a big way. However, this illustrates another parallel between

---

22. Benny Hinn, *Good Morning, Holy Spirit* (Nashville, TN: Thomas Nelson, 1990), 42.
23. Neil T. Anderson, *The Bondage Breaker*, 2nd ed. (Eugene, OR: Harvest House, 1993), 85-86.

charismatic and kundalini teachers: Both believe demonic activity is a sign of spiritual progress or accomplishment, although they explain this in different ways. As we saw in chapter 13, yogis (at least, Western yogis) teach that their sufferings—including poltergeist attacks—are signs of spiritual growth or "emergence." On the other hand, charismatics think poltergeist attacks indicate success in spiritual warfare. But such terrible deception only leads occult practitioners more deeply into activities that destroy their souls.

I doubt the demons who attacked Mr. Anderson that morning intended to interfere with his chapel message. But he played right into their hands by believing it.

SATAN DOES NOT TOUCH THE OBEDIENT

How, then, can a believer be safe from Satan? See Proverbs 1:32-33:

> the turning away of the simple will slay them,
> And the complacency of fools will destroy them;
> But whoever listens to me will dwell safely,
> And will be secure, without fear of evil.

Scripture says that the Christian who listens to and obeys God will be safe from the evil one, who will not touch him (again, see 1 John 5:18). This does not mean we can avoid temptation, suffering, illness or persecutions; indeed, we may experience these problems severely. However, poltergeist experiences—frontal attacks by demons—do not happen when one is walking in the will of God.

After the miraculous conversion of his entire family to Christianity, Rabi Maharaj reported that all poltergeist experiences ceased. He writes that as well as experiencing greater tenderness and love:

> There was another change that was not visible from the outside, but which meant even more to us. The haunting footsteps that we had thought came from Nana's spirit were no longer heard storming up and down the attic or stamping

outside our bedrooms at night. The peculiarly disagreeable odor that had often accompanied these phenomena and that we had never been able to trace had disappeared, never to return. And no longer were objects suddenly moved by some invisible force off the sink or a table or out of a cupboard to crash to the floor. We understood at last that the cause of all of these things had not been Nana's spirit, as we had supposed, but spirit beings the Bible called "demons"...[24]

Desperate charismatics, troubled by poltergeist experiences, frequently turn to leaders who claim a deliverance ministry. And it may be that sometimes God uses them, I don't know. But one thing I do know: although there is no precedent in orthodox Christianity for deliverance ministries, or "warrior" ministries like "Generals of Intercession," there are among the pagans. Consider shamans, for example.

COMPARISON WITH SHAMANIC PRACTICES

In tribal societies, shamans are believed to play an important role in battling and keeping away evil spirits that threaten families and communities. It is noteworthy that they also act as prophets and healers. In fact, it is alarming to realize just how many parallels there are between shamans and charismatics. Religious historian Huston Smith wrote:

> This section should not end without mentioning a distinctive personality type, the shaman—widespread but not universal in tribal societies—who can bypass symbolism and perceive spiritual realities directly...shamans are able to heal themselves and reintegrate their lives in ways that place psychic if not cosmic powers at their disposal. These powers enable them to engage with spirits, both good and evil, drawing power from the former and battling the latter where need be. They are heavily engaged in healing, and appear to have preternatural powers to foretell the future...[25]

24. Maharaj, 136.
25. Smith, 380.

Do you see how closely the shamanic role resembles that of the charismatic prophet? Let me demonstrate. I will copy Mr. Huston's description of shamans and substitute charismatic terminology to show that there really is no difference, at least not on these points:

> This section should not end without mentioning a distinctive personality type, the charismatic prophet—widespread but not universal in Christian circles—who can bypass religious form and perceive spiritual realities directly...prophets have supernatural gifts that place prophetic vision and Jesus' power at their disposal. The power of Jesus enables them to engage with spirits, both good and evil, having authority over the former and battling the latter where need be. They are heavily engaged in healing, and appear to have preternatural powers to foretell the future.

Can we not see the eerie similarities between charismatic prophets and shamans?

Not everyone who cries "Lord, Lord" will enter the kingdom of heaven

I could say more; more about "Joel's Army," YWAM, or other groups that are traveling along the occult highway. But I will simply point out that the day will come when Jesus will declare a solemn thing:

> Not everyone who says to Me, "Lord, Lord," shall enter the kingdom of heaven, but he who does the will of My Father in heaven. Many will say to Me in that day, "Lord, Lord, have we not prophesied in Your name, cast out demons in Your name, and done many wonders in Your name?" And then I will declare to them, "I never knew you; depart from Me, you who practice lawlessness!" (Matthew 7:21-23).

Chapter Seventeen

BOXES, BABIES
AND BATH WATER

Fear not at all; fear neither men nor Fates, nor gods, nor anything. Money fear not, nor laughter of the folk folly, nor any other power in heaven or upon the earth or under the earth.
— Aleister Crowley, satanist,
disparaging caution

God's desire to bless us is far greater than Satan's ability to deceive us. It is far healthier to focus attention on the wheat, and not the chaff, nor on the enemy sowing weeds.
— Sandy Millar, charismatic vicar,
disparaging caution

Be sober, be vigilant; because your adversary the devil walks about like a roaring lion, seeking whom he may devour.
— The apostle Peter, (1 Peter 5:8),
exhorting caution

*I*t can be difficult to talk with charismatics in a meaningful way about their experiences because they are convinced their good experiences are from God, and their bad ones prove it. They also resort to pat answers to discourage enquiry and discussion; my task now is to deal with some of these.

PAT ANSWER #1:
THE BABY AND THE BATH WATER

Despite misgivings, many Christians remain in charismatic circles because they don't want to "throw the baby out with the bath water." I'm sure they have the same fear I did: they don't want to end up in a big, dead church where no one ever talks about the Holy Spirit. They sincerely want to be where God is.

But this is a mistake.

First, what is the "baby" believers must cherish above all? By now you know what I am going to say. The baby—the light, and the pearl of our faith, that which we must treasure and protect—is truth. We are to love it (Zechariah 8:19), remain in it (1 John 2:24; 2 John 9) and work for it (3 John 8). It protects us (Ephesians 6:14). Truth is the beginning, the middle and the end of faith.

If we neglect truth, we neglect God. Pastor teacher John MacArthur underscores our responsibility to make sure we are walking in truth:

> [There are many] passages in the New Testament that command us to draw a clear line of distinction between sound doctrine and pseudo-Christianity. These verses *command* us to keep spiritually separate from those who corrupt the essential truths of the Gospel. Not only that, they attach the guilt of the false teacher's evil deeds to the one who fails to distinguish clearly between truth and error. We who love Christ should be very conscientious about interpreting and applying those commandments with the utmost care.[1] (emphasis original)

In response to Pat Answer #1 we can say that the "baby" we are to love is God's Word, and we must rescue it from bath water that is polluted by occult doctrine and practice (see 2 Corinthians 6:17).

---

1. John MacArthur, *Reckless Faith*, (Wheaton, Illinois: Crossway Books, 1994), 107.

Pat Answer #2:
God Won't Send us a Stone or a Snake

When I first questioned TB manifestations, people often dismissed my concerns by saying that when we ask for the Holy Spirit, God "will not send a stone or a snake" because Jesus said:

> Or what man is there among you who, if his son asks for bread, will give him a stone? Or if he asks for a fish, will he give him a serpent? If you then, being evil, know how to give good gifts to your children, how much more will your Father who is in heaven give good things to those who ask Him! (Matthew 7:9-11).

From these verses people conclude there is no need to worry about spiritual deception so long as they "ask for" the Holy Spirit, because God will not allow them to receive another spirit.[2]

But look at Paul's words to the Corinthians:

> I fear, lest somehow, as the serpent deceived Eve by his craftiness, so your minds may be corrupted from the simplicity that is in Christ. For if he who comes preaches another Jesus whom we have not preached, or if you receive *a different spirit* which you have not received, or a different gospel which you have not accepted, you may well put up with it! (2 Corinthians 11:3-4, emphasis added)

From this passage we know that a believer can receive a different spirit. Paul says so.

When Jesus said that God knows how to send good gifts, He did not mean that we cannot be deceived, or that He will protect us from all our mistakes and spiritual sins. If so, biblical warnings are pointless. Jesus meant that God will give good gifts to those who ask for good gifts. To ask for anything through occult practice is not to ask for a good gift.

---

2. Of course, this answer fails to take into account that charismatic practices are occult. We cannot use the words "Holy Spirit" or "Jesus" like a magic charm to summon Him whenever we think we want Him.

The Israelites, wandering in the desert, are an example for us today. They became bored with manna and lusted after other food. This angered the Lord (Numbers 11:10), but He gave them what they wanted: quail. In our day, God's ways and truth are the manna with which we are to be content. But if we prefer quail, like "new wine" thrills and spills, God will grant our request, just as He gave the Jews what they requested. But this is not a good thing:

> They soon forgot His works;
> They did not wait for His counsel,
> But lusted exceedingly in the wilderness,
> And tested God in the desert.
> And He gave them their request,
> But sent leanness into their soul
>   (Psalm 106:13-15).

In answer to Pat Answer #2 we might point out that God sends quail to those who tempt Him, and with quail comes leanness to the soul.

PAT ANSWER #3:
WE CAN'T PUT GOD IN A BOX

An Alpha leader once said to me that he "just knows" God is at work in the Toronto Blessing. He was also certain that God has "anointed" Benny Hinn in the power of the Holy Spirit. (Mr. Hinn has been known to slay people in the Spirit by blowing or waving a jacket over them.)

Even after I shared my research with the Alpha leader, he insisted there was "no doubt" about God's blessing on Benny Hinn. He voluntarily acknowledged that Mr. Hinn's teaching is "not orthodox. However," he continued to my genuine astonishment, "God doesn't require the truth. He chooses where He will show up and who He will work through." *God does not require truth?* "God will not be limited by teaching," the Alpha leader repeated. "He may, and does, sovereignly choose to bless wrong teaching." I could hardly believe what I was hearing. *God blesses wrong teaching?*

However, the Alpha leader is not alone in holding this remark-able, unbiblical view. Many charismatics say things like "The Holy Spirit can show up anywhere," apparently believing that because He can, He will. Or they say, "You can't put God in a box," or "He likes to surprise us." They believe God cannot and will not be limited in any manner, and we should not be surprised to find Him "outside the box."

However, the Bible does not teach this. There is one box we can "put God into"; or, should I say, into which He has put Himself. There is one place where He expects us to look for Him, and one place we can always find Him, no surprises. Where would that be? Where else, but in truth. The psalmist said, "The Lord is near to all who call upon Him, to all who call upon Him in truth" (Psalm 145:18).

Furthermore, we can confidently and categorically state that God cannot be found in false teaching. Why? Because He is the God of truth (John 14:6) and He cannot lie (Titus 1:2). The Holy Spirit is the spirit of truth (John 14:17) who brings truth (John 15:26; 16:13). He is not a spirit of false doctrine—how absurd! Therefore, we know that the spirit behind any teacher of false doctrine is not God's Holy Spirit.

Think about it. Would the God of truth bless false teaching just to surprise us? Or just to demonstrate His "sovereignty"? Would a holy God let His children fall under the influence of false teaching just to prove we can't put Him in a box? Would He make a point of being inconsistent, or unfaithful to His own truth? If so, how could we call Him a God of truth? We could not. In fact, we would have to call Him a liar.

Dear reader, if we believe God does not honor His own truth, we are in fact calling Him a liar.

But thanks be to God, He is faithful to His truth and promises. Indeed, if He were not, how could He judge us for falsehood and unfaithfulness? What grounds would He have to condemn anyone for lies or dishonesty? The psalmist said:

> For He is coming, for He is coming to judge the Earth.
> He shall judge the world with righteousness,
> And the peoples with His truth (Psalm 96:13).

We can respond to this Pat Answer by pointing out that *God is always faithful to His truth.* Also crucial to understand is the warning of the apostle John, who said, "Whoever transgresses and does not abide in the doctrine of Christ does not have God" (2 John 9), and, "If anyone comes to you and does not bring this doctrine, do not receive him into your house nor greet him; for he who greets him shares in his evil deeds" (2 John 10-11).

PAT ANSWER #4: HIS CHILDREN KNOW HIS VOICE

The Alpha leader continued to argue with me, saying, "I know it's God with Benny Hinn. You can't say it's the devil." When I asked how he could be so certain, he said that he has been to Toronto and "the Spirit feels the same." It appeared his confidence was based on good feelings, probably a *phos* light experience. As we have seen, untold numbers of seekers find *phos* light in the occult and believe they have met with God. They naively believe this "touch of love" is the voice of God, and they have heard Him and are following Him.

What did Jesus say about this? He said:

> he who enters by the door is the shepherd of the sheep. To him the doorkeeper opens, and the sheep hear his voice; and he calls his own sheep by name and leads them out. And when he brings out his own sheep, he goes before them; and the sheep follow him, for they know his voice (John 10:2-4).

In these verses the sheep represent God's children who hear His voice. But we must ask, is the voice the sheep hear and follow a "touch of love"? No. Jesus teaches not that God's children recognize love feelings but, rather, that they recognize truth. This is clear from His later words:

> Everyone who is of the truth hears My voice (John 18:37).

Jesus did not say He came to bear witness to love, but to truth. He said, "For this cause I was born, and for this cause I have come into the world, that I should bear witness to the truth" (John 18:37).

He came in love, but with the singular purpose of bringing truth. It is important not to confuse love with truth (see Chapter 19). Jesus' voice is the voice of truth, speaking words of truth to those who are of the truth. It's that simple.

The right response to Pat Answer #4 is a reminder that the day will come when many who now say "Lord, Lord" will realize they mistook the voice of God.

PAT ANSWER #5:
SOME HAVE MORE FAITH IN SATAN'S ABILITY TO DECEIVE THAN IN GOD'S ABILITY TO BLESS

Sandy Millar of Holy Trinity Brompton in London, England, was quoted saying:

> God's desire to bless us is far greater than Satan's ability to deceive us. It is far healthier to focus attention on the wheat, and not the chaff, nor on the enemy sowing weeds.[3]

With this and similar exhortations, charismatic leaders exhort us to open up to occult experience. "God is good, so just trust!" they say. Now I ask, where in the Bible will you find Jesus, or the prophets of God, or the apostles, saying anything like that? Can you imagine Paul saying, "Don't worry about receiving a different spirit"? Of course not. Or Jesus saying, "You don't need to be alert because God just wants to bless you"? Ridiculous. Or Peter saying, "Your adversary ranges the Earth looking for whom he may devour; but never mind, open up and receive a blessing"? Unthinkable. This is what the Bible says:

> Beloved, do not believe every spirit, but test the spirits, whether they are of God; because many false prophets have gone out into the world (I John 4:1).

> Be sober, be vigilant… (I Peter 5:8).

---

3 Sandy Millar, quoted in Richard Riss, "Twentieth Century Revival Movements," *http://www.anointed.net/Libraryroom/Revival.*

You shall not go after other gods, the gods of the peoples
who are all around you (for the Lord your God is a jealous
God among you), lest the anger of the Lord your God be
aroused against you and destroy you from the face of the
Earth (Deuteronomy 6:14-15).

Beloved Christian, your faith is not in issue if you are concerned about deceiving spirits. In fact, those who are heedless or dismissive in the face of biblical warnings bring their own faith seriously into question.

Those who are of the truth guard it jealously, and stand diligently against all that is false.

Chapter Eighteen

UNDERSTANDING SPIRITUAL ADULTERY

The Lord said also to me in the days of Josiah the king:
"Have you seen what backsliding Israel has done? She has
gone up on every high mountain and under every green
tree, and there played the harlot."

—Jeremiah 3:6

Scripture holds that unfaithfulness in sexual matters is destructive and defiling. Sexual activity before marriage is unfaithfulness to the future spouse. Marital adultery destroys the sanctity of the covenant bond and breaks a relationship.

In Christianity, issues and problems of human sexuality are used to teach spiritual truths.

An important lesson to take from the Bible is that occult activity is unfaithfulness to God, akin to fornication or adultery in the flesh. Therefore when believers take up with the occult, they destroy the sanctity of the New Covenant bond. And spiritual unfaithfulness breaks relationship with God.

Our sexuality and spirituality are important to God. He desires purity in both.

The one-flesh bond

Sexual intercourse brings the most intimate relationship possible with another person. It brings heart, soul and body knowledge, and God intends it to be reserved for the covenant relationship of marriage. The sexual act unites a man and a woman physically, emotionally and spiritually, creating a unique bond—a "one-flesh" bond—with mysterious and significant implications for the individuals, whether they realize it or not. Moses said that "a man shall leave his father and mother and be joined to his wife, and they shall become one flesh" (Genesis 2:24).

Likewise, *spiritual* intercourse brings intimacy with unseen spirit, even heart, soul and body knowledge.

The one-flesh bond between a husband and wife is powerful and enduring, but also fragile. To flourish, it must be cherished in love, honored in faithfulness and nurtured by truthfulness; then it will bring joy and contentment. If dishonored, betrayed or abused, however, misery is sure to result.

Like the bond between a husband and a wife, so the *spiritual* bond between God and those in covenant with Him is powerful and enduring, but also fragile. Scripture portrays the church as the bride of Christ: "For your Maker is your husband, the Lord of Hosts is his name; and your Redeemer the Holy One of Israel..." (Isaiah 54:5). Just as marriage is intended to bring unity and satisfaction to husbands and wives, so the covenant relationship with God is intended to bring spiritual unity and satisfaction to His people; and if the covenant is cherished, honored and nurtured in faithfulness, it will do just that.

But we humans share spiritual roots which, when watered by occult influence, cause us to betray our Maker. In darkness we stumble because we cannot see the danger.

Magick: the knowledge of good and evil

What does the Bible say about our spiritual roots? How is it that humans can be seduced by false light?

In the book of Genesis, a simple but profound story set in a garden illustrates how evil gained influence over mankind. The following verses set the stage:

> The Lord God planted a garden eastward in Eden, and there
> He put the man whom He had formed. And out of the
> ground the Lord God made every tree grow that is pleasant
> to the sight and good for food. The tree of life was also in
> the midst of the garden, and the tree of the knowledge of
> good and evil…Then the Lord God took the man and put
> him in the garden of Eden to tend and keep it. And the
> Lord God commanded the man, saying, "Of every tree of
> the garden you may freely eat; but of the tree of the knowl-
> edge of good and evil you shall not eat, for in the day that
> you eat of it you shall surely die" (Genesis 2:8-9,15-17).

Although God's purposes are largely hidden, it is clear that He
Himself placed both the tree of life and the tree of the knowledge
of good and evil in the midst of the garden. He Himself set both
the right way and the wrong way within reach of both Adam and
Eve.

These trees represent two sources of spirituality, and two spiritual powers with which man must contend. They represent two
ways of practicing religion: the way of God and the way of the serpent. And, the serpent is still telling lies when he promises that his
way does not lead to death.

God forbade Adam and Eve to eat Satan's fruit, but the serpent
deceived Eve:

> Now the serpent was more cunning than any beast of the
> field which the Lord God had made. And he said to the
> woman, "Has God indeed said, 'You shall not eat of every
> tree of the garden'?" And the woman said to the serpent,
> "We may eat of the fruit of the trees of the garden; but of
> the fruit of the tree which is in the midst of the garden,
> God has said, 'You shall not eat it, nor shall you touch it,
> lest you die.'"
> And the serpent said to the woman, "You will not surely
> die. For God knows that in the day you eat of it your eyes
> will be opened, and you shall be like God, knowing good
> and evil."

254 TRUE TO HIS WAYS

So when the woman saw that the tree was good for food,
that it was pleasant to the eyes, and a tree desirable to make
one wise, she took of its fruit and ate. She also gave to her
husband with her, and he ate (Genesis 3:1-6).

Adam—not deceived as Eve was, but with his eyes wide open—
also ate. And this single act had profound consequences not only
for Adam and Eve, but for all mankind and for all eternity. It
brought the spiritual influence of Lucifer upon them and upon
the entire human race. This is the event Christians refer to as the
Fall. It was a bad fall. An unholy fall. It led to what we might call
a spiritual divorce from God. Adam and Eve were banished from
His presence, and He said:

"Behold, the man has become like one of Us, to know
good and evil. And now, lest he put out his hand and take
also of the tree of life, and eat, and live forever"—therefore
the Lord God sent him out of the garden of Eden to till
the ground from which he was taken. So He drove out the
man; and He placed cherubim at the east of the garden of
Eden, and a flaming sword which turned every way, to
guard the way to the tree of life (Genesis 3:22-24).

WHAT GOOD, WHAT EVIL?

What, we might ask, was the knowledge of good and evil Satan
offered to Adam and Eve?

It is important to begin by understanding that when both God
(Genesis 2:15-18) and the serpent (3:4-5) spoke about knowing
good and evil, they were not talking about discerning right from
wrong. We know this was not the meaning because Scripture
teaches that man cannot tell the difference, at least not fully.

On the knowledge of good

What, then, was the "good" Adam came to know by partaking
of the serpent's fruit?

I was very interested to learn that the Hebrew word translated
"good" in Genesis 3 has no moral significance at all. Its meaning

is limited to natural or sensual experience that is pleasant, sweet, precious, peaceful or agreeable, but it does not touch on issues of moral goodness, or of righteousness before God.

In other words, the knowledge of good is about *feeling* good, not *being* good.

On the knowledge of evil

What about the "evil" that became part of man's experience through the serpent's temptation?

Significantly, the Hebrew word translated "evil" in Genesis 3 contains *both* natural/sensual *and* moral elements. It includes experiences both of sensual evils such as calamity, hunger, deformity, distress, injury and misery, and also moral evil such as wicked desires, thoughts and beliefs. Therefore, to know the evil of the serpent is to experience *both feeling* bad and *being* bad.

Furthermore, to know evil means that *being bad* makes us *feel good*. This is the grave result of the Fall, and one problem of our sin nature.

On knowing

The Hebrew word translated "knowledge" or "knowing" in Genesis 3, in the context of the forbidden fruit and the knowledge of good and evil, is from the root word *yada*, having the sense of "knowing by experience," as opposed to knowing through the mind or intellect. In Hebrew *yada* is also a euphemism for sexual intercourse. It is surely no accident that this word was used in Genesis to describe how humans can know good and evil.

The fact is that Satan is the god of occult experience, where human flesh and spirit meet occult spirit. This means that the knowledge gained by men and women in occult spiritual encounters is sensual and experiential knowledge of Satan. In the same manner a man comes to know a woman by intimate personal encounter and not through a book, so man comes to know Satan through occult experience and not through the Word.

Occult knowing is an intimate, sensual and personal experience with occult spirit. Therefore when people soak, enter trance states and open themselves up to occult love they are, whether they realize it or not, lying with God's enemy, the serpent.

This is enormously significant.

ABOMINABLE SPIRITUAL ENCOUNTERS

When we realize that occult practice involves consorting with Satan, we begin to understand why the Bible refers to it as harlotry, unfaithfulness and spiritual adultery. We understand why trafficking in spirits is abominable to God, and why He casts out those who chase after, and covet, occult experience. Our Lord cannot abide when our hearts and thoughts turn to and are taken up with His enemy. How can He do anything else but cast out a bride who purports to enter into covenant with Him and then lies repeatedly with His enemy, all the while professing faithfulness with her lips?

> To dabble in the occult is to step into a chamber of adultery where we commune with satanic spirits and become intimately known by them.

To dabble in the occult is to step into a chamber of adultery. To commune with occult spirit is to consort with the devil.

Let us learn and remember that through forbidden practices we come to know, and be known by, God's enemy, Satan. Intimately. Increasingly. Spirit, soul and body. We open up to him, invite him in, trust him, surrender to him, want more of him, worship him, love him. He makes us feel good—real good at first. We get hooked, and return to him repeatedly, again and again. He whispers lies in our ears and turns our hearts away from the God who is our spiritual husband. He works in our minds, hearts and flesh. When things start to go wrong, we try harder. We blame ourselves, our faith, our spiritual walk. We are duped. We vomit, and return to our vomit. We are ruined for the ordinary—to our increasing loss, but to Satan's increasing glee. And to the increasing wrath and jealousy of Jehovah God.

Do you see, dear reader? Do you understand? Are you willing to believe, even if you don't understand yet? Do you see that we could never have known the dangers of the occult unless a loving God stooped to tell us?

Are you willing to heed God's merciful warning? Can you hear? *Through mystic and occult practices men and women offer their souls to Lucifer for intimate spiritual intercourse, and are in grave temporal and eternal danger.* Let Moses say it again for God:

> I call heaven and Earth as witnesses today against you, that I have set before you life and death, blessing and cursing; therefore choose life, that both you and your descendants may live; that you may love the Lord your God, that you may obey His voice, and that you may cling to Him, for He is your life and the length of your days... (Deuteronomy 30:19-20).

TEMPTATIONS OF THE SERPENT

When Eve chose to taste the forbidden fruit, she was genuinely deceived. She believed it was not only good to taste, but also safe, and good for wisdom. Again:

> the serpent...said to the woman, "You will not surely die."

And:

> when the woman saw that the tree was good for food, that it was pleasant to the eyes, and a tree desirable to make one wise, she took of its fruit and ate.

See how the occult offers temptations comparable to the temptations that deceived Eve:

1. Occultists do not believe their practices lead to death. They think *they will not die*, for example that they are escaping the temporal world and becoming one with God.
2. Occultists believe their *eyes are opened:* For example, to see angels, spiritual things or deep mystic truths.

3. Whether they realize it or not, mystics teach that we *can be like God*: for example, reading minds and telling the future.
4. They experience *good (sensually) and pleasing* communion with spiritual forces.
5. They—as do we all—know evil, but they are more vulnerable to *experiencing evil in the fullest sense*, especially spiritual evils such as depression and insanity; also evil thoughts, culminating sometimes in the ultimate delusion that evil itself does not exist.
6. Occultists believe their practices *make them wise*.

As Eve was vulnerable to deception, so are we. Should we suppose we do not share her weakness? On the contrary, we must be *more* vulnerable: before the Fall, Adam and Eve were spiritually pure, but we are not.

EVIL IN HUMAN HISTORY

Evil was present in the Garden of Eden, and evil is with us today. Individually we struggle with erroneous beliefs and wrongful impulses. As a race we are plagued by war, greed, crime and brutality.

The Bible explains that all this is the influence of Satan who, for now and until God puts an end to it, is the "god of this world." God withholds His hand of judgment while He unfolds His divine purposes, purposes now being written in the history of the Earth.

Although we cannot escape physical death or the influence of evil while we are yet flesh and blood, spiritual sanctuary has always been available for men and women who willingly follow God's ways. This is difficult to understand, but God knows our weakness. To help us He not only spelled out what we need to do repeatedly in Scripture, He also illustrated the consequences of failing to heed His commands—including the consequences of spiritual adultery—through biblical accounts of men and women who went before us in time.

The first example was, of course, Adam and Eve. Their unfaithfulness defiled them, and God drove them away, out of the garden and into the world. Later, when God gave the law to Moses, He forbade the Jews to follow the practices of other nations and promised them a new garden, a Promised Land, if only they would obey Him. But they, like Adam and Eve, failed to do so. Among other things they repeated gross spiritual sins, turning to idols, mysticism and divination. Time and again God warned them. He pleaded through His prophets. But false teachers rose up in great numbers and the Israelites shut their ears to God to follow them instead. In the end, God did with them what He had earlier done with Adam and Eve: He drove them out; out of the Promised Land and into the world.

In his letter to the Corinthian church, which had fallen into mysticism and the occult, Paul wrote:

> brethren, I do not want you to be unaware that all our fathers were under the cloud, all passed through the sea, all were baptized into Moses in the cloud and in the sea, all ate the same spiritual food...But with most of them God was not well pleased, for their bodies were scattered in the wilderness. Now these things became our examples, to the intent we should not lust after evil things as they also lusted. And do not become idolaters as were some of them. As it is written, "The people sat down to eat and drink, and rose up to play" (I Corinthians 10:1-3,5-7).

Let us learn from the examples God has set before us, so we will not also be cast away by Him.

Banished, not abandoned

Although God banished Adam and Eve, He did not abandon them. When they became ashamed he clothed them with leather. He remained by them, to guide and teach them.

And so it was later when He came to work with the people of Israel. He strove with them in myriad ways over centuries. Again and again they were unfaithful, but again and again He forgave them and took them back.

In the book of Deuteronomy, Moses repeats tirelessly the same stern warnings:

> You shall not go after other gods, the gods of the peoples
> who are all around you (for the Lord your God is a jealous
> God among you), lest the anger of the Lord your God be
> aroused against you and destroy you from the face of the
> Earth (Deuteronomy 6:14-15).

The warnings most consistently repeated in the Old Testament
have to do with religious practice. (see Deuteronomy 4:2-4,15-
16,28; 5:7-9; 7:4-5, 8:19; 11:28; 12:30-31; 13:1-8,12-13; 17:2-4;
18:9-22, 29:18-21,25-27,29, being only some in the book of
Deuteronomy alone.)

Moses also warned men and women not to think they can
understand the "why" of God's commands in the area of spiritual
practice. Our part is to simply do as we are told, and this is what
it means to trust God. Moses said, "The secret things belong to the
Lord our God, but those things which are revealed belong to us
and to our children forever, that we may do all the words of this
law" (Deuteronomy 29:29). He gave to the Jews a message very
like the one God gave to Adam in the Garden:

> See, I have set before you today life and good, death and
> evil, in that I command you today to love the Lord your
> God, to walk in His ways, and to keep His commandments,
> His statutes, and His judgments...But if your heart turns
> away so that you do not hear, and are drawn away, and wor-
> ship other gods and serve them, I announce to you today
> that you shall surely perish; you shall not prolong your days
> in the land... (Deuteronomy 30:15-18).

But like Adam and Eve the Jews could not, or would not, hear.

Blind and deaf to the truth

God forbade the Jews to make statues of animals or heavenly
beings, which are false gods. But the Jews made them and worshiped
them anyway. Christians use these stories to teach about worldly
idols and temptations, but rarely, if ever, to teach about the occult.
This is a serious oversight, and the consequences are plain to see.

The lessons we need to learn from biblical accounts of idolatry have to do with spiritual matters. The history of Israel shows that men and women, who are spiritual beings, tend naturally to pursue spiritual things, but tend naturally to error and the worship of false gods.

Take, for example, the story of Micah (Judges, chapters 17–18). Micah stole some silver from his mother. He later confessed and returned it. His mother said, "I had wholly dedicated the silver from my hand to the Lord for my son, to make a carved image and a molded image" (Judges 17:3). She did this even though God had commanded, "You shall not make for yourself any carved image, or any likeness of anything that is in heaven above, or that is in the earth beneath, or that is in the water under the earth..." (Deuteronomy 5:8-9).

Micah put the idol in his home and asked a wandering Levite to live with him as his priest. By now Micah was feeling hopeful about the future, and he said, "Now I know that the Lord will be good to me, since I have a Levite as priest!" (Judges 17:13). We might ask, how could Micah make such obvious blunders and think he was pleasing the Lord, but is the same thing not happening today, also?

Micah did not renounce God. He paid lip service to Him, but worshiped a false god. Micah's error is obvious because he worshiped a statue—a tangible, visible form. Most of us are too sophisticated to make this mistake. But we make a more subtle one: We conjure up an idea or mental image—an *image-ination* so to speak—based on experience or fancy, and worship this as our god.

LUCIFER: GOD OF THE NATIONS

Satanic high priest Aleister Crowley once observed (and he had an uncanny knack for stating things the way they are) that Magick is the common denominator of world religions (see chapter 11). Mr. Crowley observed that people of all nations are practicing the same religion and serving the same god, whether they call themselves satanists, Hindus, Buddhists, Druids, witches, what have you. Their god is Lucifer, the god of mystic love, occult powers, spiritual drunkenness, manifestations, and enchantments; and also the god of all the miseries we have seen.

But there is one religion Mr. Crowley excluded from his equation, and rightly so: Christianity.

Mr. Crowley and the Bible agree that in the final analysis there are two, and only two, gods. That is, there are two powerful spirits, spirits with authority and rule over angelic beings who also desire to teach and rule human beings. Of course, where Mr. Crowley went wrong was in his judgment of which is the true God.

The Bible teaches that Jehovah, the God of Christianity, is the true God. He is the creator of all things and all beings, including Satan. (Although the devil is powerful, we must not err in thinking that he is in any way God's equal.) For this reason and many more, Christians proclaim Jehovah as the true God:

> For the Lord is great and greatly to be praised;
> He is to be feared above all gods.
> For all the gods of the peoples are idols,
> But the Lord made the heavens…
> Give to the Lord, O kindreds of the peoples,
> Give to the Lord glory and strength.
> Give to the Lord the glory due His name…
>   (Psalm 96:4-5,7-8).

PORTRAITS OF THE TWO GODS

From what we have seen so far we can paint two portraits; one of God, and the other of Satan:

Jehovah: the call of truth

Jehovah, the true God, brings love to those who have faith in Him through belief in, and obedience to, His truth. He speaks through Jesus and the Word. He is the God who set wisdom in place. He may give miracles to build faith or for His purposes, but He seeks our worship and service for the love of His truth. He insists that we need to hear His words and, further, that we should not listen to anything else. He teaches that communion with unknown spirits is defiling, is spiritual sin and is covenant-breaking. He calls to us by the voice of truth.

Jehovah comes in one name only: His own, through Jesus the Christ and His Holy Spirit. If we are faithful to Him, He will be faithful to us and we will know from His hand many sweet things, gifts that are perfect and good. His love is real and his light is true. Believing His promises leads to life—spiritual life both now and in eternity beyond the grave. To remain in His love we need to be faithful to His commands, and then He is faithful to shed His love abroad in our hearts.

Satan: the siren song of love

Satan, the serpent god, also brings love—or, we should say experiences of a light that seem like love. He brings it to those who surrender to him through occult and mystic practice. He speaks through fantasy, enchantments, visions and manifestations. He delights to tickle our ears with things we want to hear, and to enthrall us with the sensational and the supernatural. His is a siren song of love without truth.

Satan comes in many names—kundalini, Kali, Isis, Brahman, Lucifer, the Goddess, the serpent, etc.—and he will even pose in the names of Mother Mary, Jesus, God or the Holy Spirit if he can get away with it. He is behind all religions except true Christianity, and he is behind all counterfeit forms of Christianity. Satan's angels are as deceptive as he is, and will pose as mythical gods, spirits of dead people, blasphemers and even angels who love God and blow trumpets.

The serpent strives to distort our understanding of who Jesus is and why He came. He binds us to himself spiritually through a combination of delightful pleasures (good) and cruel tortures and immorality (evil). His light is dark and his love untrue; to receive it you must seek him repeatedly in the occult. He is called the father of lies because in him there is no truth. Believing his promises lead to death—spiritual deadness in this life, and the second death in the life to come.

Who is your God?

It is to you to judge if you follow the serpent or Jehovah. Both beckon, even now. Both desire your service, devotion and worship.

But if we lie in the love of Lucifer after tasting the goodness of God, how seriously we betray the One whose love is true.

Chapter Nineteen

WEAPONS OF
MASS SEDUCTION

Harlotry, wine, and new wine enslave the heart.
My people ask counsel from their wooden idols,
And their staff informs them.
For the spirit of harlotry has caused them to stray,
And they have played the harlot against their God.

—Hosea 4:11-12

*W*hy do people turn to the occult?

In matters of spiritual temptation we can learn much from examples set for us in the arena of human sexuality.

SEXUAL HUNGER, SPIRITUAL HUNGER

What needs or desires make us vulnerable to sexual seduction? Sometimes we are lonely, wanting comfort. Other times we are attracted to the beauty or influence of the lover, or excited by adventure and romance. Perhaps we fear having missed out on "the real thing." Perhaps we have excessive drive or unhealthy appetites. Perhaps we are just plain bored.

Whatever the motivation, if we believe sexual satisfaction is more important than sexual purity—or more important than our marriage vows—we can be seduced. Or, we will ourselves become seducers.

It is similar in matters of spiritual seduction. I often hear charismatics say they were feeling dry, depressed or bored, looking for more. Some envied the adventures of charismatic friends or believed their experiences were "the real thing." Many were simply curious, unaware they were flirting with the occult. Often pastors were seeking something—anything—to bring vitality to their congregations. Believers and nonbelievers alike venture into the occult because they are searching for meaning and purpose in their lives, or relief from spiritual pain and emptiness.

Whatever the motivation, if we do not understand and heed God's warnings about the occult we can be seduced, or can ourselves become false teachers.

Enter the serpent.

SEDUCERS: THE LIZARD AND THE DRAGON

The dragon god is a spiritual predator without a conscience. He has a human counterpart of sorts, the so-called "lounge lizard," a sexual predator who roams the bars looking for women.[1] The dragon and the lizard use similar techniques to obtain the willing surrender of their victims. It is helpful to consider these.

Most will agree that a "lounge lizard" is the sort of man who:

- hates rules and standards
- emphasizes love over truth
- wants us to feel, not think
- keeps changing his story
- tells women what they want to hear

Let us see what we can learn from the human sexual tempter to understand the schemes of the spiritual tempter.

THE LIZARD HATES RULES AND STANDARDS

A lounge lizard knows that to accomplish his purposes with a woman he hopes to seduce, he must first deal with her conscience:

---

1. I don't mean to suggest that women are not also guilty of sexual predation.

to stifle it or convince her to deny it. He must find a way around any standards she holds which would motivate her to resist sexual seduction or temptation.

Take the standard against adultery. Many religions, not just Christianity, recognize sexual fidelity as an objective standard to which partners in a marital relationship should submit, no matter what. But the lizard will tell you that faithfulness is not the only thing that counts; at least, not all the time. Other things are important too; your happiness, for example. This argument undermines the absolute, objective nature of the standard of fidelity. If you believe it, the rule against adultery is no longer absolute, but becomes relative: relative to your personal happiness. Because your level of happiness will change with time and circumstances, the standard changes, too. Fidelity becomes conditional and the standard becomes subjective: subordinate to your will, your desires, and your perceived needs. Influenced by the lie, you begin to accept feelings as your guide instead of the simple, safe standard of fidelity.

The lizard has other tricks in his bag. He paints strict moral codes with a brush of contempt, teaching us to mock goody-goodies and puritanical "nerds." Often the desire to please others and be accepted leads us to forsake godly standards: we exchange morality for popularity.

And so it is with the dragon when it comes to spiritual matters. But because spiritual sin is more difficult to identify, so the temptations of the serpent are more difficult to identify.

If faithfulness to God means holding to His truth is an absolute standard, and if it means rendering obedience to His commands, the dragon will tell us that other things matter too: things like personal happiness and popularity. He will tempt us to sacrifice obedience, and the primacy of place that obedience should have in our lives, to other standards. He will tell us that it is unloving to do anything else. Obedience, then, becomes conditionally important, subordinate to other considerations.

The dragon also paints those who emphasize obedience and doctrine with a brush of contempt, teaching us to condemn them as boring, legalistic or unbalanced. Often the desire to be accepted tempts us to subordinate truth to popularity.

268 TRUE TO HIS WAYS

Influenced by weak teaching and subject to wavering standards, Christians have affairs, divorce, remarry, sit under false
teaching and practice disobedience in other ways because their
consciences are dulled to godly, biblical standards. Their own
happiness and personal desires have become the measure by
which they make life decisions.

Charismatics have also taken to occult ways and, their minds
darkened by the dragon, have forsaken God's truth. They have
been seduced.

THE LIZARD EMPHASIZES LOVE OVER TRUTH

A very effective lizard-like technique is to teach "love is all that
matters." Another way to put this is, the lizard tells us that nice
feelings are loving, but that acting on moral standards is not.
Therefore, he says, we should not be guided by truth, but rather
by generous, compassionate and loving feelings. Then love usurps
the place of truth, with many consequences for our relationships.

"I love you and you love me, that's what really matters," the
woman says, and seduces a married man. "He doesn't love you," says
the lounge lizard to the lonely girl, "but I do." People break promises, lie about it and get to know someone from whom they should
stay far, far away—all in the name of so-called love. Love becomes
their standard and their guiding light. And at first it seems okay. It
"feels right" for a time, although pain is the usual consequence.

The dragon uses similar "love" teachings to seduce believers into
spiritual error. He wants us to think our faith is "founded on love."
He minimizes doctrine in favor of "love, peace and unity." Thus love
usurps the place of truth, and Satan's messengers get to look righteous, holy, loving and good. "Love and unity" become our guides
instead of the simple, absolute standard of fidelity to God's truth.

How right this seems! But it is not right, and we must be alert to
the wiles of the serpent. We must consider all things biblically, not
being misled by an appearance of righteousness which lacks the
power thereof. To err by emphasizing love over truth has serious
consequences both for our faith, and for our relationship with God.

Scripture tells us that the works of God are *truth and justice*. It
is not His love but His *Word*—His revelation of truth—which must
form the foundation of faith. To depart from truth is not loving.

Satan wants us to worship the "rule" of love.

In Christian circles the love-is-all-that-matters seduction technique has proved very successful. I do not mean to belittle people's efforts to be loving. I simply mean to say that love is no standard, and Jesus never said it was. We are not to be guided by love, but by truth.

Charismatics who emphasize love say things like "God is more concerned about our heart," "God just wants us to be loving, and to love our neighbors," or, "by love we can overcome evil." Rick Joyner closes his book *The Final Quest* with a supposed word from God that, "Love will be the power that destroys the works of the devil. And love will be what brings My kingdom."Not so. John, in the closing book of the Bible, wrote:

> Then I heard a loud voice saying in heaven, "Now salvation, and strength, and the kingdom of our God, and the power of His Christ have come, for the accuser of our brethren [the devil], who accused them before our God day and night, has been cast down. *And they overcame him by the blood of the Lamb and by the word of their testimony…*" (Revelation 12:11). (emphasis added)

Charismatics are not alone in proclaiming love as the standard; it is the call of virtually all religions. A Hindu mystic cries, "O Mother, make me mad with Thy love. What need is there for knowledge or reason?" (see chapter 20). Unitarians and Buddhists teach the importance of love. Singers sing about it; there is a song entitled, "All We Need is Love." Psychologists write about our need for love, even our need to love ourselves. John Lennon and Yoko Ono staged a "love-in" for the world to see. A Muslim Sufi wrote:

> The whole purpose and meaning of creation is to discover the secret of Love. The experience of love is the most fulfilling and important experience we can have, the highest of all values… We are here to be in communication with one another and explore the mystery of Love.[2]

---

2. Helminski, 42, 45.

Even satanists talk about the importance of love. The Great Beast Aleister Crowley wrote in his master treatise, the *Book of the Law*, that "There is no law beyond Do what thou wilt. Love is the law, love under will."[3] Human will, says Crowley, must be guided by love, for *love is the law.* Hmmm—a satanic priest who teaches love?

Is this one area where ancient wisdom and worldly philosophy, charismatics, rock stars, other religions and satanists all have it right? Is the whole world right, and Christianity wrong? Will love unite us all? Conquer the devil? Give meaning to life? Is love the answer? Makes sense. After all, if we truly loved each other, there would be no war, rape or crime. There would be no unloved children, no abused animals, no violence between spouses and no hate crimes; no theft, no bullies, no murder and no suicide. We obviously need more love. Who could deny it?

To proclaim love as your rule and standard sounds good and righteous and caring, and no doubt comes from a genuine desire to be good and righteous and caring. But the trouble is, it doesn't work. World religions have taught love for many centuries, but it hasn't worked yet. And the Bible says it will never work.

It will never work because the human heart is naturally incapable of true love. The human heart is sickly, feeble and deceptive (see Jeremiah 17:9) and prone to great evil. Human "love" is fickle, and easily descends to selfishness or perversion. To follow the way of "love" becomes a justification for following the way of the self, not the way of God. And this leads us straight to Crowley's conclusion, namely that love is the law—love under will.

Furthermore we must ask, what are we talking about when we say "love"? Do we mean feelings of compassion, or fond feelings that help us and others feel good about themselves? There is nothing wrong with this in and of itself, but we must ask, what kind of a standard—what kind of a law—can such feelings really be? They are subjective, fluctuating and unreliable. We cannot measure love, except by subjective assessment of our personal feelings and desires, and by our own—usually mistaken—estimation of the needs and desires of others.

---

3. Crowley, *The Book*, II, p. 50.

I am not saying that genuine self-sacrificing love cannot be found among human beings. There is much love in the world, among families and peoples of all faiths and nations. There are many people guided by genuine, altruistic desires who do good for others. But what I am saying is that *love is not the law*. If it were, we would need to accept the rule of the human heart, like satanist Aleister Crowley did. But our hearts are hard, says Scripture, harder than we can understand, and deceitful above all things. And this, of course, is why our efforts to be loving do not succeed. This is why fallen man, even with his well-meaning religions of love, has never been able to change the world.

Jehovah wants us to worship the rule of truth

Christianity differs from other religions because it teaches that men and women who want to be loving first need to know and believe God's objective, reliable, unchanging truth.

The Bible teaches that the world is the way it is because men and women have hard hearts, hearts fundamentally depraved by sin in ways we cannot understand, which inevitably reject the very truth that can bring us into God's light and love. This is a mystery, but as we have seen (chapter 4) Jesus came to bring the truth we need. He came in love bringing truth. Mercy required Him to do so, because the world walks in darkness without it.

Therefore truth, not love, is the answer. Truth, not love, is the law. Jesus taught in numerous ways and by different parables that His truth is so important, so vital, that it is the foundation upon which we must build our lives, and it must be the measure of all our practices. Given this, the reverent, accurate articulation of truth—that is, doctrine—must be of primary importance to believers.

John MacArthur says:

> The great preacher C.H. Spurgeon said, "My harshest words are far more full of love than the smooth words of soft-speaking ministers who say, 'peace, peace,' when there is no peace. Do you think it is any pleasure for me to preach like this?"

272 TRUE TO HIS WAYS

> Sound, biblical doctrine therefore underlies all true wis-
> dom and authentic faith. The attitude that scorns doctrine
> while elevating feelings or blind trust cannot legitimately
> be called faith, even if it masquerades as Christianity. It is
> actually an irrational form of unbelief. God holds us
> accountable for *what we believe* as well as *how we think*
> about the truth He has revealed.[4] (emphasis original)

We must conclude, then, that "love is the law" is the dragon's
siren call. Truth is the law of God and must be the law of His
people, also, if they will be faithful to Him.

The place of love

What place, then, does love have in Christian faith? A great place.

Jesus commanded us to, above all, love God and our neighbor.
Furthermore, the Bible teaches—and His children know from
experience—that God *is* love. He gives love, is moved by love,
moves us to love and teaches us about love. He sheds His love
abroad in our hearts. From Him we learn that forgiveness makes
love complete, that love requires mercy, that love is tender and
gentle and much more. He commands us to grow in love.

It must be noted, Paul also said to have truth without love
makes one as a clanging symbol or an empty gong. But Scripture
teaches that the way to be loving, and to grow in love, is by learning and growing in understanding of God's truth, and by obeying
all His commands. The apostle Paul taught that love is the *fulfill-
ing* of the law—not the law itself (Romans 13:10). It is a *fruit* of
godliness, not a *root* of godliness. And, love rejoices in the truth
(1 Corinthians 13:6). Love is the final and crowning accomplishment of God's work in a faithful heart—a heart that has learned
to hate sin and cherish truth.

THE LIZARD WANTS US TO FEEL, NOT THINK

Lust shuts off our brains, and alcohol lowers inhibitions. That's
why the lounge lizard says, Make 'em hungry, get 'em drunk. If he
can *excite our feelings*, he can prevent sound thinking.

---

4. MacArthur, *Reckless Faith* , p xiii.

Likewise the dragon aims to get us hungry—hungry for occult encounter. And he aims to get us drunk—drunk on manifestations and enchantments, so we focus on feelings and forget how to think. He wants to get us excited about experiences and miracles and things that titillate the flesh.

Our heavenly Father, however, would *excite our minds,* because through reason we grow in the knowledge of truth and develop a godly conscience. Jesus said, "You shall love the Lord your God with all your heart, with all your soul, and with *all your mind.* This is the first and great commandment" (Matthew 22:37-38). It is by minds renewed through truth that we are transformed to know God's will. Paul wrote to the Romans, "be transformed by the renewing of your mind, that you may prove what is that good and acceptable and perfect will of God" (Romans 12:2).

If a godly heart is developed by exercising the mind to understand God's Word, we can be certain that Lucifer will discourage the pursuit of doctrinal clarity. That's one reason he gets us chasing after experience. You will recall from chapter 7 the following charismatic teaching which reverses the way to genuine godliness and actually despises the gift of reason:

> Satan's Temptation: That Man Descend to Reasoned Knowledge...Had I been living only out of reason, I would have rejected the Toronto blessing. Since I was trained to live out of my heart and out of revelation, I have embraced it.

This writer has swallowed the bait of Satan hook, line and sinker.

Both the lizard and the dragon discourage thinking, demanding trust without enquiry to override natural caution and fear. They hate questions, because good questions encourage intelligent thought—and might even lead to answers! "Just trust!" they say. "Throw caution to the wind!" Predictably, satanist Aleister Crowley also belittles reason and enquiry, and urges us to set fear aside in the quest for occult experience. In *The Book of the Law* he wrote:

> Also reason is a lie; for there is a factor infinite & unknown; & all their words are skew-wise.

> Enough of Because! Be he damned for a dog!
> But ye, o my people, rise up & awake!…
> A feast every day in your hearts in the joy of my rapture!
> A feast every night unto Nu, and the pleasure of uttermost delight!…
> Dost thou fail? Art thou sorry? Is fear in thine heart?
> Where I am these are not.[5]

Man's natural suspicion and fear of the occult should be respected, not ignored. Reason and alertness are precious, God-given tools which enable us to avoid spiritual seduction.

THE LIZARD KEEPS CHANGING HIS STORY

Like any accomplished lizard does with his victims, Satan keeps us confused by changing his story, fudging the facts and telling everybody a different story of love and faith. As a result there are many different versions of "truth" in the world: a myriad of religions, myths and imaginations.

Of course, God's truth is the target. The dragon wants us to love myths: there are hundreds, even thousands, to choose from. Or we are invited to invent our own—whatever works for us. These myths may or may not include fanciful stories about Jesus; after all, it serves Satan well to distort the truth about the Son of God.

We have seen that occultists do not acknowledge the absolute nature of truth. They teach the story that it is experiential, evolving or irrelevant. Many believe "truth" is being mystically revealed to humans and through humans in the progression of time. Another story is that truth—objective truth—is an illusion. Yet another is that we become truth—and hence, divine like God—through meditation and attaining "higher consciousness." Modernists turn to ancient wisdom, and charismatics think they have discovered something new. Yogis think vibrations are lighter now, aboriginals worship animal spirits and New Agers seek truth within: hundreds of different stories about truth. How can it be? Only Crowley called it all what it really is—the worship of

---

5. Crowley, *The Book,* II, 33-34.

Lucifer (chapter 11). Few recognize the inherent contradiction: if the story keeps changing, it wasn't true to begin with.

Charismatics have been misled by those who teach that truth evolves. Earlier (chapter 7) we saw the teachings of Bill Hamon, who believes truth is revealed and established through the subjective experiences of the "new prophets":

> Coming Into Present Truth. Many individuals from various backgrounds are coming into the present truth of what God is doing in this day and hour. They include those with no church background…These individuals are coming into a full Christian heritage, rich in "know-so" salvation…the experiential truths which God has taken more than 450 years to restore to the corporate Church, individuals can now receive within a short period of time…The trumpet for advancing is about to sound again. Your generation will be challenged to establish the greatest truth and the most revolutionary reality that has ever been revealed to the Church.[6]

Satan's truth is like shifting shadows. His prophets teach all sorts of contradictions believed to be wisdom. But God's truth is unchanging, singular and trustworthy. Jesus said:

> Therefore whoever hears these sayings of Mine, and does them, I will liken him to a wise man who built his house on the rock: and the rain descended, the floods came, and the winds blew and beat on that house; and it did not fall, for it was founded on the rock. Now everyone who hears these sayings of Mine, and does not do them, will be like a foolish man who built his house on the sand: and the rain descended, the floods came, and the winds blew and beat on that house; and it fell. And great was its fall (Matthew 7:24-27).

God alone is faithful; with Him there is no shifting or turning.

---

6. Hamon, *The Eternal Church*, 10, 12.

276 Tʀᴜᴇ ᴛᴏ Hɪs Wᴀʏs

Tʜᴇ ʟɪᴢᴀʀᴅ ᴛᴇʟʟs ᴜs ᴡʜᴀᴛ ᴡᴇ ᴡᴀɴᴛ ᴛᴏ ʜᴇᴀʀ

The lounge lizard needs a woman to be vulnerable and open to his advances before he can have his way. So he woos, flatters and tells her what she wants to hear. He speaks words of love and knows how to make her *feel* loved. But he does *not*, in fact, love her. He simply wants to use her, to get her for his own purposes. He tries to please her, but certainly not for her sake.

And so it is with the dragon god. Urging us to open up to him and "just trust," the serpent tells us everything will be all right. It's an age-old seduction technique: "Trust me, and feel my arms of love." He will make us feel better, he promises. Just let him have his way. But he does not, in fact, love us. He is seducing us.

Many are the promises that appeal to human flesh. Healing, miracles, occult powers, psychic ability, love, bliss, peace, oneness with the universe, wisdom, supernatural visions and psychic powers—all these are promised through occult practice. On the other hand, no one wants to hear about standards, rules or unbending truth; and how much less about hell, judgment or a God of wrath! In fact, the unvarnished truth of God has great potential to offend and Satan takes advantage by whispering sweet nothings we like to hear.

One of these sweet nothings is a very tall tale about truth, an occult teaching common in many different faiths which holds that because God is both love and truth, then love and truth are essentially the same thing and, therefore, God's truth is "in love." The story is that when we find love, we have found truth; and not only truth, but God Himself. This teaching is common in cults and occult religions where gurus, spiritually enabled to awaken love in the hearts of devotees, are revered as prophets of God and "Truth." Occultists often capitalize the words love and truth, as you may have noticed in quotations throughout this book, because they believe love, truth and God are all one and the same; a perfect, mystic One. How close this seems to biblical teaching! But, it is occult thinking because it is about finding truth, or God, in subjective experience.

Charismatics, perhaps misled by *phos* light experiences, have also become confused about the place of love and truth in Christianity, and this has culminated in the widespread propagation of a false gospel based on similar occult thinking. It is difficult to explain, but I will try. The proponents of this gospel hold that Jesus, who is both Love and Truth, makes Himself known to man in and through love and truth, and that we can reveal Jesus to others through loving them as well as through Scripture. The Bible is useful for truth, they think, but truth should not be over-emphasized because then we forget the love part of the equation and become "unbalanced." In this view, Jesus is a mystic Word, a mystic, loving Truth. It may not be articulated exactly like this, but look carefully and you will find this teaching all around. A common expression of it is the desire to "bring Jesus' love to the nations," when it is actually His words of truth that we are commanded to bring.

The reader may be tempted to take issue. After all, God is both love and truth, the Bible tells us so. But, it pleases God to distinguish the two for man's sake and, as we have seen (chapter 6), before man can know God's love, he must first receive words of truth by intellectual apprehension. Yes, we also receive His words in our hearts: His precious Word can cause our hearts to swell with great joy. But, it is essential to realize that God's Word is first presented to our minds and must engage the intellect. Jesus came to bring *logos*-truth, not a mystic love-truth. He told Pilate, "For this cause I was born, and for this cause I have come into the world, that I should bear witness to the truth. Everyone who is of the truth hears My voice"(John 18:37). His voice is no experiential touch of love: that is occult. His voice is contained in words of *logos*-truth. If fact, I do not think Scripture ever says that Jesus came to "bring love."

To further illustrate the false, charismatic gospel, consider a letter written to me by a pastor who believes my emphasis upon truth is unbalanced. He believes that to be loving toward others is the first duty of every Christian not only because our Lord commanded love, but also — and here the occult thinking creeps in — because "it is only through loving and humble obedience that the Truth is revealed." Note the capitalization in "Truth." Note also the belief that revelation of "Truth" comes through subjective experience: in this case, loving relationships. Tragically, this pastor is teaching a false gospel, one that ignores man's need for *logos*-truth. It also promotes reliance upon works. Even worse, it exalts man because it assumes his loving obedience can be so perfect and so humble, it actually reaches divine proportions: what faith this requires in one's own righteousness!

Why do many of us prefer tall tales? Because words of truth offend, that is why. Jesus said many would be offended, including the Pharisees who, like those who promote another gospel, are false teachers with great faith in their own righteousness. But, He also said that those who love Him will keep His words (John 14:24), and those who are not offended by Him are blessed indeed (Matthew 11:6). Strive, therefore, to hear the truth, and follow not after tall tales that tickle your ears!

RESIST SEDUCTION: CLING TO TRUTH

Israel's mighty God, betrayed again and again, used the prophet Hosea to illustrate the spiritual harlotry of His people:

> Then the Lord said to me, "Go again, love a woman who is
> loved by a lover and is committing adultery, just like the
> love of the Lord for the children of Israel, who look to other
> gods and love the raisin cakes of the pagans" (Hosea 3:1).

The adulterous woman in this verse exemplifies the unfaithful nation of Israel, and remains an example for us today. Angry, God warned Israel:

> My people are destroyed for lack of knowledge. Because
> you have rejected knowledge, I also will reject you from
> being priest for Me; because you have forgotten the law of
> your God, I also will forget your children (Hosea 4:6).

These warnings, spoken to Israel, are also for us. If we forget God and stray from words of knowledge, He will forget us. Therefore, dear one, cling fast to His words, that you will be able to stand fast against occult seductions.

Chapter Twenty

~

KILLING US SOFTLY,
WITH HIS SONG

O Lord God, help us now to really worship You…May the attractions of these crude things be gone, and may You catch us away to Yourself. We do not ask to be entranced or to see an angel in shining apparel, but we do ask that by faith we may see Jesus.

—Charles Haddon Spurgeon

God is looking for those who will worship Him in spirit and in truth (John 4:23). This is no vague, unimportant statement. It clearly explains the prerequisites for genuine worship: one must be "in spirit" through spiritual rebirth, and "in truth" through faith that is founded upon believing and accepting God's Word. The Levitical laws taught by Moses were intended to demonstrate, among other things, that we cannot approach God or please Him unless our worship is pure—pure in spirit and pure in truth.

PRAISING EXPERIENCE

Songs of mystics focus on the pleasures of *phos* light experience, and the devotees' longing for it. Lyrics are often invocational, inviting the Spirit to come, as in the following song written to Kali:

O Mother, make me mad with Thy love.
What need is there for knowledge or reason?
Make me drunk with the wine of Thy love.
O Mother, who steals the hearts of the bhaktas! Drown me
    in the sea of Thy love.[1]

Charismatic lyrics also express longing for, and pleasure in, manifest presence. From a Christian rock group:

I feel lonely without hope
I feel desperate without vision
You wrap around me like a winter coat
You come and free me like a bird[2]

Contrast the lyrics of the charismatic group against the words of a psalm, where the writer seeks not presence, but truth:

Oh, send out Your light and Your truth!
Let them lead me;
Let them bring me to Your holy hill
And to Your tabernacle.
Then I will go to the altar of God,
To God my exceeding joy;
And on the harp I will praise You,
O God, my God
    (Psalm 43:3-4).

Charismatics often emphasize singing—praise and worship—over teaching because during singing the spirits manifest and experiences happen. Singing is a form of invocation, especially if it becomes hypnotic. Here is what one charismatic pastor said:

We have not yet formulated our doctrines into a "state-ment of faith." Our greatest values are in the area of praise

---

1. Quoted in "Another Visit," Ch 1.
2. Delirious, "Obsession," CD, *Cutting Edge*.

and worship. We want to facilitate the presence of God in our midst…I do know of many lives that were significantly changed in Toronto. What happens there is legitimately of the Spirit.[3]

To seek blessings through spiritual presence is, of course, the *occult* way. Contrast the truly biblical lyrics of an old hymn, "Trust and Obey":

> When we walk with the Lord in the light of His Word,
> What glory He sheds on our way!
> While we do His good will He abides with us still,
> And with all who will trust and obey.

I do not think I have ever seen a charismatic song on the importance of obedience. But many express significant spiritual pain. One would almost think it is a normal part of the Christian walk:

> When all around has fallen, your castle has been burned
> You used to be a king here, now no-one knows your name
> You live your life for honor, defender of the faith
> But you've been crushed to pieces and no-one knows your
>   pain…
> When tomorrow has been stolen and you can't lift your head
> And summer feels like winter, your heart is full of stone…[4]

This songwriter believes himself a "defender of the faith," but at the same time feels his heart is full of stone. He describes feeling "crushed" and "burned"— bereft of the peace of God. This is a false Christian witness. Such pain is the inheritance of a soul alienated from God, not one that abides in His will.

---

3. Bruce/Lorraine Friesen, interview by Jack Krayenhoff, "A church named 'Lion of Judah' outgrows its site," *Sunday Magazine,* January, 2004.
4. Delirious, "When All Around Has Fallen," CD, *Cutting Edge.* Over the years the lyrics of this charismatic rock group have become increasingly mystic, and increasingly unhappy.

OCCULT INFLUENCE IN WORSHIP

Charismatic songs are so popular, they can be found in almost every church. Songs produced by Vineyard, Arrow in the Hand, and Latter Rain are simple and pleasant. They talk about love, submission and rivers of grace. They maintain a semblance of orthodoxy. And, to be fair, they also sing happy lyrics. But many believers find charismatic songs unsatisfactory. They long to sing the old hymns again; not because they are old, nor because they are hymns, but simply because they contain deeper truths and are more faithful to truth.

Somebody once said that much of the problem with charismatic music is not what is said, but what is unsaid. Popular musician Robin Mark acknowledges this, but unfortunately believes it to be a good thing:

> As the church began to tap back into the well of worship…we began to see songs with simple phrases…These are new days and God is doing new things…I think it's fair to say that some modern worship is more "touchy feely" than grounded in biblical theology. But God is after our hearts as well as our minds. We need a balance between right and proper theology and the intimacy of relationship as children of our Heavenly Father. No matter how "sound" a hymn might be, God is not impressed by our brainpower and intellect, but rather by our attitude of heart.[5]

Mr. Mark errs in that, for one, he holds a mystic view of God as a "well of worship" to be "tapped into." For another, he calls for a balance between "intimacy" and "theology," which is really a sacrifice of truth to accommodate experience. Satan hates truth: it gets in the way of his work. So who is most pleased—the god of experience or the God of truth—when songwriters go simple on theology?

---

5. Robin Mark, "Innerview—Days of Elijah," *Servant Magazine-A Ministry of Prairie Bible Institute*, Issue 69, 2004, 10.

There is not only a lack, but also a distortion of truth in some charismatic lyrics. For example one song says the church will "rise up like the dawn." I fear this is a reference to the false charismatic teaching about the end-time power of the church. Another says there is "truth in every circumstance"—an occult and pantheistic view. Still another says, "Your love is the anchor," but as we know it is not love, but truth, that anchors us; love is the serpent's siren song to lead us away from the Word.

Also disturbing is that despite appearances, many charismatic songs are not written for, or to or about the true God. They were written for, and to and about the god of the occult. Of course, many do not realize this. However, lyrics penned in praise of Satan, which extol the delights of occult enchantments, must—when the truth is known—be foul on the lips of a believer. And how much more so to the ear of God!

True, many lyrics are ambiguous. One writer celebrates "being under the influence of love" which could be a reference to spiritual intoxication or just a slightly inept expression of joy. Following are other lyrics that may reflect occult experience:

"I will soar with you" (in mystic enchantment);

"Strip away my weaknesses" (in occult washing);

"The power of the Lord is moving in this place" (manifestations are starting to happen);

"Be still for the glory of the Lord is shining all around" (mystic spirit);

"In faith receive from Him" (just trust and open up);

and:

"I've given in to his control" (occult submission).

As believers repeatedly sing lyrics which sugarcoat, omit or distort doctrine, their understanding will be affected and discernment blunted. For if our minds are washed and renewed by truth, then what will error do but defile us and undermine the foundations of our faith?

TRUTH IN WORSHIP

Well-written songs explore many Christian truths, including the mysteries of sin and salvation, God's sovereignty, our weakness and folly, our need for forgiveness, God's great mercy and love and many others. In thoughtful contemplation of truths like this the Christian heart is prepared for and rises in worship. John Stott said, "Only as we hear again what God has done are we ready to respond in praise and worship."[6] He explains:

> The Psalter was the great hymnbook of the Old Testament church, and the Psalms are still sung in Christian worship today. It is instructive, therefore, to learn from this source what true worship is. The basic definition of worship in the Psalter is to "praise the name of the Lord," or to "ascribe to the Lord the glory due to his name." And when we begin to inquire what is meant by his "name," we find that it is the sum total of all that he is and has done. In particular, he is worshiped in the Psalms as both the Creator of the world and the Redeemer of Israel, and the Psalmists delight in their praises to give lengthy catalogs of God's works of creation and redemption.[7]

UGLINESS IN WORSHIP

We might expect that if charismatic worship is occult, demonic activity will occur. And so it does, in congregations deeply involved in occult practice.

Highly charismatic worship leaders often arrange lengthy times of worship, sometimes even asking the congregation to chant things like "awake, awake," or "fall on me now, fall on me now." Such repetition may induce a semi-hypnotic trance, an altered state

6. Stott, 32.
7. Stott, 30.

which opens the mind to the demonic. Michael Green gives the following eyewitness testimony:

> I think of one person I know who became uncontrollably afflicted with shaking, motor movements of the arms and grinding of the teeth during a protracted time of worship. This was the utterly unexpected evidence of demonic attack, which proved to be both multiple and long lived and went back to ancestor infestation and Hindu background and worship.[8]

Mr. Green found this attack to be "utterly unexpected" because he is unaware of the dangers of charismatic practice. Note how he attributes the problem to the person's background, not to the occult nature of a "protracted time of worship." In fact, he thinks it is the beauty of such worship which causes Satan to manifest! He says that during praise and worship, "the spirits will be stirred into rebellion and opposition."[9] This is yet another example of the strange belief that poltergeist experiences mean the Holy Spirit has arrived.

Mr. Green recalls other episodes:

> I think of another who gave no sign of demonization until during praise and worship uncontrollable mockery arose in them; with another it was inability to pray; with another it was uncontrollable laughter at holy things.[10]

It is terrible that these things are happening in congregations that claim to worship in the name of Christ. The sheep are being led into the clutches of a cunning spiritual enemy who is, as a once popular song put it, killing us softly with his song.

---

8. Green, 136.
9. Green, 136.
10. Green, 136.

Chapter Twenty-One

A Pure and Spotless Bride

*Christ also loved the church, and gave Himself up for her,
that He might sanctify her, having cleansed her by the
washing of water with the word, that He might present to
Himself the church in all her glory, having no spot or wrinkle
or any such thing; but that she should be holy and blameless.*
—Ephesians 5:25-27 NASB

Jesus is not only Savior to those who trust Him—a reality wonderful in itself—He is friend, king, brother, Lord and also a departed bridegroom who will at some point in the future return to Earth and gather the church, like a bride, unto Himself.

THE SYMBOLISM OF JEWISH BETROTHAL AND MARRIAGE CEREMONIES

Under the Mosaic Covenant, God prescribed ceremonies which serve as types, or symbols, to illustrate how He would deal with the Christian church under the New Covenant. Jewish wedding traditions are richly symbolic of the relationship between Jesus as bridegroom and the church as His bride.

In ancient Israel if a young man saw the girl he wanted, or if a father saw the girl he wanted for his son, he would go to her with a marriage proposal. An important part of the proposal was the price to be paid by the bridegroom; it was intended that he should pay dearly for the bride of his choice. If the terms were suitable, the young man and woman would drink a cup of wine together. This sealed the covenant between them; they were now betrothed. Henceforth the couple would be referred to as husband and wife, although the marriage would not be consummated for a time to come. Meanwhile, their covenant bound the young people to certain tasks and responsibilities. The husband was charged with preparing a place to live—either a room in his father's house or a separate dwelling. He could not return to fetch the bride until their new home was complete. When the groom's father declared all to be in readiness, the betrothed young man, with little warning to his wife, would head for her house to take her away and bring her back to the place he had prepared beforehand. He and his friends would shout and make a great noise as they neared the home of the bride.

For the willing young woman the promise of this future event—being fetched and taken away by a man who wanted and cherished her—held great romance. She wanted to be ready when she heard his shout and knew that his arrival was imminent, and kept her oil lamp lit in case he came in the middle of the night. Needless to say, she was also expected to keep pure, with serious penalties should she fail to do so. She wore a veil whenever she left the house so other men knew she was spoken for.

When at last the young man arrived, he would steal his bride away and take her joyfully to their new home. Into the private chamber they would go, shutting the door on the rest of the world, to begin a new life together.

The covenant proposal of the lamb

Bible readers will recognize the significance of Jewish betrothal and wedding traditions for the Christian church. Allow me to illustrate this with word pictures drawn from Scripture, starting with the Passover supper.

In chapter 26 of Mathew's Gospel we see Jesus seated at a large table, ready to partake of a ceremonial meal with His disciples. He contemplates the events soon to come, and looks around at his disciples. They (except Judas) will be the first members of the new covenant church, His soon-to-be-betrothed bride. The time is Passover. Jesus knows the price He must offer for His bride, and He is willing to pay it.

The price is His own life; Himself as the sacrificial Lamb.

The gift of his life is the highest price any man could pay. Yet the life of Jesus is infinitely more precious and valuable than that of any other. He is unique, begotten by God yet born of woman, and the only man to live who knew no sin. The price of His life is so inestimably high, so eternally sufficient, it will actually be enough to rescue His bride—that is, all men and women who believe on Him—from bondage to sin and death. It will clothe them with radiant garments of righteousness and holiness, garments without which they would be unable to enter the places He will prepare for them in heaven:

> None of them can by any means redeem his brother,
> Nor give to God a ransom for him—
> For the redemption of their souls is costly,
> And it shall cease forever—
> That he should continue to live eternally,
> And not see the Pit (Psalm 49:7-9).

The sacrifice of Jesus is not only costly, it is incredibly merciful because the bride Jesus will die for is not pure, not sweet and not beautiful. In fact, she is defiled by lust and sin, blind to her own folly and by nature hostile to her Groom.

By her very nature this bride cannot anticipate the joy of intimacy with Jesus; she thinks the idea foolish and unnecessary. She does not desire her Groom, and to be faithful to Him is beyond her natural ability. Furthermore, she does not understand the lengths to which Christ Jesus must go—and will and did go—for her, nor how utterly dependent she is upon Him to make her beautiful and willing. Indeed, she does not know what true beauty is, nor appreciate it. This bride is rude, ignorant and unclean! Yet still, Jesus will die for her. In obedience to His heavenly Father, He will do everything asked of Him to win this wretched church and to present it to Himself a pure and spotless bride:

> Christ also loved the church, and gave Himself up for her,
> that He might sanctify her, having cleansed her by the wash-
> ing of water with the word, that He might present to
> Himself the church in all her glory, having no spot or wrin-
> kle or any such thing; but that she should be holy and
> blameless (Ephesians 5:25-27 NASB).

Willing to suffer punishment unimaginable, and to spill His blood in agony so His bride can be made clean, our Lord Jesus sits at the Passover table and looks around with great love at His disciples. Knowing He must express deep and mysterious truths with words and symbols that can lead to a right understanding, He breaks bread and gives it to them, saying:

> Take, eat; this is My body (Matthew 26:26).

By this act and these words Jesus is telling the disciples that He will die—that is, give His body to be broken—to pay the price necessary to purchase them for Himself. Then He takes a cup of wine and, after offering thanks to God, He gives it to the disciples, urging them to accept:

> Drink from it, all of you. For this is My blood of the new
> covenant, which is shed for many for the remission of sins
> (Matthew 26:27-28).

By this act and these words Jesus is building on the symbolism of the marriage covenant. He is not only telling them that He will spill His blood for them, but He is also showing them the significance of this sacrifice, namely redemption and salvation.

Lastly, because Jesus knows that through death and resurrection He will shortly be leaving the disciples to prepare a place for them in heaven, He says:

> But I say to you, I will not drink of this fruit of the vine
> from now on until that day when I drink it new with you
> in My Father's kingdom (Matthew 26:29).

By these words our Lord promises to return and fetch the disciples home with Him to heaven. Earlier He had already told them:

> Let not your heart be troubled; you believe in God, believe
> also in Me. In My Father's house are many mansions; if it
> were not so, I would have told you. I go to prepare a place
> for you. And if I go and prepare a place for you, I will
> come again and receive you to Myself; that where I am,
> there you may be also (John 14:1-3).

Just how this will happen is explained in Paul's first letter to the Thessalonians:

> For this we say to you by the word of the Lord, that we who
> are alive and remain until the coming of the Lord will by no
> means precede those who are asleep. For the Lord Himself
> will descend from heaven with a shout, with the voice of an
> archangel, and with the trumpet of God. And the dead in
> Christ will rise first. Then we who are alive and remain shall
> be caught up together with them in the clouds to meet the
> Lord in the air. And thus we shall always be with the Lord
> (1 Thessalonians 4:15-17).

Thus it is that although the bride of Christ lost her Groom to death, at the same time she gained more than she could ever have imagined: a promise and a hope to carry her through to His next coming. The sacrifice of Himself not only paid the high price needed to obtain this undesirable, unwilling bride it also, joy of joy and wonder of wonders, defeated death itself and laid the foundation for His later work—work which would include making her willing and radiant, and then returning to take her home with Him. The death that claimed our Lord could not hold Him, and the waiting bride—who

292 TRUE TO HIS WAYS

must for now be content with the seal of the Holy Spirit indwelling and sanctifying her to make her ready—will receive her Groom back at some point in the future, at the time when God says that all is ready and Jesus may return to snatch her away and take her to places that He will have prepared beforehand.

We who are not beautiful, not pure, not faithful; we who have done nothing, known nothing and contributed nothing; we can know Him not only in this life, but will know Him even better in the life to come, forevermore and without ceasing! Praise be to God, what an awesome mystery! What a revelation to fill our hearts with awe.

JUDGING RIGHTLY

How, then, shall the people of Christ remain faithful until He returns?

It is essential for a bride to distinguish correctly between things that are godly and things that defile, so she can keep herself accordingly. This requires understanding and discernment, and the deliberate choice to turn away from forbidden practices and liaisons.

Judging self

Before we judge others, we must first judge ourselves. For example, we must judge our faith with soberness. We must judge our actions, deeds and words. Even our thoughts matter: those which are defiling we must take captive, for we are to think on things that are honest, true, pure, lovely and of good report (Philippians 4:8).

> Therefore "Come out from among them and be separate," says the Lord. "Do not touch what is unclean, and I will receive you" (2 Corinthians 6:17).

Most importantly, perhaps, it is crucial for believers to understand their own sinfulness. Is this a negative teaching? Is this only going to depress us? No. It is always good to know the truth. The believer awakened to the reality of the dark things in his heart discovers that his new insight brings a joy more sweet than bitter, for it tramples pride anew. It also illuminates our need for salvation, and awakens dependence upon the work that Jesus did; all things that grow our faith. It restores us to a right relationship with God.

John Piper said in a sermon:

> O the perils of not knowing our sin! There is a great sadness that comes from not being saddened by knowing our sin. There is a great pain that comes to the soul and to the marriage and to the family and to the church and to the world from not tasting the pain of knowing our own sin. There is a great self-destruction that comes from not experiencing the self-devastation of knowing our sin. There is an eternal loss that comes from not losing our pride in the knowledge of our sin. If there is any hope and any faith and any joy and peace, any love, it will come from knowing our sin. So get to know your sin![1]

Those who judge themselves rightly purify themselves for the Groom. So let the bride examine herself, never judging herself righteous on her own account.

Judging others, judging activities

The bride of Christ must watch how she spends her time, and the things she reads, watches and hears. This is all part of guarding her heart—her inner being—and keeping herself pure. Her soul is God's territory.

She must judge her teachers carefully. If the mind is washed by truth, it is also darkened by false teaching, made unclean in ways we cannot fully understand. If adultery is as much a sin of thought as of deed (Matthew 5:28), then filling the mind with falsehood is as much a sin as soaking in occult spirit. The bride must flee from both. She must not taste honey from the corpse; she must not even touch it.

---

1. John Piper, Sermon: "The Importance of Knowing Our Sin," April 1, 2001.

Judging our church body

Finding godly fellowship means judging the pastors or leaders of your congregation for faithfulness to God's truth and faithfulness to His ways. If they are godly, you should find others, also godly, for fellowship in the congregation and may rely upon their leadership. However, if they are not faithful to truth you must reconsider.

The bride of Christ must avoid spiritual fellowship, and perhaps also personal fellowship, with the unfaithful (not with unbelievers, but those who profess Christianity falsely [1 Corinthians 5:9-13]). It is especially dangerous and defiling to associate with those who walk under the influence of occult spirits. We are to separate ourselves unto Jesus, and to be a peculiar people. We are to avoid fellowship with works of darkness indeed we should expose them (Ephesians 5:11). To wink at occultism among those who call themselves brothers and sisters is to collaborate in their deeds. To associate with the unfaithful is to choose them over the Groom and is itself unfaithful.

I'll be honest: The search for godly companionship and for a faithful congregation can be discouraging. Nevertheless, God has promised that if we will turn from our ways, He will raise up leaders to teach and lead us in truth:

> "Return, backsliding Israel," says the Lord, "and I will not cause My anger to fall on you; for I am merciful," says the Lord, "and I will not remain angry forever. Only acknowledge your iniquity, that you have transgressed against the Lord your God, and have scattered your charms to alien deities under every green tree, and you have not obeyed My voice," says the Lord... "And I will give you shepherds according to My heart, who will feed you with knowledge and understanding" (Jeremiah 3:12-13,15).

I returned to God's ways, and He led me to a small church and group of believers committed to the whole of God's Word without apology or compromise. We are praying for Christians everywhere, that they will return to truth and that God will give them faithful shepherds. It is a joy to meet and worship with serious believers who walk in godly paths.

Awaiting the Groom:
keeping Him in our thoughts and esteem

As she waits, as she keeps herself pure for a good and noble groom, a faithful Jewish bride makes a deliberate effort to remember him and to keep him uppermost in her hopes and thoughts. Out of sight does not mean out of mind. She contemplates things about him that she loves and admires. She hopes for a life to be lived with a trustworthy man who loves her, and whom she loves in return. These thoughts and efforts honor the husband.

And so it is—or should be—with the bride of Christ. In the absence of our Lord we need to make a deliberate effort to remember and esteem Him, especially since the natural mind is easily distracted. For this reason our worship and preaching must be God-centered, not man-centered. Man-centered teaching focuses on what we want, or what we think we need—a "financial miracle," or a house, or healing, etc. These things are not wrong in themselves, but the bride who sets her heart on treasures like these has set her heart on things that fade away, things which do not and cannot prepare her for eternity with Jesus. Our Lord said:

> Jesus said, "As the Father loved Me, I also have loved you; abide in My love. If you keep My commandments, you will abide in My love, just as I have kept My Father's commandments and abide in His love. These things I have spoken to you...that your joy may be full" (John 15:9-11).

Do not lay up for yourselves treasures on Earth, where moth and rust destroy and where thieves break in and steal; but lay up for yourselves treasures in heaven, where neither moth nor rust destroys and where thieves do not break in and steal. For where your treasure is, there your heart will be also (Matthew 6:19-21).

Preaching that esteems our Lord focuses upon who He is and the truths He asks us to cherish. A young Charles Spurgeon opened his morning sermon some 150 years ago by saying:

It has been said by someone that "the proper study of mankind is man." I will not oppose the idea, but I believe it is equally true that the proper study of Gods' elect is God; the proper study of a Christian is the Godhead. The highest science, the loftiest speculation, the mightiest philosophy, which can ever engage the attention of a child of God, is the name, the nature, the person, the work, the doings, and the existence of the great God whom he calls his Father.

He added:

And, whilst humbling and expanding, this subject is eminently *consolatory.* Oh, there is, in contemplating Christ, a balm for every wound; in musing on the Father, there is a quietness for every grief; and in the influence of the Holy Ghost, there is a balsam for every sore...

It is by contemplating and cherishing the things of God that the human soul is purified and made whole, faithfully kept for the return of Jesus Christ.

THE PROMISE OF THE GROOM

Our God left us with precious promises to keep our faith and hope alive—promises of a new heaven and a new Earth, of peace and safety for man and beast and of everlasting, loving intimacy with the Groom:

In that day I will make a covenant for them with the beasts of the field, with the birds of the air, and with the creeping things of the ground. Bow and sword of battle I will shatter from the Earth, to make them lie down safely.

I will betroth you to Me forever; yes, I will betroth you to Me in righteousness and justice, in lovingkindness and mercy; I will betroth you to Me in faithfulness, and you shall know the Lord (Hosea 2:18-20).

And the Spirit and the bride say, come, Lord Jesus, come!

Glossary

Age of Aquarius   In astrology, New Age and occult thought, the coming stage in the evolution of human spirituality that will be characterized by experiential revelation of new "truths" as man moves to "higher consciousness."

Brahman   The Hindu name for "God" as formless and ubiquitous, neither personal nor impersonal; variously understood as the essence of the unknowable, ultimate reality or the "oneness" of all that is.

Chakra(s)   (Hindi) "Energy centres" on the body through which kundalini "power" or "energy" flows. In Hindu thought chakras can become "blocked" by repressed memories, emotional wounds, etc.

Guru   (Hindi) Literally, "teacher"; one considered to have attained union with Brahman who can initiate others in the yogic way. He or she is worshiped as an earthly incarnation of Brahman and a vehicle of divine energy and wisdom.

Kali   Hindu goddess associated with kundalini/shakti. Believed to be a consort of the god Shiva.

Kriya(s)   (Hindi) Manifestations of awakened kundalini, including uncontrollable body movements, weeping, laughing, feelings of "electricity" in the body, spiritual intoxication and vocalizing a variety of animal sounds. There are many kriyas, paralleled by manifestations in charismatic experience.

Kundalini   (Hindi) Literally, "coiled one"; kundalini (also "shakti"; the "serpent force") is variously considered to be the energy of God, the power of a Hindu god or goddess (Kali or Shiva), a latent, primordial energy residing in man, the "power" of

the subconscious, or a universal energy which descends
upon a spiritual seeker through yoga or meditation.
Kundalini is symbolized by a serpent with 3 1/2 coils sleeping at the base of the spine which, when awakened, brings
men and women into *yoga*—union with God. The
"Kundalini" is known to bring feelings of intense spiritual
bliss, especially during early practice; but if awakened
improperly, great suffering. Practitioners believe kundalini
brings spiritual cleansing, healing and higher knowledge;
however, over time kundalini practices lead to moral, spiritual and physical disintegration.

**Kundalini
Awakening**   Religious initiation experience in Hinduism; often referred
to as a "baptism," it usually feels like a "force" rising up or
awakening in an individual, in varying degrees of intensity.
Some experience it as a mystic force falling upon them,
awakening their "spiritual perceptions."

Mantra   In occult practice, a word, phrase or sound repeated to
induce a mystical state or invoke a god.

Maya   The word used in Hinduism to explain reality and the universe; it is intended to teach that reality—i.e., all of God's
creation and His creatures, and natural human consciousness of time and matter—is actually an illusion, only perceived as "real" by those who are spiritually immature, and
who rely upon the reason and the natural senses to understand truth. In Hinduism "truth" is found only through
yoga, and salvation from temporal trials and suffering
comes through "enlightenment" when, as a result of communion with occult forces, the seeker has fully "realized"
that reason is a lie.

Samadhi   (Hindi) A blissful state of altered consciousness usually
imparted by a guru—by touch but also through prayer,
breath, a look or symbolic action such as waving clothing.
It can also be achieved through meditation or other
Eastern practices. In Samadhi the worshiper may feel
extraordinary love in his heart and may see visions of
angels, experience healing and emerge with psychic gifts.
Associated with kundalini awakenings.

Shakti   (Hindi) Literally "power," used as a synonym for kundalini.

**Shaktipat or
shakti pat**   (Hindi) Literally "power transfer" or "power touch," this
term described the touch of a guru, usually to a person's
forehead, which produces supernatural effects and is used
to awaken kundalini/shakti.

Siddhi(s)   (Hindi) Supernatural gifts or powers which, among other
things, enable the initiate to see into the spiritual realm
(e.g., see angels and demons), perform miracles and know
the secrets of others.

Yoga   (Hindi) Literally, "yoking," a religious practice for attaining
union with God, or Brahman. Yoga is intended to arouse
or awaken kundalini.

Appendix

[printed verbatim from the Web;
copyright waived by authors—see below]

NATIONAL SCHOOL OF THE PROPHETS
28 January 1999

On Jan 28th, 1999, Thursday evening, Cindy Jacobs read a transcript from a most unusual meeting which took place the preceding Tuesday. In this meeting, several prophetic voices from around the nation got together for an entire day of seeking God and sharing with each other what the Spirit of God has been speaking to them privately regarding our nation. Present at this meeting were Cindy Jacobs, Chuck Pierce, Barbara Weintroble, Bobby Byerly, Jim Lafoon, Bill Hamon, Rick Joyner, Hector Torres, John and Paula Sanford, Dutch Sheets and others. I believe Paul Cain was also present. During this time, this word came forth from the combined prophetic streams represented.

The National School of the Prophets was a conference for equipping the prophetic ministry in the Body of Christ for the next century. This meeting was a first of it's kind in that several major national and international prophets came together to in an unprecedented way to share with each other the "burden of the Word of the Lord". Never before had these prophetic streams joined into one before - and they did so with amazing unity and oneness. There was an absolute lack of competition and striving - but an overwhelming of preferring others. This conference demonstrated to me the beginning of the unity God is bringing in His Body world-wide and the awesome terror that His bride will be when we move together in the Unity of the Spirit. It was truly an privilege to witness this. Amen.

Blessings upon all of you.

Randy Gingrich

P.S. Since this is a Word from God for our nation, please feel free to distribute this to whoever you feel needs to read it.

Subject: CINDY JACOBS WORD TO THE NATION

Word To The Nation — Read by: Cindy Jacobs

National School of the Prophets Conference Colorado Springs, Colorado

Thursday evening, January 28, 1999

This is a description of a prophetic word delivered to the United States of America by a group of prophets, including Cindy Jacobs, Dutch Sheets, John and Paula Sandford, Jim Laffoon, Hector Torres, and Bill Hamon. The setting was the January 28 evening session of the "National School of the Prophets" conference, hosted by the Wagner Institute for Practical Ministry, held in Colorado Springs, Colorado, January 28-30, 1999.

This is a summary and transcript of part of the prophetic word given. The first part is condensed and paraphrased; the second part is direct quotation, edited for readability. This transcript will be refined and extended later as time permits.

The notation [Speaker] is used in the following transcript to describe when the speaker changes to a new person. Also, a few general descriptions are interjected using [square brackets].

[Condensed Portion] [Cindy Jacobs] I pray and thank You, Father, for Your guidance. We knew there was something new You wanted to do now. As we have been praying, this is a night of history where You want to turn things in the heavenlies. I am humbled before You. I feel like the least of the least, to be able to stand before You and Your people tonight. I ask for help, for You to put Your words in my mouth, for this nation, for our cities, and I thank You for giving me that.

There was an amazing time in a Tuesday night meeting before this conference. God has called this School for such a time as this, because we are needy, and because we want to hear the word of the Lord. And we believe that God has given us at least a word to share.

Tuesday night we were working together, tag-team, leading this prayer time, Chuck Pierce, Barbara Weintroble, myself, with Bobby Byerly.

We need to turn to Acts 4, to receive the word from Acts 4, or we will be overwhelmed by the evening's word. I don't want to send us into a spasm of panic, but the Lord wants to take us there [in Acts] together so that we could bear to hear the word, and go beyond it to what the

Lord wanted us to do with the word and how to help prepare the nation.

Would everyone please pray: Father, give me ears to hear. Give me eyes to see. Give me an open heart, oh God, in the name of Jesus.

Acts 4:32-34 (New King James Version) "Now the multitude of those who believed were of one heart and one soul; neither did anyone say that any of the things he possessed was his own, but they had all things in common. And with great power the apostles gave witness to the resurrection of the Lord Jesus. And great grace was upon them all. Nor was there anyone among them who lacked; for all who were possessors of lands or houses sold them, and brought the proceeds of the things that were sold." And take particular note of verse 33: "great power" and "great grace." This is Mega-super-natural power and Mega-super-natural grace, beyond, as it were, a "normal" grace.

I am weeping for the miracle anointings of power, like John G. Lake, Katherine Kuhlman, Smith Wigglesworth. The ones like these of this generation are in this audience. God is coming with resurrection power, something we've never seen before, it's great, it's awesome, it's mega! I love that miracle anointing.

Mega power, resurrection power, creative power. The Lord had been grieved with the previous generation, because they did not handle that power right. Because of it, He decided that for a whole forty years He would not give that same anointing. But it's up, beloved, and He's giving it now.

Let's talk about great grace. This was a time of persecution. They were in a prayer meeting because they were receiving persecution. But there is a mega-grace that was poured upon this early Church; no matter what the devil did, there just were more of them. There was great, great, great grace. I promise there is great grace rolling into this room.

It can only come if His Presence is manifested. It is the sufficiency of His grace. His grace is that which is sufficient. I can feel the virtue of God being loosed, going out of me, into you. There is a comfort and healing in the great grace. Bigger than we have ever known. It's something that martyrs know, it's something that mammas and dads know when their children are being buried alive in other countries, and each one of the children shouts out, "Do not deny the faith!" It is that kind of grace.

Please stand to your feet. I want you all to receive it because it will stain you, and fear will not come upon you, because we are not going to be a fearful people. Fear is not a part of who we are! You receive that, and you believe that, you receive the word of the Lord! I release great power, and in the name of Jesus, great grace! It's coming in another wave, stand and just take it, receive it. It's His love, His manifested Presence, it is who He Is. Nothing will separate you from the Love of God which is in Christ Jesus. Please sit.

So we see that because of great power and great grace, the believers were mixed with unity of heart, nor was there anyone among them who lacked, for all who were possessors of houses or lands sold them and brought them.

So God is moving us into a new position in the Body of Christ, greater than we have known, greater than we can imagine.—- The Presence of God is getting heavier and heavier in this room. He is here! His Presence is here.

We are going to move into a different dimension than we have known. We are going to move a higher place in our faith, a higher place in our understanding, a higher place with Him, in heavenly places. We're going to look down on the word tonight, seated in heavenly places. The Lord wants to say tonight, come up, come away My beloved, come away with Me. Come away! Even a strong word is the mercy of God.

Imagine holding the Carpenter's hand, so that you will not be afraid.

[Direct Quotation Portion] [Cindy Jacobs] As we prayed, God began to speak to us many things about this great grace, and I'm not going to go completely through that meeting except to say, the very next day we met with a number of prophets that had come together. We have some here tonight, not all of them are here that were at the meeting.

We came specifically to get a word of the Lord for the nation. It's interesting how as we began to share, God began to give a consensus of heart, I believe, to a word that came. That one reason we were having trouble getting a word about Y2K, or getting a word about the coming days that we could say was a definitive word, was because, and I think Dutch has shared this part, it says in Corinthians we prophesy in part, each of us. I prophesy in part.

We prophesy in part, but when we come together, we prophesy in whole; it's a very different anointing.

And that the Lord would not give a national word without a national voice of the whole. That we've come to a new time, and we've come to a new day, where He is not going to release Himself unless we come together.

Talk about Isaiah 65:8: "As the new wine is found in the cluster, ... that I may not destroy them all." We sensed what was coming was dark; and it took the strength and the anointing of the company of prophets, of us coming together, seeking the Lord's face, and knowing each other by the Spirit. The Lord had also given us a scripture, before we came as we were praying, if you'll turn to Ezekiel 43. Are you with me? I'm still just basking in that Presence, aren't you? Sweet, thank you Lord.

Ezekiel 43:1-2: "Afterwards he brought me to the gate, the gate that faces towards the east. And behold, the glory of the God of Israel came from the way of the east. His voice was like the sound of many waters; and the earth shone with His glory." The Lord spoke to us that now we were the voice of many waters, that we had come from different streams, some of these prophets, a number of them had never met each other, had heard of each other, but never ever flowed together in the same stream, very divergent streams, very unusual streams, different, some seers, some prophet-evangelists, some prophetic teachers, some prophet-apostles, different things, coming together, and God met us there.

God began to knit our hearts together, and the revelatory gift just shot out the ceiling, what we began to hear from the Lord. The revelation God began to speak to us, some things, I know if different ones began to teach, like Jim Gault began to teach, but it wasn't Jim Gault teaching us, we knew it was the Lord, because Hector Torres had the same thing, and as we came together, this one had this piece and this piece and this piece, and then we would go just Oh, Wow, we saw it come together, and then God would move another place and begin to manifest another way, and yes, we'd all been hearing about humility and what He wanted to do, and James Ryle had this to say, and another had this to say, and we were taken a place higher and higher that we had never been before. There was something greater than all of us in our midst, because we had come together in unity, and the blessing of God manifested in our midst.

And as Acts 13 was being shared about, it was so beautiful. [We] began to talk about the church in Antioch, that there is a return to the Antioch church, and how these people in verse 1 were from different ethnicities, different backgrounds, some had more money than others, but God brought them together, and they ministered to the Lord, and as they ministered to the Lord, the Holy Spirit said. Not one prophet or another, the Holy Spirit said. And you know, I have been in those meetings. In fact, even from the night before when we prayed, God was flowing with His anointing so much, the next day we couldn't remember who initiated a thing, who really in a way had this word or that, or what piece they had; it was "the Holy Spirit said!" You hear me? And God is bringing us to a new day and a new hour where it's going to be, "the Holy Spirit said!" Amen?

And we are crying out to God that that is so, even this night.

Finally in the day, John Sandford began to share something that he has shared with me in private, and I won't go into the whole thing, but essentially that God takes counsel with his people and his prophets, that he doesn't move in a vacuum. And it's much deeper than that, forgive me John, but think about this: perhaps on the Mount of Transfiguration, with Moses and Elijah and Jesus, it was a council come together to discuss the Cross, to strengthen Jesus, but a discussion of this, that He brought these incredible prophets together. Do you think in heavenly places where it says there are 24 elders around the throne, maybe those just aren't symbolic figureheads. Maybe there's a council of eldership in heaven, could it be? It could be.

And if there is that in heaven, then there needs to be that in earth. That there are things that God is looking at in the way of nations and places, and He is looking for a people to take counsel with.

I have done this privately many times in prayer, probably many of you have. I remember one very dire prophetic word that came out before the last election, from reputable sources, [who] sent it around different places. Finally I was so troubled by it that I fasted three days, (and I didn't know I would ever tell anyone this). At the end of the third day I came before the Lord, just by myself very early in the morning, and I began to take counsel with God concerning this nation. And I began to say, Lord, what will the nations say? Will they say that a million-plus men can humble themselves in Washington, D.C., and You not see? And I just began to remind the Lord. And it was a very intense thing, I don't know how to explain it to you. But at the end of the time, I knew that it changed. I knew it was canceled. Didn't tell anybody, didn't even tell Mike. Didn't tell anybody I did that. It was between

God and me. He told me "I want you to do this, take counsel with Me," and so I just did it. Probably many of you could tell stories.

But as we began to pray and we began to worship, a sensing came in our midst, the Lord was calling us up together in His throne room. It was such a holy moment, I do not have words to describe it to you. I don't know how everybody else felt. But God began to share how the Lord was putting like chairs in heavenly places, and we were coming up together. That He would speak to us about the judgments and the things to come, to take counsel together. It was such a holy moment. None of us knew how to do this! None of us. I don't know how they felt, I certainly didn't feel very spiritual about it, I mean, I just felt kind of afraid. I wanted to be right before God. [Looks at the other prophets.] What do you think, didn't you guys, some of you, feel the same way?

And then the Lord spoke a word, of which I'm going to read some of that in a minute. And it had to do with an alliance between Communism and Islam. How many of you can say that you have seen something like that coming? Let me see your hands.

Yeah. That's what I thought. Much of what we're going to share is not going to surprise you.

And as we were there in the middle, we realized that meant war, and the Lord had spoken some words about war even to me recently, and I felt like the Lord said to me, "Present your very own son and daughter in the midst of this council. Present your grandchildren. Present your own flesh and blood, in the middle, for it is these who die in war." And I began to cry out to God, "God, it wasn't that generation who did these things. Don't lay it to their charge." And I knew as a nation we were going to lose sons and daughters. And then the Lord began to tell us, "Pray for this nation as if you were going to lose that child. I want you to think about your very own flesh and blood, and I want you to think about putting them there in that council chamber." And I began to weep. Now, not all of us are weepers. Thank God, Jim Gott's a weeper, because the next thing I knew, he was flat on his face next to me, and we just wept in chorus. It wasn't a pretty sight. God began to speak to us. In a moment I'm going to read these words to you, and then, afterwards, I want to share with you the next thing, and I want tell you where we're going, so that you can bear it, you know what? because I love you, but God loves you more. He will not give us more than we can bear. Beloved, he will not. Take heed, if you have a strong word, then you need to ask God how to give it and how to prepare the heart for it. Because God does not take lightly those who abuse His sheep. You are the sheep of His pasture, that He gave His very life for. Prophets, take heed.

And so as we wept, I felt the Lord saying, in different ways we've gotten this word in listening, there's bitterness that flows in the prophetic stream. And there's hurts and there's woundedness, and so there is not what is needed to turn this until we are made whole, and we cleanse this stream. And after this word we're going there.

Would you that were in the meeting, that would like to come to the platform, please come and stand with me. [Several men and women prophets began to join Cindy Jacobs on the platform, to stand in a line behind her.] There may be something, if we can get another mike up here, that one might want to interject. This is not everything that was said. It's what I got up early and just recalled, asking the Lord to show me. Not everyone in the meeting has approved this; everyone has seen it. It's not that they didn't want to [approve it], they just didn't get back with everyone. However, I think almost everyone here did read it and did say yes, we believe this is what the Lord was saying. Now, Bobby heard it because I read it in a meeting.

And before I read this word, I'm going to ask my pastor if he will pray for me, okay?

[Dutch Sheets] Lord, we just thank you now for Your strong anointing that is upon Cindy right now and upon each one of us, to flow with what she is doing, and to give her the ability to share these words, under a true and pure anointing of your Holy Spirit. And Lord, that we would have prophetic ears to hear, Lord, that there would be a canopy anointing that hovers over this entire room. So Lord, we claim that now, and I just speak release over Cindy in boldness, and even the tender heart of God and the bold heart of God, wrapped in one, to bring forth this word in the way you want it done. I just speak protection blessing over you and your household, and over your anointing in Jesus's name.

[Cindy Jacobs] Jesus! [She took a deep breath and began.] A report of words that came to the gathering of elder prophets, January 27, 1999. An alliance will form between Communism and Islam. A second prophetic word came from 1988 which said there will be an alliance between Communism and Islam more evil than anything we have previously known. Europe particularly needs to cry out to God. If

Europeans cry out, God will hear them in their day of trouble, and American intercessors are to be a great help to them in that time.

A word came that war is coming, and that many of our young men and women will die on this soil, and foreign soil, if we do not cry out to God.

What is coming on the world is so serious that Y2K will pale in comparison. It's all right to prepare for Y2K provided that preparation is not a heaping up solely for our personal needs without considering the plight of neighbors. If storing is done selfishly, it will be like sifting sands that slip through our fingers. The Church is not to fall into fear and panic, but to seek His face and presence. Y2K issues will be different in various regions. Some will be harder hit than others. Each area needs to raise up a prayer shield and gather apostles, prophets, and intercessors to pray to hear from God.

Acts 11:27 says "And in those days prophets came from Jerusalem to Antioch. Then one of them, named Agabus, stood up and showed by the Spirit that there was going to be a great famine throughout all the world, which also happened in the days of Claudius Ceasar. Then the disciples, each according to his ability, determined to send relief to the brethren dwelling in Judea. This they also did, and sent it to the elders by the hands of Barnabas and Saul." (New King James Version) This scripture indicates they heard a specific word for their region and prepared. We must intentionally seek the Lord together in each city and region, not only for ourselves, but as to what the Lord would require us to do for other regions. Some, like Judea, will be harder hit than others.

Our cities need to be established as cities of refuge. Large cities can do this by boroughs. This is done in intercession through establishing the Watch of the Lord with 24-hour prayer and praise. We must rebuild the walls of our cities, like Nehemiah, establishing 12 gates of prayer and praise.

1999 will be a year of heaping up, but be a good steward of what God is giving you, because it is provision for the year 2000. In some sense, 1999 is the sixth year of heaping up before the seventh year of sabbath rest.

Y2K is a man-made problem which will cause a disruption of communication like the Tower of Babel, and for a season, communication will be shut off. Y2K itself will not be the major shaking, but the shakings will come with the domino effect. Prayer can soften the fall of these dominos.

The Lord spoke strongly of economic shakings. Several dreams have been given to various prophets about disaster striking the nation, and in particular the east coast. The Lord was showing that we are not ready in any measure for what is coming and that it will be titanic in proportion.

One of His last words to us was because of our prayers and standing in the gap, (this was as we were in that prophetic council before the Lord,) it seems that because of the tears and deep intercession of the prophets and others, that complete destruction will be averted, but He is still going to spank America. This could not be averted.

In the coming shaking, so many things will be happening to those in the Church that those who are in the Church who have been against spiritual warfare are going to realize their need to stand up and fight against the enemy.

The accuser is coming with a fresh onslaught. There will be Islamic terrorist attacks which will particularly hit children. [She stopped and cried.] School buses and shopping malls will be hit. It will only be perhaps 10 to 20 but it will put tremendous fear and even terror into the heart of the nation. This fear will boomerang especially against those Christians who are in militia organizations, but will focus against all Christians and cause a persecution of the Church.

Another word specifically for Colorado Springs is that in time of war or attack we will be one of the primary first targets, and we are not ready in the Spirit. Our walls are broken down, and we do not have the prayer coverage we need to withstand the onslaught. Complacency needs to be broken, and prayer watches and coverage put in place to rebuild the walls of the city. We are vulnerable to attack.

God spoke to us deeply about the need for humility. Those of us from Colorado Springs confessed our sin of pride, that we had believed our own P. R. and public relations. Many have been hearing from God of the need for brokenness and humility.

And I think Dutch is going to perhaps touch on this tomorrow night. Another word that we agreed upon is that the Lord is angry at the Church for not praying for President Clinton, even though we are commanded to in 1 Timothy 2:1-3. It had not been God's will for the things that happened to him and by him, and these things may not have occurred at all if we had really cried out to God for him rather than condemned him. It was shown to us how much warfare surrounds the Presidency, and that even the strongest Christian leader could not stand under such an onslaught without heavy intercession and prayer covering. We entered into repentance for our sinfulness.

Are there any of the other prophets that would like to give an amplification to this? Anything you'd like to say, please feel free to. Anything? John, did you want to?

This is John Sandford.

[John Sandford] Such councils are held for decision making. The decision was given, that the dire prophecies would be withheld, but that there would be discipline, and Jim Laffoon spoke of that discipline.

[Jim Laffoon] It was really clear to me that as we were in the council of the Lord, the Lord spoke clearly to me that although that the dire judgment could be prolonged and even averted, through prayer and crying out to God, a certain form of discipline was going to come on the nation that would not be averted. I think if we pray and cry out, some of the more horrible things we've heard of will be averted; [but] there will be some form of dealing. Both brother Chuck [Pierce] and I independently, through visions that God spoke to us, felt like we have an economic safety zone through the end of September, but beginning the last quarter of this year, which is October, we both have deep uncertainties about the stock market and the economy. We're not saying by that, the stock market's going to crash on October 1, but our sense is we're coming into a danger zone the last quarter of this year, economically, and that somewhere in this last quarter, or the first quarter, that we're going to see major, major shakings in the economy that won't be cured overnight. And that we just need to take that into consideration in our planning.

[Hector Torres] In Proverbs 24:6 it says that with strategy, the battle shall be fought, and in the multitude of counsel there is safety. And I believe that there are people here from many cities, even many nations of the world, and I believe that God has given this word so that you can take this back with you, to know that this is part of the strategy that God is saying the Church needs for these last days. We need to come into humility, we need to come into repentance, we need to come into prayer, we need to build those gates in our cities, and begin to praise and worship the Lord, and to fight the battle. And when it says in the multitude of counsel there is safety, I believe that it is speaking of the

Church coming into unity, coming into a oneness of mind, coming into a place of coming together for prayer, for intercession, and to seek, as Jeremiah 29:7 says, to seek the peace of the city to which I've called you, and pray for it unto the Lord, for in it's peace you will have peace. God says that He is the God of peace, and that we are to be peacemakers, and the Bible says that the God of peace will soon crush Satan under our feet. So we need to come in a spirit of peace, a spirit of love, and we need to come in a spirit of humility, seeking in counsel how we are to prepare the strategy for our own regions and our own cities.

[Cindy Jacobs] This is Paula Sandford. That was Hector Torres.

[Paula Sandford] We talked about how it was so important for us to keep our focus on the Lord, on the Lord's love for us, no matter what is going on around us. If our comforts are disrupted, if we have anxieties, we need to continually refocus on the Lord, because He is the same Lord that He has always been. And if He allows discipline, if He sends discipline upon us, His discipline is always for our good. He is love. And if we start focusing on our discomforts and our fears, and feeding those, then we're going to cease to receive, to take into ourselves what the Lord wants to write upon our hearts in love.

[Bill Hamon] It was made fairly clear to us that the greatest thing we have to fear is fear itself. And that Christians above all should not have a spirit of anxiety or fear. We've been praying and believing for God for the miraculous. All of us want to see the miraculous, but we don't want to be in a position to need the miraculous. We all want to see God feed the 5,000 supernaturally, but we don't want to be in a position where we can't feed them otherwise. And we're going to see some fulfillment of prophecies and things that God has declared for these last days, but God has to set the stage for it to happen. And the main thing that we sense is that we must keep the joy, the peace, and what's going to make the difference in the Christians is they are going to see us full of joy, full of peace, full of comfort, sharing our last morsel of food with them, giving and receiving, and they are going to see Christianity like they have never seen it before. Amen?

And what Cindy read there at the very beginning, was what several of us sensed, and what I sensed was what God showed me in 1992, that there was going to be an East-West war. This wasn't something that God planned, but something the devil planned. He told us to go to all the Pacific Rim nations, and we started traveling to the Pacific Rim nations in '92, we went to twelve nations on several continents, but we went to the Pacific Rim nations, Korea, Japan, and Philippines, and Malaysia, and several of them, clear to Australia, the Pacific Rim, all the way around, mainly, right off the coast of China.

Now God showed me in a vision that China had plans to rise up and join alliance with a couple of Islam nations, I don't know how many but a couple of them, and then a couple of old Communist nations would join forces. It would be like when Japan and Germany and Italy joined in an alliance to go against the rest of the world in the Second World War. China and these two other nations and the two communist nations would join in an alliance, to go against the West, and it would end up being an East-West war.

Everywhere I went I gave the Word of the Lord. I was in Hong Kong just a little while before they were to be taken over by China, and gave the Word of the Lord, and gave them a four-year thing that was going to happen according to the Word of the Lord, when China took over. And God was saying that we can completely avert it [the war] by prayer, we can make it less, or if we don't win it by prayer, we will have to fight it, and our sons and daughters will have to fight in that war. And it will be a world war, it is not Armageddon, it has nothing to do with any biblical prophecy about war per se, it's something planned of the devil. But we can stop it.

And it was strange, God gave me a burden and a passion everywhere I went; we did warfare! In Singapore, (I believe it was in Singapore, Malaysia,) we had 200 pastors up on the front, we went to war in the Spirit for 45 minutes, we battled in the Spirit and sent some big gun shells over into these areas.

But God has never has had a passion in me or charged me to really talk too much in the United States, but I know we have to do some praying, but I believe now is the time. I believe now is the time, Amen? And we need to realize we are in a war right now. The moment Christians forget they are in a war they start losing the war. And we are in a war. The devil never gives up. And we need to realize we're going to battle. But I want you to fortify yourself, and you fortify yourself with that third phrase, that you love not your life unto death. Hey, you're already dead, your life is hid with Christ in God, what have you got to fear? Amen? The worst that can happen is that you starve to death and die and go to heaven! Or they shoot you or you die some other way. What have you got to lose? Loose yourself from fear! Come on, I said loose yourself from fear! I said loose yourself from fear! Hallelujah! Amen! 365 times in the Bible it says "Fear not." Every time God starts to speak to anybody about a big enterprise He starts out with "Fear not," "Fear not," "Fear not," "Fear not," "Fear not," "Fear not." Fear is of the devil. Perfect love casts out fear. So we want to be people of courage, people of boldness. And I remember the first prophecy that ever came across in the prophetic presbytery in 1953, and part of the prophecy said, "In the last days, I'll send you forth in the 11th hour, and you will stand as one full of courage, and thousands around you will be full of fear, but you will stand to be a light and a signal." And I believe that God is raising up saviors on Mount Zion, and we're to be that light and that person, Amen.

[John Sandford] Something of great historic significance has happened, and that is that this is the first time, at least in American history, that the recognized prophets, or at least some of them, have gotten together from different streams in unity. And we are so aware that God doesn't want to speak through one any more. He wants to speak through the body of Christ.

And what that filters down [to] is that in this call we have made for you to do things in your community, it is a call for unity in the communities, not for just one voice in the community, but for a corporate voice. I received a scripture that said, "Eight Levites stood and cried out to God." We need eight Levites in every community. You realize we mean more than eight! It's a corporate time. God needs his people to respond, not just one voice.

Sources

1. Books

Anderson, Neil T. *The Bondage Breaker*, 2nd ed. Eugene, OR: Harvest House, 1993.

Barnes, Albert. *Barnes Notes on the New Testament*, 8th ed. Grand Rapids, MI: Kregel Publications, 1975.

Brooke, Tal. *Lord of the Air*. Eugene, OR: Harvest House, 1990.

Coleman, Robert E. *The Master Plan of Evangelism*, 45th ed. Old Tappan, NJ: Spire Books, 1987.

Conway, David. *Magic, an Occult Primer*, 2nd ed. New York: Bantam Books, 1972.

Crowley, Aleister. *The Book of the Law*. Orig. 1904. York Beach, ME: Samuel Weiser, 6th ed. 1989.

Frangipane, Francis. *The Jezebel Spirit*. Cedar Rapids, IA: Arrow, 1991.

Friend, Thomas W. *Fallen Angel: The Untold Story of Jimmy Page and Led Zeppelin*. Titusville, FL: Gabriel Publications, 2002.

Green, Michael. *I Believe in Satan's Downfall*. Great Britain: The Guersney Press, 1981.

Hamon, Bill. *The Eternal Church*. Arizona: Christian International, 1981.

Hamon, Bill. *Prophets and the Prophetic Movement: God's Prophetic Move Today*. Destiny Image, 1990.

Helminski, Kabir. *The Knowing Heart: a Sufi Path of Transformation*. Boston, MA: Shambhala Publications, 1999.

Hinn, Benny. *Good Morning, Holy Spirit*. Nashville, TN: Thomas Nelson, 1990.

Joyner, Rick. *The Final Quest*. New Kensington, PA: Whitaker House, 1996.

LaSor, William Sanford. *Men Who Knew Christ: Great Personalities of the New Testament*, 2nd ed. Glendale, CA: G/L Regal Books, 1971.

Levi, Eliphas. *The History of Magic*. Orig. 1013. Trans. A. E. Waite, London, Great Britain: Ryder & Company, 1969.

Logan, Daniel. *The Reluctant Prophet.* Garden City, NY: Doubleday, 1968.

MacArthur, John F. Jr. *Charismatic Chaos.* Grand Rapids, MI: Zondervan, 1992.

MacArthur, John F. Jr. *Reckless Faith.* Wheaton, Il: Crossway Books, 1994.

Maharaj, Rabi R., with Dave Hunt. *Death of a Guru: A Remarkable True Story of One Man's Search for Truth.* Eugene, OR: Harvest House, 1984.

Martin, Walter R. *The Kingdom of the Cults*, 15th ed. Minneapolis, MN: Bethany Fellowship, 1974.

Michaelsen, Johanna. *The Beautiful Side of Evil.* Eugene, OR: Harvest House, 1982.

Montgomery, Ruth. *Strangers Among Us.* New York: Fawcett Crest, 1979.

Mookerjee, Ajit. *Kundalini: the Arousal of the Inner Energy.* New York: Destiny Books, 1982.

Owen, John. *The Holy Spirit: Abridged and Made Easy to Read by R.J.K. Law.* Edinburgh: Banner of Truth Trust, 1998.

Packer, J. I. *Evangelism & the Sovereignty of God.* Downers Grove, IL: InterVarsity, 1961.

Packer, J. I. *Rediscovering Holiness.* Ann Arbor, MI: Servant Publications, 1992.

Randles, Bill. *Making War in the Heavenlies: A Different Look at Spiritual Warfare.* Great Britain: St. Matthews Publications, 1996.

Randles, Bill. *Mending the Nets: Themes from 1st John.* Cambridge, Great Britain: St. Matthews Publishing, 2000.

Randles, Bill. *Weighed and Found Wanting: The Toronto Experience Examined in the Light of the Bible.* 2nd ed., Cambridge, Great Britain: St Matthew Publications, 1996.

Stearn, Jess. *A Prophet in His Own Country: The Story of the Young Edgar Cayce.* New York: William Morrow & Company, 1974.

Smith, Huston. *The World's Religions.* New York, NY: Harper, 1991.

Smith, Warren. *Deceived on Purpose: The New Age Implications of the Purpose-Driven Church.* 2nd ed. Magalia, CA: Mountain Stream, 2004.

Spurgeon, Charles Haddon. *Spurgeon on Prayer & Spiritual Warfare.* New Kensington, PA: Whittaker House, 1998.

Spurgeon, Charles Haddon. *The Best of C. H. Spurgeon.* Grand Rapids, MI: Baker Book House, 1945.

Stewart, James S. *The Wind of the Spirit.* Nashville, TN: Abingdon, 1968.

Stott, John R.W. *Your Mind Matters: the Place of the Mind in the Christian Life.* Downers Grove, IL: InterVarsity, 1972.

Summers, Father Montague: *The History of Witchcraft and Demonology.* Orig. 1925. Secaucus, NJ: Castle Books, 1992 ed.

Suster, Gerald. *Crowley's Apprentice: The Life and Ideas of Israel Regardie.* York Beach, ME: Samuel Weiser, 1990.

Websters New Collegiate Dictionary. 3rd ed.

White, John. *When the Spirit Comes With Power: Signs & Wonders among God's People.* Downers Grove, IL: InterVarsity, 1988.

2. Web locations: Articles, no author information

"Another Visit to Sinti Brahmo Samaj." *http://www.kathamrita.org/kathamrita/k1sec12.htm.*

"Awakening the Sleeping Kundalini." *http://www.geocities.com/HotSprings/Villa/1555/bab1.htm#awakening.*

"Breaking Curses, Spells and Incantations." *http://home.datawest.net/esn-recovery/free/prayer10.htm.*

"Enter the Elijah Mantle." *http://pub35.ezboard.comm/bigulp.*

"Human Subtle System (Tree of Life)." *http://www.adishakti.org/subtle_system/kundalini.htm.*

"Kundalini: Risker & Information." *http://www.kundalini.se.* English: click on "Kundalini Network & Information" near bottom of page.

"Questions and Answers about Gail's Experience." *http://www.well.com/user/bobby/extra/q&agail.html.*

"Spells to Remove a Curse." *http://www.paralumun.com/spellscurse.htm.*

"The Way of Cain: New Teachings in the Christian Church—Where Are They Leading Us?" *http://www.apologeticsindex.org/r06a22.html.*

"What is Kundalini?" *http://www.geocities.com/HotSprings/Villa/1555/bab1,htm#whatiskundalini.*

3. Web locations: Books, Articles, Testimonies, etc.

Alphabetical according to (1)author last name, or (2)author first name, or (3)sponsoring organization, or (4)other.

Abramelin the Mage, edited by S. Liddell MacGregor Mathers. *The Sacred Magic of Abramelin the Mage.* *http://www.esotericarchives.com/abramelin/abramelin.htm.*

Anandamaya. "The Blue Man." *http://www.sadhanaashram.org/experiences.html.*

Anderson, Dirk. "Great Signs and Wonders II—The Party Has Begun." *http://www.intowww.org/articles.*

Arnott, Carol. *Spread the Fire Magazine.* "Does the 'Inner You' Need Healing?" Vol. 6, Issue 5: 2000. *http://www.tacf.org/stf/archive/6-5.*

Arnott, Carol. *Spread the Fire Magazine.* "Women—The Anointing Makes Room For You." *http://www.tacf.org/stf/archive/4-4/feature4.html.*

Azusa, Bill. *@aol.comhttp://members.aol.com/Azusa/azusaindex.html.*

Bailey, Ruth A. "The Ascending Goddess: Kundalini Shakti." *http://www.aloha.net/~ruth/Chapter6.html.*

Barnes, Jill. *http://www.niksula.cs.hut.fi/ahuima/toronto/testimony.html.*

Bates, Dorothy; "The Goddess Kundalini Arrives in the West, Spiritual Poetry by Dorothy Bates." *http://www.kundalinni-support.com/poetry1.html.*

Bentley, Todd. "Opening Our Eyes to the Angelic Realm." *http://www.elijahlist.com/words/display_word.html?ID=1785.*

Cady, H. Emilie, edited by R.L. Miller. *Lessons in Truth for the 21st Century.* Abib Publishing, 1999. *http://website.lineone.net/~newthought/lessons.4.htm, 5.*

Campo, Garald. "New Aeon Magick." *http://www.ecauldron.com/newaeon02.php.*

Ching Hai. "Samadhi." *http://www.godsdirectcontact.com/teachings/AZsamad.htm.*

Cindy Jacobs et al, "Word to the Nation." Rocky Mountain Awakening, National School of the Prophets. *http://www.awake.org/testimony/nsop.htm.*

Claiborne, David. "Goetia." *http://heru-ra-ha.tripol.com/topics/goetia.html.*

Dental miracles: *www.surewordministries.com/dentalmiracles.html.*

Dixon,Patrick. "Signs of Revival." *http://www.patrickdixon.co.uk/signs/Signs-1.htm.*

Dream interpretation: *http://www.lapstoneministries.org.*

Durrance, Alfred L. "Intercessory and Soaking Prayer." *http://durrance.com/FrAl/intercessory_and_soaking_prayer.htm.*

Energy Ball Man. "When the Serpent Bites." *http://www.kundalini-suport.com/serpent.html.*

Enget, Ron. "Fresh Fire Falls on Beulah, North Dakota." *http://groups.yahoo.com/group/Rivermail_list/message/2286?source=.*

Fitch, Ed. "Pagan Ritual for Basic Use." *www.angelfire.com.*

Garry. *http://www.angels-and-demons.com.*

Global psychics.
http://www.globalpsychics.com/lp/Tips/remove_curses.htm.

Gray, Adrian. Campelltown, New S. Wales, Australia.
http://www.tacf.org/stf/archive/2-4/testimonies.html.

Greg. *http://members.iinet.net.au/~gregga/toronto/testimonies/*
northamerica/na-on-2.html.

Greig, Gary; Virkler, Mark; Virkler, Patti. *Sound Doctrine through
Revelation Knowledge.* Lamad Publishing, 2003.
http://www.cwgministries.org/books/Sound-Doctrine.pdf.

Hall, Larry. Sword of the Spirit Apologetics. "The Toronto Cursing is No
Laughing Matter!" *http://www.luciferlink.org/wtoro.htm.*

Inessa King Zaleski. "Siddhis: Supernormal Perceptual States."
http://www.cabiz.net/heartlink/siddhis1.htm.

Jacobs, Cindy. "A Word of Exhortation." *www.generals.org/articles.*

Jacobs, Cindy. "Restoring the Spirit of Elijah."
http://www.generals.org/articles reports words/.

Jafree. "Who is Jafree? The Personal Life & Teachings of Jafree!"
http://www.enlightenedbeings.com/about_jafree.html.

Jordan, James and Denise. Fatherheart ministries.
http:// www.fatherheart.net.

King, Patricia (Pat Coking). *http://www.extremeprophetic.com.*

Kundalini-support forum. *http://www.kundalini-support.com./forums.*

Master Sadhana Ashram. *www.sahanaashram.org.*

Multidimensions.com. *http://www.multidimensions.com.*

Niger, Missa. "La Messe Noir."
http://www.thefirewithin.dk/library/blackmass.htm.

Oates, Gary & Kathi. "Tucson Area Christian Fellowship."
http://www.tacf.us/pr06.htm.

Paramhansa Yogananda. "Samadhi."
http://www.yoganandarediscovered.com/jaitruth/Csamadhi.html.

Petrie, Alistair. "Lion on the Wall: Prophetic Dream—Wednesday, May
29th/02—4:00 a.m." *Watchman, South Africa.*
http://www.christiannet.co.za/watchmansa/wall.htm.

Philpott, Kent; Miller Avenue Baptist Church. "Warrior Angels."
http://www.w3church.org/WarriorAngels.html.

Pierce, Chuck. "A Gospel for the New Year (Jewish calendar)."
http://www.generals.org/articles.

Piorek, Ed. *Spread the Fire Magazine.* "Marinated in God." Vol. 2, Issue 3, 1996. *http://www.tacf.org.*

Re samadhi: *http://www.aiis.com.au/AISS%20Subweb/hot%20news.htm.*

Riss, Richard. Interview with Pastor Wendell Smith, *www.anointed.net/Libraryroom/revival.*

Riss, Richard. "Twentieth Century Revival Movements." *http://www.anointed.net/Libraryroom/Revival.*

Sacred Word Trust. "shaktipat info." *http://shaktipat.info/.*

Sanada, Solomae, Living Spirit Foundation. "What is Kundalini?" *http://www.geocities.com/HotSprings/Villa/i555/bab1.htm#whatiskundalini.*

Sandford, John. *Spread the Fire Magazine,* June 1996, Vol. 2, issue 3. *http://www.tacf.org.stf/archive/.* Site altered, other information not available.

Scotland, John. Liverpool, England. *http://www.tacf.org/stf/archive/2-4/testimonies/html.*

Scott, Moira H. "What Is Ecstatic Ritual? A Short Introduction." *http://www.angelfire.com/ms3/caer_arianrhod/Ecstatic.htm.*

Sorger, Matt. "The Coming Healing Revival." *http://www.elijahlist.com/healing_columns/052303_Sorger.htm.*

Spiritual Emergence Network, California Institute of Integral Studies (SEN@CIIS). *http://www.ciis.edu/comserv/sen.html.*

Sri Chinmoy. "Kundalini the Mother-Power." *www.srichinmoylibrary.com/kundalini-mother-power.*

Sri Kalki Bhagavan, "Cosmic Reality is One: the Wise Perceive It In Many Ways." *http://www.skyboom1.tripod.com/index27.html.*

Sri Kalki Bhagavan. "Siddhis and the chakras; transcript of a workshop by Dharma Dharini Bhagavad Dasa." *http://skyboom1.tripod.com/index27.html.*

TantraMag.Com. "Kali, the Terrible Face of God," *http://sivasakti.com/local/art-kalie.html.*

Taylor, Chad. "Repentance, Reconciliation, and Renewal: The Keys of Revival." *http://www.consumingfire.com/rrandr.htm.*

Terpstra, Charles J. "Pentecostalism's View of the Christian Life." *http://www.prca.org/current/Articles/Pentecostalism4.htm.*

Thompson, Stephanie; Reiki Blessings Academy. "Higher Education in Holistic Healing for the Body, Mind & Spirit!" *http://www.reikiblessings.homestead.com/kundalini~ns4.html.*

Venice Voodoo. "Herbs and Roots."
   http://www.venicevoodoo.com/herbs.html.

Walters, Kathie. "Faith!" *(www.goodnews.netministries.org);*
   http://www.elijahlist.com/gospels/display_gospel.html?ID=1842.

Warner, Sandy. *http://www.thequickenedword.com.*

Way of Life Literature, "Confusion about the Latter Rain."
   http://www.wayoflife.org/fbns/endtimesconfusion.htm.

Wisner, Kerry. "The Ancient Egyptian Calendar and Festivals Part Two:
   Celebration of the Festivals."
   www.inkemetic.org/Library/calnfest2.htm.

Wolfe, Burton H. "Introduction to the Satanic Bible."
   http://www.beyondweird.com/satanic-Bible.html.

Woods, Cathy. "Some Characteristic Symptoms of Awakened Kundalini."
   http://www.cit-sakti.com/kundalini/kundalini-manifestations.htm.

4. Articles, Other

Carter, C., *Union Leader*, Manchester. Site not available for publication.

Endtime Revivals Unmasked, video. By God's reddende ark, no further
   information available.

Hells Bells 2, DVD. Directed by Erik Hollander. Cleveland, OH: Reel 2
   Real Ministries, 2004.

Hill, John. *Coming to Grips with Deliverance.* Self-published pamphlet,
   Victoria, B.C., undated.

Krayenhoff, Jack. "A church named 'Lion of Judah' outgrows its site."
   (Interview with L. and B. Friesen) *Sunday Magazine*, January 2004,
   sundaymagazine.org.

Krayenhoff, Jack. "Whatever happened to the 'Toronto Blessing'?"
   (Interview with D. Hixson) *Sunday Magazine*, June 2003,
   sundaymagazine.org.

Callaway, Phil. "Innerview — Days of Elijah," (Interview with Robin
   Mark) *Servant Magazine-A Ministry of Prairie Bible Institute*, Issue
   69, 2004, *sundaymagazine.org.*

Piper, John. Sermon: "The Importance of Knowing Our Sin." April 1,
   2001.

TRUE TO HIS WAYS

Psalm 119:9-16

How can a young man cleanse his way?
By taking heed according to Your word.
With my whole heart I have sought You;
Oh, let me not wander from Your commandments!
Your word I have hidden in my heart,
That I might not sin against You.
Blessed are You, O Lord!
Teach me Your statutes.
With my lips I have declared
All the judgments of Your mouth.
I have rejoiced in the way of Your testimonies
As much as in all riches.
I will meditate on Your precepts,
And contemplate Your ways.
I will delight myself in Your statutes;
I will not forget Your word.

True to His Ways
Order Information

Order on-line from author's Canadian Web site:
  Go to truetohisways.com
  Further information available there

Telephone orders direct from author:
  Call (250) 386-8689. Leave a message, we'll call back
  (Canada & US)

Order from ACW Press:
  1200 HWY 231 South #273
  Ozark, AL, USA 36360
  Toll-free (800) 931-BOOK [931-2665])

You may also order through Amazon.com or through your local bookstore.

Book Price: Canada $19.63
**   U.S. $17.00**

Shipping & Handling
(applies to orders from author and ACW Press):

Direct from author: go to truetohisways.com

U.S. Orders: (through ACW Press)	$3.95 ($ US) for the first book and $1.50 for each additional book within US, Canada and Mexico. International orders add $6.00 for the first book and $2.00 for each additional book.

Prices subject to change
The author is taking no profit from this book